T0305074

Eurasian Economic Integration

Eurasian Economic Integration

Law, Policy and Politics

Edited by

Rilka Dragneva

University of Birmingham, UK

Kataryna Wolczuk

University of Birmingham, UK

Edward Elgar

Cheltenham, UK • Northampton, MA, USA

Published by
Edward Elgar Publishing Limited
The Lypiatts
15 Lansdown Road
Cheltenham
Glos GL50 2JA
UK

Edward Elgar Publishing, Inc.
William Pratt House
9 Dewey Court
Northampton
Massachusetts 01060
USA

A catalogue record for this book
is available from the British Library

Library of Congress Control Number: 2013942239

This book is available electronically in the ElgarOnline.com Law Subject
Collection, E-ISBN 978 1 78254 476 0

ISBN 978 1 78254 475 3

Typeset by Columns Design XML Ltd, Reading
Printed and bound in Great Britain by T.J. International Ltd, Padstow

Contents

List of contributors		vii
Preface		viii
List of abbreviations		ix
Table of cases		xi
Table of legislation		xiii

1. The Eurasian Customs Union: framing the analysis   1
    Rilka Dragneva and Kataryna Wolczuk

PART I   LEGAL AND INSTITUTIONAL FRAMEWORK OF THE ECU

2. The development of Eurasian economic integration   15
    Julian Cooper
3. The legal and institutional dimensions of the Eurasian
    Customs Union   34
    Rilka Dragneva
4. Russia, the Eurasian Customs Union and the WTO   61
    Richard Connolly

PART II   THE ECU AS VIEWED FROM THE MEMBER STATES

5. Russia and the Eurasian Customs Union   81
    Julian Cooper
6. Russia, the Eurasian Customs Union and the Asian dimension   100
    Silvana Malle
7. Belarus: player and pawn in the integration game   119
    Matthew Frear
8. Kazakhstan and Eurasian economic integration: quick start,
    mixed results and uncertain future   139
    Nargis Kassenova

PART III THE ECU AND ITS RAMIFICATIONS FOR THE
EUROPEAN UNION

9. The impact of the Eurasian Customs Union on EU–Russia
   relations   163
   Hiski Haukkala
10. Eurasian economic integration: implications for the EU Eastern
    policy   179
    Laure Delcour and Kataryna Wolczuk
11. Commitment, asymmetry and flexibility: making sense of
    Eurasian economic integration   204
    Rilka Dragneva and Kataryna Wolczuk

Appendix 1 *Regional integration initiatives and organizations in*
              the post-Soviet space   222
Appendix 2 *Post-Soviet countries' applications and accessions*
              to the WTO   224

Index   225

Contributors

Dr Richard Connolly, Lecturer in Political Economy, Centre for Russian and East European Studies, University of Birmingham, UK

Professor Julian Cooper, Professor of Russian Economic Studies, Centre for Russian and East European Studies, University of Birmingham, UK

Dr Laure Delcour, Senior Research Fellow, Institute of International and Strategic Relations (IRIS), France

Dr Rilka Dragneva, Senior Lecturer, School of Law, University of Birmingham, UK

Dr Matthew Frear, Visiting Lecturer in East European Politics, Centre for Russian and East European Studies, University of Birmingham, UK

Professor Hiski Haukkala, Professor of International Relations, School of Management, University of Tampere, Finland

Dr Nargis Kassenova, Associate Professor, Director of the Central Asian Studies Centre, Department of International Relations and Regional Studies, KIMEP University, Kazakhstan

Professor Silvana Malle, Professor Emeritus, Director of the Centre for International Studies, Department of Economic Science, University of Verona, Italy

Dr Kataryna Wolczuk, Reader in Politics and International Studies, Centre for Russian and East European Studies, University of Birmingham, UK

Preface

This volume is the result of the close research collaboration of scholars who share a long-lasting and deep interest and fascination with legal, political and economic developments in the post-Soviet world. Using an interdisciplinary methodology, we seek to contribute to the understanding of the complex and controversial moving target of Eurasian economic integration.

The majority of the volume's contributors are based at the University of Birmingham or have benefited from research cooperation with the Centre for Russian and East European Studies (CREES). Previous drafts of some of the chapters in this volume were presented as papers at the CREES Annual Conference, June 2012, at Cumberland Lodge, Windsor Great Park, UK. We thank the French Institute of International Relations (IFRI) for their kind permission to adapt and reprint Nargis Kassenova's chapter on Kazakhstan, originally published as part of IFRI's *Russie. Nei.Reports* (No. 4, November 2012).

We would like to express our gratitude to the publishing team at Edward Elgar for their support and efficiency in the delivery of this book. We also thank Roman Wolczuk for his thorough feedback on several of the chapters and Matthew Frear for the language editing of the contributions.

The work on this volume was facilitated by the editors' ESRC research grant Nr ES/J013358/1 'Russia and the EU in the Common Neighbourhood: Export of Governance and Legal (In) Compatibility'.

We dedicate this book to our children, Rosalyn, Yulia and Roman, who have patiently watched (and endured) it develop since its inception at a playground in Windsor Great Park in June 2012.

Rilka Dragneva and Kataryna Wolczuk
March 2013

Abbreviations

APEC	Asia-Pacific Economic Cooperation
ASEAN	Association of Southeast Asian Nations
AVE	ad valorem equivalent
bcm	billion cubic metres
CACO	Central Asian Cooperation Organization
CAEU	Central Asian Economic Union
CARICOM	Caribbean Community
CET	common external tariff
CIS	Commonwealth of Independent States
CPRF	Communist Party of the Russian Federation
CSTO	Collective Security Treaty Organization
CU-95	Customs Union of 1995
DCFTA	deep and comprehensive free trade area
EBRD	European Bank for Reconstruction and Development
ECU	Eurasian Customs Union
EDB	Eurasian Development Bank
EEC	Eurasian Economic Commission
EEU	Eurasian Economic Union
EFTA	European Free Trade Association
ENP	European Neighbourhood Policy
ENPI	European Neighbourhood and Partnership Instrument
EU	European Union
EvrAzES	Eurasian Economic Community
FDI	foreign direct investment
FEZ	free economic zone
FTA	free trade area
FTZ	free trade zone
GDP	gross domestic product
GUAM	Georgia, Ukraine, Azerbaijan and Moldova
HEEC	High Eurasian Economic Council
HOCU	Highest Organ of the Customs Union
Mercosur	*Mercado Común del Sur*
NAFTA	North American Free Trade Agreement
NATO	North Atlantic Treaty Organization

PCA	Partnership and Cooperation Agreement
RAM	recently acceded member
RTA	regional trade agreement
OECD	Organisation for Economic Co-operation and Development
OPEC	Organization of the Petroleum Exporting Countries
OSCE	Organization for Security and Cooperation in Europe
SCO	Shanghai Cooperation Organization
SES	Single Economic Space
UNCTAD	United Nations Conference on Trade and Development
USA	United States of America
USRB	Union State of Russia and Belarus
USSR	Union of Soviet Socialist Republics
WB	World Bank
WTO	World Trade Organization

Table of cases

Ekonomicheskii Sud Sodruzhestva Nezavisimykh Gosudarstv,
Konsul'tativnoe zaklyuchenie Nr 01-1/3-05 po zayavleniyu
Integratsionnogo Komiteta EvrAzES o tolkovanii chasti 2 stat'i 1,
chasti 1 stat'i 14 Dogovora ob uchrezhdenii EvrAzES ot 10 oktyabrya
2000 goda, Economic Court of the CIS, Consultative Resolution
Nr 01-1/3-05 on the application of the Integration Committee of
EvrAzES for interpreting Section 2, Article 1 and Section 2, Article 14
of the Treaty on the foundation of EvrAzES of 10 October 2000, 10
March 2006 ....49, 56

Ekonomicheskii Sud Sodruzhestva Nezavisimykh Gosudarstv, Opredelenie
Nr 01-1-E/2-10 po zayavleniyu Pravitel'stva Respubliki Belarus' k
Pravitel'stvu Rossiiskoi Federatsii, Economic Court of the CIS, Ruling
Nr 01-1-E/2-10 on the application of the Government of Belarus
against the Government of the Russian Federation, 20 April 2011 56

Kollegiya Suda Evraziiskogo ekonomicheskogo soobshchestva, Reshenie
po zayavleniyu otkryogo aktsionernogo obshchestva 'Ugol'naya
kompaniya "Yuzhnyi Kuzbass"' ob osparivanii punkta 1 Resheniya
Komissii Tamozhennogo soyuza ot 17 avgusta 2010 goda Nr 335,
Collegium of the Court of EvrAzES, Decision on the application of
Yuzhnyi Kuzbass against Section 1 of the Decision of the Commission
of the Customs Union of 17 August 2010 Nr 335,
5 September 2012 57

Kollegiya Suda Evraziiskogo ekonomicheskogo soobshchestva, Reshenie
po zayavleniyuobshchestva s ogranichennoi otvetstvennost'yu
"ONP"ob osporivanii resheniya Komissii Tamozhennogo soyuza ot 18
Oktyabrya 2011 goda Nr 819', Collegium of the Court of EvrAzES,
Decision on the application of ONP against Decision of 18 October
2011 Nr 819 of the Commission of the Customs Union, 15 November
2012 57

Apellyatsionnaya palata Suda Evraziiskogo ekonomicheskogo
soobshchestva. Reshenie po zayavleniyu otkryogo aktsionernogo
obshchestva 'Ugol'naya kompaniya "Yuzhnyi Kuzbass"', Appeals
Chamber of the Court of EvrAzES, Decision on the application of
Yuzhnyi Kuzbass, 29 November 2012...57

The decisions of the Economic Court of the CIS are available on its website: http://sudsng.org/database/deed.

The decisions of the Court of EvrAzES are available on its website: http://sudevrazes.org/main.aspx?guid=20341.

Table of legislation

International agreements

Soglashenie o statuse Ekonomicheskogo suda Sodruzhestva Nezavisimykh Gosudarstv, Agreement on the status of the Economic Court of the CIS, 6 July 1992..............56

Ustav Sodruzhestva Nezavisimykh Gosudarstv, Charter of the CIS, 22 January 1993......16, 42

Dogovor o sozdanii Ekonomicheskogo soyuza, Treaty on the creation of the Economic Union, 24 September 1993 16

Soglashenie o sozdanii zony svobodnoi torgovlya, Agreement on the creation of free trade area, 15 April 1994 16

Soglashenie o Tamozhennom soyuze mezhdu Rossiiskoi Federatsiei i Respublikoi Belarus, Agreement on the Customs Union between the Russian Federation and Belarus, 6 January 1995................. 18, 37

Soglashenie o Tamozhennom soyuze, Agreement on the Customs Union, 20 January 1995 ....18, 37

Dogovor ob ugloblenii integratsii v ekonomicheskoi i gumanitarnoi oblastyakh, Treaty on Deepening Integration in the Economic and Humanitarian Sphere, 29 March 1996 48

Dogovor o Tamozhennom soyuze i Edinom ekonomicheskom prostranstve, Treaty on the Customs Union and the Single Economic Space, 26 February 1999 18

Soglashenie o pravovom obespechenii formitovaniya Tamoxhennogo soyuza i Edinogo ekonomicheskogo prostranstva, Agreement on the Legal Guarantees for the Formation of the Customs Union and the Single Economic Space of, 26 October 1999...................48–9

Dogovor ob uchrezhdenii Evraziiskogo ekonomicheskogo soobshchestva, Treaty on the foundation of EvrAzES, 10 October 2000, amended 25 January 2006 and 6 October 2007 ('The EvrAzES Treaty') 19, 38, 40, 43, 48–9, 56

Soglashenie mezhdu Evraziiskim ekonomicheskim soobshchestvom i Sodruzhestvom Nezavisimykh

Gosudarstv o vypolnenii Ekonomicheskim Sudom Sodruzhestva Nezavisimykh Gosudarstv funktsiii Suda Evraziiskogo ekonomicheskogo soobshchestva, Agreement between EvrAzES and CIS on the Economic Court of the CIS performing the functions of the Court of EvrAzES, 3 March 2004 56

Dogovor o Komissii Tamozhennogo soyuza, Treaty on the Commission of the Customs Union, 6 October 2007, amended 9 December 2010 ....21, 38, 50, 52

Protocol o poryadke vstupleniya v silu mezhdunarodnykh dogovorov, napravlennykh na formirovanie dogovorno-pravovoi bazy Tamozhennogo soyuza, vykhoda iz nikh i prisoedineniya k nim, Protocol on the procedure for entry into force of the international agreements directed to forming the treaty basis of the Customs Union, the exit from them and accession to them, 6 October 2007 ('The 2007 Protocol')..............38, 40, 43–4

Soglashenie o edinom tamozhenno-tarifnom regulirovanii, Agreement on Common Customs and Tariff Regulation, 21 January 2008 53

Dogovor o Tamozhennom Kodekse, Treaty on the Customs Code of the Customs Union, 27 November 2009 ....2, 22, 43, 45–6, 64, 125

Soglashenie ob ustanovlenii i primenenii v Tamozhennom soyuze poryadka zachisleniya i raspredeleniya vvoznykh tamozhennykh poshlin (inykh poshlin, nalogov i sborov), imeyushchikh ekvivalentnoe deistvie, Agreement on establishment and implementation within the Customs Union of a procedure for recording and distributing import customs duties, 20 May 2010 23

Dogovor ob obrashchenii v Sud Evraziiskogo ekonomicheskogo soobshchestva khozyaistvuyushchikh sub'ektov po sporam v ramkakh Tamozhennogoo soyuza i osobennostyakh sudoproizvodstva po nim, Treaty on the application of commercial subjects to the Court of EvrAzES in relation to disputes within the customs union and the particulars of the judicial process, 5 July 2010 57

Dogovor o funktsionirovanii Tamozhennogo soyuza v ramkakh mnogostoronnei torgovoi sistemy, Treaty on the functioning of the Customs Union in the multilateral trade system, 19 May 2011 47, 64–5

Dogovor o zone svobodnoi torgovli,
Treaty on the free trade area,
18 October 2011
*Dogovor o Evraziiskoi
ekonomicheskoi komissii,*
Treaty on the Eurasian
Economic Commission, 18
November 2011 ('The Treaty
on the EEC')....25, 40, 50, 53–5

**Decisions of the Interstate
Council of EvrAzES**
*Reshenie Nr 2 'Ob obespechenii
priemstvennosti organov
upravlenii integratsiei',*
Decision Nr 2 'On ensuring the
continuity of the organs
governing integration', 31 May
2001 48
*Reshenie Nr 3 Polozhenie o
Mezhgosudarstvennov Sovete
Evraziiskogo
ekonomicheskogo
soobshchestva,* Decision Nr 3
approving the Regulation of the
Interstate Council of the EEC,
31 May 2001 38
*Reshenie Nr 122 'Statut Suda
Evraziiskogo
ekonomicheskogo
soobshchestva',* Decision
Nr 122 'Statute of the Court of
EvrAzES', 27 April 2003 ('The
2003 Statute')........................56
*Reshenie Nr 152 'Prioritetnye
Napravleniya razvitiya
EvrAzES na 2003–2006 i
posleduyushchie gody',*
Decision Nr. 152 'The
Priorities for developing
EvrAzES for 2003–2006 and

the following years', 9
February 2004 20
*Reshenie Nr 346 Appendix 'Doklad
o formirovanii pravovoi bazy
tamozhennogo soyuza',*
Decision Nr 346 Appendix,
Report on the formation of the
legal basis of the customs
union, 6 October 2007 21
*Reshenie Nr 378 'O formirovanii
tamozhennogo soyuza i
edinogo ekonomicheskogo
prostranstva v ramkakh
Evraziiskogo
ekonomicheskogo
soobshchestva',* Decision
Nr 378 'On forming the
customs union and single
economic space within
EvrAzES', 10 October
2008..........................38, 49, 52
*Reshenie Nr 502 'O proekte novoi
redaktsii Statuta Suda
EvrAzES',* Decision Nr 502
'On the draft of a new Statute
of the Court of EvrAzES', 5
July 2010 ('The 2010
Statute') 57

**Decisions of the Interstate
Council of EvrAzES (Highest
Organ of the Customs Union)
(HOCU)**
*Reshenie Nr 1 'O formirovanii
pravovoi bazy tamozhennogo
soyuza v ramkakh Evraziiskogo
ekonomicheskogo
soobshchestva',* Decision Nr 1
'On the formation of the legal
basis of the customs union
within the framework of
EvrAzES', 6 October 2007...43

Reshenie Nr 10 'O formorovanii Edinogo tamozhennogo tarifa tamozhennogo soyuza i prisoedinenii tamozhennogo soyuza k Vsemirnoi torgovoi organizatsii', Decision Nr 10 'On the formation of a Common customs tariff of the customs union and the accession of the customs union to the WTO', 9 June 2009 23

Reshenie Nr 14 'O Doklade o khode realizatsii Plana Deistvii po formitovaniyu tamozhennogo soyuza v ramkakh Evraziiskogo ekonomicheskogo soobshchestva', Decision Nr 14 'On the Report on the progress of implementation of the Plan of Activities for the formation of the customs union within the framework of EvrAzES', 27 November 2009 43

Reshenie Nr 15 'O voprosakh organizatsii deyatel'nosti Komissii tamozhennogo soyuza', Decision Nr 15 'On issues of the organization of the activities of the Commission of the Customs Union', 27 November 2009 ('Decision Nr 15') 39, 49, 50

Reshenie Nr 17 'O Dogovore o Tamozhennom kodekse tamozhennogo soyuza', Decision Nr 17 'On the Treaty on the Customs code of the customs union', 27 November 2009 46

Reshenie Nr 20 'O voprosakh deyatel'nosti Sekretariata Komissii tamozhennogo soyuza', Decision Nr 20 'On the activity of the Secretariat of the Commission of the Customs Union', 27 November 2009 22

Reshenie Nr 21 'O smete raskhodov Komissii tamozhennogo soyuza na 2010 god', Decision Nr 21 'On the expenditure of the Commission of the Customs Union for 2010', 27 November 2009 22

Reshenie Nr 35 'O Plane deistvii po formirovaniyu Edinogo ekonomicheskogo prostranstva Respubliki Belarus', Republiki Kazakhstan i Rossiiskoi Federatsii', Decision Nr 35 'On the Plan of action for the formation of a SES between Belarus, Kazakhstan and the Russian Federation, 19 December 2009 24

Reshenie Nr 54 'O smete raskhodov Komissii tamozhennogo soyuza na 2011 god', Decision Nr 54 'On the expenditure of the Commission of the Customs Union for 2011', 5 July 2010 22

Reshenie Nr 73 'O podkhodakh k kodifikatsii zakonodatel'stva Tamozhennogo soyuza i Edinogo ekonomicheskogo prostranstva, vklyuchaya predlozheniya po realizatsii Deklaratsii o formirovanii Edinogo ekonomicheskogo prostranstva Respubliki

Belarus', Respubliki
Kazakhstan i Rossiiskoi
Federatsii ot 9 dekabrya 2010
goda', Decision Nr 73 'On the
approaches to the codification
of the legislation of the
Customs Union and SES,
including proposals on the
implementation of the
Declaration on the formation of
SES', 15 March 2011 45
Reshenie Nr 97 'O Proekte
Deklaratsii o evraziiskoi
ekonomicheskoi integratsii',
Decision Nr 97 'On the draft
Declaration for Eurasian
Economic Integration', 19
October 2011.........................30
Deklaratsiya o evraziiskoi
ekonomicheskoi integratsii,
Declaration on Eurasian
Economic Integration, 18
November 2011....................30

**Decisions of the High Eurasian
Economic Council (HEEC)**
Reshenie Nr 1 'O Reglamente
raboty Evraziiskoi
ekonomicheskoi komissii',
Decision Nr 1 'On the Rules of
Work of the Eurasian
Economic Commission', 18
November 2011 ('The Rules on
the EEC')....................41, 53–5
Reshenie Nr 5 'O chislennosti
departamentov Evraziiskoi
ekonomicheskoi komissii',
Decision Nr 5 'On the number
of departments of the EEC', 19
December 2011 26

**Decisions of the Commission of
the Customs Union**
Reshenie Nr 499 'O shtatnom
raspisanii Sekretatiata
Komissii Tamozhennogo
soyuza', Decision Nr 499 'On
the staff of the Secretariat of
the Commission of the
Customs Union', 8 December
2010 22
Reshenie Nr 636 'O proekte
Deklaratsii o formirovanii
Evraziiskogo
ekonomicheskogo soyuza',
Decision Nr 636 'On the Draft
Declaration for forming a
Eurasian Economic Union', 19
May 2011 28
Reshenie Nr 803 'O proekte
Deklaratsii o formirovanii
Evraziiskogo
ekonomicheskogo soyuza',
Decision Nr 803 'On the Draft
Declaration for forming a
Eurasian Economic Union', 23
September 2011 29

**Decisions of the Council of the
Eurasian Economic Commission**
Reshenie Nr 30 'O reorganizatsii
Evraziiskogo
ekonomicheskogo
soobshchestva', Decision
Nr 30 'On the Reorganization
of EvrAzES', 25 April
2012 41
Reshenie Nr 82 'Ob uchastii
Kyrgyzskoi Respubliki v
Tamozhennom soyuze
Respubliki Belarus',
Respubliki Kazakhstan i
Rossiiskoi Federatsii',

Decision Nr 82 'On the
participation of the Kyrgyz
Republic in the Customs Union
between Belarus, Kazakhstan
and Russia', 12 October
2012 ....27, 40

*Reshenie Nr 104 'O realizatsii
osnovnykh napravlenii
integratsii'*, Decision Nr 104
'On the implementation of the
key directions of integration',
26 November 2012 45

*Reshenie Nr 120 'O vnesenii
izmenenii v Reglament raboty
Evraziisskoi ekonomicheskoi
komissii'*, Decision Nr 120 'On
introducing changes in the
Rules of the EEC', 18
December 2012 41

**Decisions of the Collegium of the
Eurasian Economic Commission**

*Reshenie Nr 233 'O realizatsii
osnovykh napravlenii
integratsii'*, Decision Nr 233
'On implementing the main
directions of integration', 20
November 2012....................30

*Reshenie Nr 7 'O vnesenii
izmenenya v Reshenie Komissii
Tamozhennogo soyuza ot 17
avgusta 2010 Nr 335'*,
Decision Nr 7 'On amending
Decision Nr 335 of 17 August
2010 of the Commission of the
Customs Union', 23 January
2013 57

The international agreements
concluded within the CIS are
available in Russian from the
Register of legal acts and other
documents of the CIS (*Edinnyi
reestr pravovykh aktov i
drugikh dokumentov
Sodruzhestva Nezavisimykh
Gosudarstv*), http://
cis.minsk.by/reestr/ru/
index.html#reestr/create.

The international agreements and
decisions of EvrAzES are
available in Russian on its
website, http://
www.evrazes.com/docs/base.

All international agreements and
decisions of bodies of the
Eurasian Customs Union are
available in Russian on the
website of the Eurasian
Economic Commission, http://
www.eurasiancommission.org
(http://www.tsouz.ru for
documents issued prior to 19
May 2013). They are also
published thematically in the
legal archive of the Eurasian
Business Council (*Evraziiskii
Delovoi Sovet*),
http://www.customs-union.com.

1. The Eurasian Customs Union: framing the analysis

Rilka Dragneva and Kataryna Wolczuk

Regionalism – that is, the tendency for states to form regional groupings – has attracted considerable attention as a major force for global change. The proliferation and diversity of the regional integration regimes across the world has spawned major debates, focusing on the various designs, motives and modalities of participation and varying rates of integration. The 'new regionalism', mainly involving non-Western and often non-democratic states at various levels of economic development, greatly enriched the knowledge of regional integration in becoming the focus of the so-called 'second wave' of literature on regionalism. Research on the design and effects of regional institutions has benefitted considerably from the increased number of case studies. Scholars of international law and international relations have examined the diversity of regional integration regimes with particular reference to the mechanisms of coordination they use and the extent to which they resort to binding, legalized commitments in structuring cooperation.[1]

However, developments in the communist bloc were treated as a distinct phenomenon and were not fully embraced by the literature on new regionalism. The East-Central European states rushed to join the European Union (EU) and NATO, even before their accessions were duly absorbed into the fold of European studies with their distinct analytical perspectives associated with the 'old' regionalism.[2] In contrast, the post-Soviet states featured only occasionally in comparative studies of regionalism.[3]

---

[1] See, for example, Special Issue 'Legalization and World Politics' (2000) 54(3) *International Organization*.

[2] Enlargement fuelled the perception of the EU as a normative power, which differs from other cases of regional integration.

[3] Recently some comprehensive analysis of Eurasian integration (including aspects of the Eurasian Customs Union) in light of the political economy of

With the dissolution of the Soviet Union and its single economic system, the ongoing economic interdependencies between the newly independent republics meant that they faced the challenge of setting up new – this time international – economic relations among themselves, while engaging in state-building and trying to overcome the negative economic effects of the break-up. Over the next two decades, the region witnessed a stream of initiatives directed towards economic integration – some within the framework of the Commonwealth of Independent States (CIS), others outside it (see Appendix 1). These projects were characterized by weak and ineffective institutional frameworks and delivered limited economic results. They generated high volumes of international agreements and a multitude of high-profile political meetings, but failed to make much impact. The declarative and ultimately insubstantial initiatives resulted in fatigue and scepticism amongst observers of post-Soviet developments.

When, in 2007, Russia, Kazakhstan and Belarus announced their intention to set up a customs union within the Eurasian Economic Community (hereafter 'Eurasian Customs Union' or ECU), there was little reason to believe that the initiative would fare better than its predecessors. Only five years later, however, the organization has proved itself a more credible integrative mechanism, thereby meriting renewed attention to economic integration in Eurasia.

Firstly, there have been significant practical developments in setting up a customs union: a common customs tariff was agreed upon in January 2010, a common customs territory became effective as of 1 July 2010 (6 July for Belarus), and internal physical border controls were eliminated in January 2011. A common Customs Code of the Customs Union, containing the bulk of customs regulation, was adopted and upon its entry into force replaced the respective domestic legislation of the member states of the ECU.

Secondly, the customs union project was supported by a more effective legal and institutional framework compared with previous initiatives. The set-up of the ECU provides for supranational delegation, an identifiable and transparent legal basis, and binding third-party dispute resolution. Thus, it is presented as a 'new style' project – one that appears to rely on a modern, rule-based legal and institutional framework in delivering economic benefits.

---

regionalism has begun to emerge: see Alexander Libman and Evgeny Vinokurov, *Holding-Together Regionalism: Twenty Years of Post-Soviet Integration* (Palgrave Macmillan, 2012); Evgeny Vinokurov and Alexander Libman, *Eurasian Integration: Challenges of Transcontinental Regionalism* (Palgrave Macmillan, 2012).

Thirdly, Eurasian integration has been a fast-moving and ambitious project. The economic cooperation agenda has developed from a customs union to a single economic space which was launched in January 2012. Importantly, the process of preparing for a Eurasian Economic Union to become effective as of January 2015 is currently under way.

Fourthly, the ECU has been presented not in terms of past-oriented discourses about shared values and history, but one that offers a future-oriented modernization agenda and tangible economic benefits, and incorporates best international practice in the field.[4] Importantly, and unlike previous frameworks in the post-Soviet world, the ECU must operate in harmony with the commitments which are associated with Russia's accession to the World Trade Organization (WTO), which took place in August 2012.

Finally, the ECU is seen as the nucleus for attracting other former Soviet republics to the project. Deepening of integration is happening alongside its widening. While Tajikistan has expressed interest, Kyrgyzstan is already negotiating accession, although their ultimate membership is far from certain. With its intense focus on Ukraine as a potential member, the ECU has put itself into direct competition with the EU's policy in its Eastern neighbourhood.

Therefore, Eurasian economic integration has been a dynamic process leading to actual domestic changes and appearing to rely on EU-style, legalized mechanisms of coordination, with implications for the EU's own policy in the post-Soviet space. In the confident words of one of the intellectual architects of Eurasian integration, the Russian economist and current adviser to President Putin, Sergei Glaz'ev:

> [T]he fast development of Eurasian integration process calls for amazement in observers, bewilderment in the remaining countries of the CIS, and a desire for further deepening of integration and general development in its members.[5]

The emergence of the ECU has inevitably sparked a reawakening of interest in the region, yet the reaction has not necessarily been of the kind that Glaz'ev anticipated. Businesses have had to respond to the changed

---

[4] Rilka Dragneva and Kataryna Wolczuk, 'Russia, the Customs Union and the EU: Cooperation, Stagnation or Rivalry?', *Briefing Paper REP BP 2012/01* (Chatham House, August 2012).

[5] Sergei Glaz'ev, 'Rubezhi dostignuty, tseli opredeleny, zadachi postavleny' (2012) 12 *Evraziiskaya Integratsiya: Ekonomika, Pravo, Politika* 9, 10.

customs formalities in everyday transactions. As various company publications and surveys show, there has been a keen interest in making sense of the new regulatory framework and its particular implications for trade.[6]

Policy-oriented responses and analysis have only gradually followed. For many, including the EU, the project represents a 'great mystery'.[7] Understandably, given the past record, there is a great deal of scepticism as to whether the ECU is something to be taken seriously at all. The EU has largely sought to ignore the new regime (despite some engagement at the technical level), not recognizing it as a formal regional actor to which individual member states have ceded control over customs policy and other matters, primarily because of the lack of WTO membership of its two member states, Kazakhstan and Belarus. The question of international recognition is critically connected with the issue of whether the ECU can be regarded as what it purports to be – a developed regional economic grouping formed on a voluntary basis with a credible economic rationale. Certainly, well-respected analysts have been sceptical as to the extent to which the ECU is capable of delivering economic benefits to its members.[8]

For many, the creation of the ECU serves political ends and amounts to nothing else but a neo-imperial vehicle for Russia's domination of the post-Soviet countries. In the words of US Secretary of State, Hillary Clinton, in December 2012, acceptable labels such as 'customs union' or an 'economic union' do not conceal Russia's regional power ambitions.[9]

---

[6] For example, Galina Dontsova, 'Assessment of How the Customs Union is Working', *The Moscow Times*, 29 November 2011, reporting on an Ernst & Young survey of major foreign investors. Most large law and accounting firms have published overviews and news updates of legal developments related to customs regulation in the ECU region.

[7] Olga Shumylo-Tapiola, 'The Eurasian Customs Union: Friend or Foe of the EU?', *The Carnegie Papers* (Carnegie Endowment for International Peace, October 2012).

[8] Lucio Vinhas de Souza, 'An Initial Estimation of the Economic Effects of the Creation of the EurAzES Customs Union on Its Members', *Economic Premise No.47* (World Bank, January 2011); David Tarr, 'The Eurasian Customs Union among Russia, Belarus and Kazakhstan: Can It Succeed Where Its Predecessor Failed?', *FREE Policy Brief Series* (Stockholm Institute of Transition Economics, 11 May 2012).

[9] Charles Clover, 'Clinton Vows to Thwart New Soviet Union', *The Financial Times*, 6 December 2012; Dumitru Minzarari, 'Russia is Building Diplomatic and Military Tools to Prevent Western Resistance to its Eurasian Union', *Eurasia Daily Monitor*, 11 December 2012, http://www.jamestown.org/programs/

This claim relates closely to concerns that Russia's 'smart hegemony' through the use of such labels masks the spread of 'bad governance' and the deterioration in democratic standards across the region. As some commentators have argued, this has been a 'primitive' policy initiative from an economic point of view and, ultimately, an attempt by Putin's Russia to set itself as 'an independent centre of power that does not intend to strengthen ties with modern democracies but to rally around itself countries with political systems less advanced than its own'.[10] The spectre of the Soviet Union has not been put to rest, despite President Putin's assurances that the Eurasian project is not a restoration of the USSR but a vehicle for a functional economic cooperation like other regional groupings.[11] As Putin's press secretary pointed out in response to Secretary Clinton, '[w]hat we see on the territory of the ex-Soviet Union is a new type of integration, based only on economic integration. Any other type of integration is totally impossible in today's world'.[12]

Thus, the question is not only about whether Russia – given its past history, regional hegemony and global ambitions – can engage in genuine economic integration with smaller states. Certainly many other regional economic integration groupings, such as NAFTA or Mercosur, exhibit strong asymmetry in membership too. It could be argued that asymmetry may not be such an issue if tamed by a stable and transparent set of rules governing the interactions. The question is also about whether Russia and its partners can 'do rules' – that is, engage in rule-based integration. Given the concerns about domestic standards of the rule of law in these countries, the claim to a new style, rule-based regional integration merely fuels scepticism. Do rules and respect of sovereignty for partner countries prevail when Russia's interests are at stake? After all, crude energy-related arm-twisting has often ended up as Russia's preferred negotiating method with the post-Soviet states. Similarly, would the new common regulation contribute to a business-friendly environment? Or would it amount to yet another mechanism for redistribution of resources between neo-patrimonial networks and oligarchs as well as the extraction of rents by corrupt state officials?

edm/single/?tx_ttnews%5Btt_news%5D=40227&cHash=ad94243ad3ff38007951bf72fc08cf4a (accessed 13 February 2013).

[10] Vladislav Inozemtsev, 'Keeping Russia from Turning Back', *The Washington Post*, 6 November 2011.

[11] Vladimir Putin, 'New Integration Project for Eurasia: A Future which is Being Born Today', *Izvestiya*, 3 October 2011.

[12] Cited in Clover, above note 9.

It is not surprising that given the history of the region and the high geopolitical stakes of the ECU's potential expansion, the debate has been politically charged and subject to strong views and stereotypes. Yet it also suffers from a polarization of views in which the ECU is branded as insignificant and doomed to inconsequential collapse, on the one hand, or as the omnipotent tool of Russia's intentions for the region, on the other. While both perspectives have validity, their use as a normative lens for understanding the ECU offers a limited and skewed interpretation of the complex processes that have taken place. Given its scholarly and policy salience, it is critical that the ECU is examined in a comprehensive, clearly structured and theoretically informed manner. While academic analysis of various aspects of Eurasian integration is slowly building up, it does not yet present a systematic analysis of developments.

This volume seeks to address this academic gap in examining the development, architecture and implications of the Eurasian Customs Union. In particular, it focuses on the following questions:

1.   What are the factors relating to the scope, mode and pace of cooperation that characterize the project? What developments have taken place and what is the institutional architecture built around them? How does the ECU compare in those terms with other regional integration initiatives?
2.   What are the key driving forces behind the ECU? How can its origin be explained and how do theoretical frameworks help us to understand it?
3.   What are the likely implications of the ECU for its existing and prospective members, and also for key international players with stakes in the region, such as the EU?

In conducting such an analysis, we encounter two broad challenges – an analytical and an empirical one. We will outline them in turn and explain how we address them.

In engaging in an analysis of the development of the ECU, we draw on the analytical tools used by international law and international relations scholars in examining the regional integration efforts between states: why they cooperate, what mechanisms of coordination they use, and why they resort to binding, legalized commitments in structuring cooperation. Yet, in approaching Eurasian integration we are only too conscious of the problems of trying to neatly fit it into existing theoretical frameworks.

Given Russia's hegemonic position in the post-Soviet space, realism at first glance appears to be a particularly attractive analytical perspective. In international relations and international law this perspective rests on several assumptions: that states are the primary actors in the international system; their preferences are exogenous and fixed; and the anarchic nature of the international system determines that states compare relative power and zero-sum struggle. With the realists' main focus being on the variation of power and interest, international law is viewed as the embodiment of interests and is made effective through the balance of power. Legal rules that 'work' are those that emanate from the interests of strong states and bind the weak ones.[13]

We find this perspective instructive in certain ways. Given the nature of statehood in post-Soviet states, the locus of decision-making power is firmly at the state level (with a very limited role for societal actors). Similarly, traditional conceptions of power are paramount in Russia's regional behaviour. Yet, in this volume, we go beyond a purely *realist* (and often ideologically driven) paradigm limited to highlighting Russia's hegemonic ambitions. Asymmetry undoubtedly is a strong feature of Eurasian integration, but it is unhelpful to oversimplify Russia's motivation and underestimate the political, economic, administrative and international challenges that the formation of the new regime entails for the biggest country in the region. Also, one cannot ignore the role of other member states. Even if the input of Kazakhstan and Belarus in the institutional design of Eurasian integration is likely to be constrained, domestic preferences and capacity for reform in all member states matter enormously for the architecture, legitimacy and the implementation of the common regime.

The *rational functionalist* or *institutionalist* perspective, as defined in the international law and international relations literature,[14] views international agreements as a way of addressing perceived needs. Functionalists assume rational actors who design institutions on the basis of the outcomes anticipated. As Keohane states, 'institutions can be accounted for by examining the incentives facing actors who created and maintain

---

[13] See summaries of the realist perspective in Judith Goldstein et al., 'Introduction: Legalization and World Politics' (2000) 54(3) *International Organization* 385; Beth A. Simmons, 'Compliance with International Agreements' (1998) 1 *Annual Review of Political Science* 75; Kal Raustiala, 'Form and Substance in International Agreements' (2005) 99 *American Journal of International Law* 581.

[14] Goldstein et al., ibid.; Barbara Koremenos, Charles Lipson and Duncan Snidal, 'The Rational Design of International Institutions' (2001) 55(4) *International Organization* 761; Andrew Guzman, 'The Design of International Agreements' (2005) 16(4) *European Journal of International Law* 579.

them'.[15] International institutions help to satisfy particular concerns in international relations, such as reducing uncertainty and transaction costs; ensuring credibility of commitments while maintaining flexibility; generally balancing policy benefits with maintaining policy discretion. Recently there has been a growing interest in why states enter into legalized, binding agreements as opposed to purely political, soft forms of cooperation. Abbott and Snidal argue that the diversity and asymmetry between nations, sovereignty sensitivities, conditions of uncertainty and complexity, and the level of negotiation and implementation costs are critical factors for the choice between hard and soft forms of cooperation.[16]

This volume is informed by a broad functionalist perspective, which explains the emergence of regional integration groupings and the extent to which they use legal mechanisms for coordination as a response to the calculation by member states of policy benefits and (loss of) policy discretion. We note, however, that much of the comparative analysis of integration initiatives uses a set of abstract, stylized preferences and indicators. While some of the functionalist arguments will be applicable to our case, there are clear tensions in applying them to the post-Soviet context.[17] Further, as Simmons points out, functionalist explanations have been mostly systemic, focusing on international market failure and collective action.[18] Yet they omit critical factors located in the domestic arena yet related to the design of international institutions as well as compliance with obligations (both in terms of domestic interests and domestic capacity).

The *liberal* international framework identifies domestic groups and actors as key actors who use the state as a means to their pre-existing ends. The state interacts with these actors in a complex process of

---

[15] Robert Keohane, *After Hegemony: Cooperation and Discord in the World Political Economy* (Princeton University Press, 1984) 80.

[16] Kenneth W. Abbott and Duncan Snidal, 'Hard and Soft in International Governance' (2000) 3 *International Organization* 421.

[17] James McCall Smith, 'The Politics of Dispute Settlement Design: Explaining Legalism in Regional trade Pacts' (2000) 1 *International Organization* 137, for example, developed a model seeking to explain the variations in the juridicization of dispute resolution in different regional integration groupings using a functionalist perspective. High levels of asymmetry between member states is one of the key factors accounting for low levels of legalization. He notes, however, that the case of the CIS is a clear exception (the CIS Court by design exhibited strong features of legalization), suggesting 'potential tension between the structure of political power and their institutional design'.

[18] Simmons, above note 13.

representation and regulation. State interactions depend on the aggregation of domestic preferences. Hence, domestic interest groups and the nature of domestic representation, as well as state-society relations, matter. Regime type, for example, is found to be important – democracies or countries with independent judiciaries are more likely to comply with international obligations. Similarly, domestic groups with preferences for compliant behaviour can exercise a compliance pull.[19]

The usefulness of this perspective is underscored by the analysis of 20 years of post-communist transformation processes, which means that the examination of this domestic dimension is absolutely imperative. Thus the emphasis is on the specificity of state-society relations in the ECU member states. These relations do not exhibit a Western-style separation but develop in the context of state capture, personalized presidencies, authoritarian conditions, and penetration by neo-patrimonial networks.[20] It is clear that a proper consideration of the nature of state-society relations in ECU countries requires extensive reliance on the approaches of area studies: in-depth empirically grounded, context-sensitive analysis of the processes, actors, preferences and emergent interactions and structures.

A further important difficulty of researching Eurasian integration relates to the conditions of legality in post-Soviet countries. The legal and regulatory sphere falls short of the standards of the rule of law promoted by (and expected by) Western actors and extralegal forms of coordination have proved to be dominant.[21] It is not that formal law and institutions are missing. It is rather that they are used strategically and selectively, intermediated (or supplemented) by a set of social and political coordination mechanisms.

Thus, the analytical approach adopted here draws on key aspects of the perspectives mentioned but adjusts them to take into account the conditions of weak rule of law characterizing its member states, semi-authoritarian political regimes, and a complex geopolitical context. This

---

[19] Simmons, ibid.; A.-M. Slaughter, 'International Law in a World of Liberal States' (1995) 6 *European Journal of International Law* 503.

[20] Susan Stewart, Margarete Klein, Andrea Schmitz and Hans-Henning Schröder (eds), *Presidents, Oligarchs and Bureaucrats. Forms of Rule in the Post-Soviet Space* (Ashgate, 2012).

[21] Kathryn Hendley, 'Legal Development in Post-Soviet Russia' (1997) 13(3) *Post-Soviet Affairs* 228; Richard Sakwa, 'The Dual State in Russia' (2010) 26(3) *Post-Soviet Affairs* 185.

is also required because the initiative is a rare example of a 'holding-together integration',[22] that is when the states pursuing economic integration previously were part of a single state. To explore Eurasian integration, the volume relies on a systematic interdisciplinary analysis of the member states' motivations – economic, geopolitical, or domestic power-driven. In this exploration we intentionally eschew the language of variables while studying economic integration in Eurasia, in order to avoid being straightjacketed by economic rationalism. We argue that we cannot understand and explain the ECU developments without integrating insights from area studies, particularly in relation to understanding the nature of commitment and capacity for implementation, as well as the important legacies that characterize developments in the region.[23] Therefore, in addition to making an empirical contribution in bringing the ECU to academic light, the book seeks to contribute to the development of an interdisciplinary framework to explain Eurasian integration as a relatively rare case of advanced economic integration pursued outside the well-studied context of Western liberal democracies and rule of law.

Our empirical challenges are closely connected to the already noted nature of statehood and state-society relations. Policy-making and preference formation in post-Soviet countries are not easy to research. As far as countries like Belarus and Kazakhstan are concerned, examining preference formation requires detailed analysis of the domestic political context and the rationale for presidents Lukashenko and Nazarbaev, respectively, to engage in Eurasian integration, as Frear and Kassenova show in this volume. Thus, the country contributions seek to map out the official moves and track records of participation, identify important domestic factions which matter (directly or indirectly), as well as spell out the factors that influence or constrain policy choices. Furthermore, given the early days of the ECU's existence and very limited academic research on the subject, it is essential to analyse its legal and institutional design. This design is complex and convoluted, yet critical for understanding the ECU. Therefore, this volume includes the detailed presentation of the legal framework of the Eurasian Customs Union, which has not been undertaken elsewhere.

The empirical scope of the analysis needs to be explained too. As noted at the beginning, the primary interest here is the Eurasian Customs

---

[22]   As described by Libman and Vinokurov, above note 3.

[23]   Drawing on area-based knowledge is in line with the second wave of regionalization literature. See Alberta Sbragia, 'Review Article: Comparative Regionalism: What Might It Be?' (2008) 46 (Annual Review) *Journal of Common Market Studies* 29.

Union, which was agreed upon in 2007 and entered into life in 2010. Given the practical changes that have already taken place, as well as the reform of domestic customs legislation that has followed, we expect that this will be a durable regime with important domestic and international implications. Yet, as will be examined in Chapters 2 and 3, the analysis of the ECU takes us back to the past and into the future. The ECU is developing on the basis of several contractual integration regimes set up in 1995 and the framework of the Eurasian Economic Community set up in October 2000. Thus, any discussions cannot be limited to developments in the late 2000s but must go back to the 1990s in order to understand fully the current processes. Similarly, given the fast-moving nature of integration and the extent to which it is likely to affect arrangements within the ECU, we refer to the Single Economic Space and the planned Eurasian Economic Union and examine developments up to the end of 2012.

Finally, in terms of the empirical focus, the volume examines the formation and design of the regime rather than the governance of integration, something which dominates European Studies. We do not seek to assess the balance between intergovernmentalism and supranationalism, or the functioning of the institutions and implementation across different policy fields in the member states. It is too early for this given that institutions such as the Eurasian Economic Commission or the Court of the Eurasian Economic Community were created only in January 2012. Our analysis also sends a warning signal against superficial comparison and underlines the importance of the careful formulation of research agendas and choice of analytical tools when studying the ECU.

Economic integration in Eurasia is a rapidly developing project and its eventual format is far from clear. This makes analysis a difficult task, with some of the forward-looking elements of the volume vulnerable to the vagaries of unpredictability. The justification for embarking on such an analysis, beyond the evident economic and political importance of these developments, is the need for a critical scrutiny of the ongoing process of economic integration in Eurasia, in light of the highly politicized view of the initiative. The analysis puts the new project on the map of international law and regionalism, thereby advancing our understanding of the political and economic forces shaping the regional international order.

The volume is divided into three parts. The first part of the book examines the development and legal design of the ECU and consists of three chapters. In Chapter 2 Julian Cooper presents the origin of the ECU and provides an essential empirical background to the subsequent chapters. Rilka Dragneva examines the legal and institutional framework of the ECU in Chapter 3, and Richard Connolly deals with the implications of Russia's membership of the WTO for the ECU in Chapter 4.

The second part of the volume examines the relative role and the preferences of the ECU's members. The objective has been to offer an insight into the key identifiable domestic interests in the Eurasian integration process, the factors affecting it, key sensitive issues that have structured the integration agenda and, where possible, its initial reception and results. Russia's role is examined by Julian Cooper in Chapter 5. Silvana Malle, in Chapter 6, continues to focus on Russia but analyses how the ECU relates to the Asian vector of Russia's domestic and external policies. Matthew Frear analyses the 'integration behaviour' of Belarus in Chapter 7, and Nargis Kassenova examines Kazakhstan in Chapter 8.

In the last part of the volume we address some of the key implications of the emergence of the ECU for the region, and more specifically for the EU. Chapter 9, by Hiski Haukkala, examines the implications for the relationships between the EU and Russia itself. In Chapter 10 Laure Delcour and Kataryna Wolczuk examine the implications of the ECU for the EU's Eastern policy. Finally, Chapter 11 develops the empirical findings of the volume into a number of analytical generalizations with regard to the origins and design of the ECU, against the backdrop of theoretical perspectives referred to in the volume.

PART I

Legal and institutional framework of the ECU

2. The development of Eurasian economic integration

Julian Cooper

1. INTRODUCTION

It is now over 20 years since the break-up of the first self-proclaimed socialist country, the USSR, and the simultaneous end of the planned economy and communist rule. During these intervening years, 15 independent states have developed and consolidated – three, since May 2004 – as members of the European Union (EU). Almost from the outset, the new states, excluding the three Baltic nations, declared an interest in retaining economic and other links within the framework of the Commonwealth of Independent States (CIS). At various times during the 1990s there were moves in the direction of a greater degree of economic integration, but in reality little progress was made. After the year 2000 a momentum built up for integration with real substance. By 2010 a tripartite Customs Union had been formed, soon followed by a project to form a Single Economic Space. This chapter is devoted to an overview of these developments in the direction of Eurasian economic integration (see also Appendix 1), with a focus on actors, decisions and institutions. It will also consider the pre-conditions for successful integration in the territory of the ex-USSR, in particular the Soviet inheritance and the activities over more than 20 years of the CIS as an institutional framework. Examination of this issue is important for gaining an understanding of the specific features of this new endeavour for regional economic integration and the ways in which it differs from similar processes in other parts of the world.

2. THE EARLY YEARS

The CIS was formed on 21 December 1991 by the signing of the Alma Ata Declaration by all the presidents of the former republics of the Soviet

Union, with the exception of the three Baltic states and Georgia.[1] This gathering was convened by the President of Kazakhstan, Nursultan Nazarbaev, who was concerned that the Central Asian republics had been excluded from the original meeting of the leaders of Belarus, Russia and Ukraine on 8 December, which had declared the foundation of a new commonwealth as a successor to the USSR. It was envisaged at the outset that the CIS would seek to maintain a high level of economic cooperation between the newly independent countries, including the preservation of long-established common infrastructures for electric power, transport and communications. From January 1993 the CIS operated in accordance with a formal Charter, which was ratified by the summer of 1994 by all countries except Turkmenistan, which adopted the formal position of associate member from 2005, and Ukraine, which acted as a full member even though it never ratified the Charter. The Charter declares the CIS to be a voluntary body of independent and equal states, possessing no supranational authority. According to Article 4, the spheres of joint activity of the member states shall include 'cooperation in the formation and development of a common (*obshchee*) economic space, common European (*общеевропейского*) and Eurasian markets, and customs policy'. This is supplemented by Article 19, which sets out the directions of cooperation, which include 'the formation of a common economic space on the basis of market relations and free movement of goods, service, capital and labour'.[2]

Having adopted a Charter, the CIS moved quickly to agree measures for economic integration. In September 1993 the leaders of nine member countries signed in Moscow an ambitous treaty on the creation of an economic union. Turkmenistan and Georgia signed later; Ukraine opted only for associate status. The treaty set out a phased process of integration: a progression from a multilateral free trade association, to a customs union, then a common market with free movement of goods, services, labour and capital, and culminating in a monetary union.[3] No timescale was envisaged – an understandable reticence given the economic difficulties facing many of the member countries at that time. This declaration of intent was soon followed by an agreement in April 1994 to form a free trade area (FTA).[4] This was signed by the presidents of all

---

[1] Georgia joined the CIS in December 1993, but left unilaterally in August 2008, a decision that took official effect for the CIS as a whole a year later.

[2] Charter of the CIS, 22 January 1993.

[3] Treaty on the Creation of the Economic Union, 24 September 1993.

[4] Note that in the usual terminology of the CIS the term 'zone' is used, but here the more common 'area' is preferred.

countries except Turkmenistan.[5] However, the agreement had no practical impact as Russia failed to ratify it. In its absence trade relations between CIS member countries were regulated by a complex set of bilateral agreements, many of which were ineffective.[6]

Before it became evident that the free trade area was a non-starter, at least for some time, the President of Kazakhstan, Nursultan Nazarbaev, proposed a more ambitious option. Speaking at Chatham House in London in early 1994, he called for the creation of a fully fledged Eurasian Union of States, an Eastern equivalent of the European Union. In late March he spoke on the same topic at a meeting at Moscow State University and began to promote the idea in the press.[7] In October of the same year he presented a draft document on the formation of a Eurasian Union, as he now termed it, to a meeting of the CIS heads of state in Moscow.[8]

It was recognized that the CIS had become an organization with centrifugal forces at work, with countries reforming and developing in different ways. Nazarbaev envisaged a Union in which not all countries would necessarily participate, but only those making a voluntary choice to pursue a policy of enhanced integration. The main decision-making body would be a Council of Heads of State with decisions taken on a four-fifths majority of member states. For developing economic integration a central role would be played by a supranational Economic Commission. But the Union would not only be concerned with economic issues; it would also work towards common policies on science, education, culture, ecology and defence, although only Russia would possess nuclear weapons. Finally, it was proposed that the capital of the Union should be located in a city near the border of Europe and Asia, possibly Kazan or Samara.

The heads of state discussed the document with some reluctance, under 'other business', not before an unsuccessful attempt by the new president of Belarus, Aleksandr Lukashenko, to have the matter removed from the agenda. According to one informed press report, the only leader backing

---

[5]   Agreement on the Creation of a Free Trade Area, 15 April 1994.

[6]   Julian Cooper, 'Russia's Trade Relations with the Commonwealth of Independent States', in Elana Wilson Rowe and Stina Torjesen (eds), *The Multilateral Dimension in Russian Foreign Policy* (Routledge, 2009) 172–3.

[7]   Roi Medvedev, 'Stanovlenie evraziiskogo proekta Nursultana Nazarbaeva', *Ezhenedel'nik*, Nr 23, 6–12 June 2012.

[8]   *Reshenie po predlozheniyu respublika Kazakhstana o formirovanii Evraziiskogo Soyuza Gosudarstv (vmeste s proektom evraiskogo soyuza)*, 21 October 1994, http://www.lawmix.ru/abro/8037 (accessed 29 January 2013).

Nazarbaev was Askar Akeev of Kyrgyzstan.[9] The final document politely thanked the Kazakh leader for his efforts and agreed that his ideas would be taken into account in considering further moves towards integration. Clearly, it was too early for projects for integration of this scale and ambition, still too reminiscent of the USSR, but Nazarbaev had sown seeds which were to bear fruit some 15 years later.

With CIS-wide initiatives for economic integration foundering, more limited regional projects developed instead. In 1994 Kazakhstan entered into a more modest arrangement with neighbouring countries, Kyrgyzstan and Uzbekistan, forming a Central Asian Union, with the aim of creating a common economic space. It was joined in 1998 by Tajikistan, becoming the Central Asian Economic Union.[10] In January 1995 Russia, Belarus and Kazakhstan agreed to form a customs union and in the following year Russia and Belarus signed an agreement, which came into force in 1997, on the formation of a so-called Union State. That there existed a lack of unity within the CIS was shown clearly in October 1997, when a number of countries seeking a more European orientation formed a new regional grouping, GUAM (Georgia, Ukraine, Azerbaijan and Moldova).[11]

As more stable and effectively functioning market economies began to evolve by the late 1990s, Russia and some other CIS countries began to show a new interest in economic integration. As noted, a tripartite customs union was agreed in 1995 and in the middle of the following year Kyrgyzstan also signed up to the initiative, followed by Tajikistan in 1997. However, this remained little more than a declaration of intent, with limited action to develop a real, functioning union. It was recognition of this that probably informed an agreement of the five heads of state in February 1999 to move with more determination towards establishing a customs union and a common economic space. To put this decision into effect, on 10 October the following year a formal agreement

---

[9]   Boris Vinogradov, 'Opyat' soyuz – po Evraziiskii? Pochemu Moskva otvergaet ideyu Nazarbaeva', *Izvestiya*, 28 October 1994, 4. Boris Eltsin is reported to have seen much that was positive in the idea of a Eurasian Union but did not think that a new Union would have support at a popular level. However, he considered some of the ideas potentially useful for future integration, a stance reflected in the final agreed document.

[10]   Annette Bohr, 'Regionalism in Central Asia: New Geopolitics, Old Regional Order' (2004) 80(3) *International Affairs* 485, 486.

[11]   Uzbekistan joined this group in April 1999 but left in 2005. In 2006 it became the GUAM Organization for Democracy and Economic Development.

was signed in Astana to establish a new international economic organization, the Eurasian Economic Community, usually known as EvrAzES (in English, EurAsEC).[12] That the title was a Kazakh proposal would be a plausible assumption. The agreement came into force at the end of May 2001 after ratification by the parliaments of the member states. In May 2002 Moldova and Ukraine gained the status of observer, followed by Armenia in January 2003. Uzbekistan signed a protocol of accession in January 2006 but in October 2008 ceased to participate in its activities.

3. THE EURASIAN ECONOMIC COMMUNITY

According to its founding document, the heads of states of the member countries recognized the necessity of coordinating their actions in the process of integrating into the world economy and the international trade system. The World Trade Organization (WTO) was not explicitly mentioned, but from the context it is clear that the task of accession to it was an important consideration. The central purpose of EvrAzES was defined as the effective advancement of the creation of a customs union and a single economic space (*edinoe ekonomicheskoe prostranstvo*).[13] Its supreme decision-making body is an Interstate Council (*Mezhgossovet*) of heads of states and government, and the standing executive body is an Integration Committee (*Integratsionnyi Komitet*), both chaired on a rotating basis for a term of one year by each country in turn according to its designation in Russian, the working language of EvrAzES.

At the level of the Interstate Council, decisions are taken by consensus. The Integration Committee has to meet at least once every three months, each member country represented by a deputy prime minister. In the absence of agreement, decisions are taken on the basis of a two-thirds majority vote, each member country having a quota of votes determined by its share of the Community's budget.[14] Day-to-day activity is entrusted to the Secretariat of the Integration Committee, with a full-time general secretary appointed for a three-year period. This post has been

---

[12]   See http://www.customs-union.com and http://www.evrazes.com/about/history (accessed 25 January 2013) for details of the formation of EvrAzES.

[13]   Treaty on the Foundation of EvrAzES, 10 October 2000. It is worth noting a difference in terminology. As noted above, in the early 1990s it was usual to refer to a 'common' (*obschee*) economic space, but in recent years it has become a 'single' (*edinoe*) space, the latter suggesting a higher degree of integration.

[14]   Russia: 40 votes; Belarus and Kazakhstan: 20 each; Kyrgyzstan and Tajikistan: 10 each.

occupied since October 2007 by Tair Mansurov, a former Communist Party official, then diplomat, of Kazakhstan. The main posts in the Secretariat are filled on a quota basis according to the share of each country in the total budget of the Community, other posts on a contract basis. Part of the Secretariat is located in Almaty, the rest in Moscow. There is also an Inter-Parliamentary Assembly consisting of delegated members of national parliaments. It meets in St Petersburg and is tasked with parliamentary cooperation and the voluntary harmonization of national legislation. Russia has 28 delegates, Belarus and Kazakhstan each have 14, and Kyrgyzstan and Tajikistan 7 each. Finally, there is a Court of EvrAzES, based in Minsk, charged with dealing with economic disputes arising from the activity of the Community.

During the initial period EvrAzES was mainly concerned with its own institutional consolidation but by 2003 it was in a position to set out a programme of activities for the years ahead. These were codified in a document based on a report supplied by Nazarbaev of Kazakhstan on the priority directions of work of the Community for 2003–06 and beyond.[15] It was agreed that the development of a customs union would be a major priority, moving towards common customs duties and trade practices in accordance with the basic rules and norms of the WTO. There would also be coordination of negotiating positions with respect to member countries gaining accession to the WTO. The document set out an ambitious programme of measures to achieve coordinated policies in relation to economic management, budget and tax matters, energy, agriculture, industry, transport, the control of borders, social issues and migration. The goal of securing the free movement of capital was declared, plus that of moving towards a common financial market, culminating in the establishment of a common currency.[16]

Developments since 2004 have, to a large extent, been in accordance with this programme document. Between 2004 and 2007 a number of basic conceptual documents were approved, covering such policy spheres as transport, agriculture and industry, foreign exchange, social and international policy, and the elaboration of interstate targeted programmes. These documents set out many detailed measures for securing better policy harmonization, but in most cases they have remained at the level of intentions, with little practical implementation. Finally, in October 2007, serious measures were at last adopted to realize the

---

[15]   Decision Nr 152 of the Interstate Council of EvrAzES, 9 February 2004.
[16]   Ibid.

Community's foremost goal, the forming of an effectively functioning customs union.

4. A CUSTOMS UNION WITHIN THE FRAMEWORK OF EVRAZES

At an informal meeting of EvrAzES heads of state in August 2006 it was decided to prepare a set of documents for the establishment of a Customs Union of Belarus, Kazakhstan and Russia (hereinafter 'Eurasian Customs Union' or ECU). This comprehensive set of agreements was finally approved at a formal meeting in Dushanbe on 6 October 2007. It included a decision to establish a Commission of the Customs Union, to be located in Moscow, and measures for the creation of a single customs area and union to be phased over the years 2007 to 2010.[17]

However, on one important issue there was an explicitly acknowledged difference of opinion. This was on the way in which decisions would be taken within the Union. Kazakhstan favoured one vote per country with decisions taken normally by a simple majority, except on some predetermined 'sensitive' questions which would be resolved by consensus. But Russia and Belarus wanted a system of weighted votes, giving Russia 57 per cent and Belarus and Kazakhstan each 21.5 per cent, so that Russia would have a built-in majority. Most decisions would be taken by a two-thirds majority, except for some on issues of principle that would be resolved by consensus.[18] The issue was resolved by the three heads of state: the Kazakh position was rejected and the Russian-Belarus stance was incorporated into the final document.[19] Perhaps as a concession to Kazakhstan, the same October 2007 meeting approved the appointment of the above-mentioned Tair Mansurov as the general secretary of EvrAzES, replacing Grigorii Rapota, a Russian. In addition to the formation of the ECU, it was decided to prepare for the next stage of integration, the creation of the Single Economic Space (SES). Thus the agenda was set for more recent developments.

One of the first tasks was to establish the Commission of the Customs Union, located in Moscow. This began work in early 2009 and its first decision was to appoint as Secretary Sergei Glaz'ev, a well-known Russian economist and political figure, already serving as deputy general

---

[17] Decision Nr 346 of the Interstate Council of EvrAzES, Appendix, Report on the Formation of the Legal Basis of the Customs Union, 6 October 2007.

[18] Ibid.

[19] Treaty on the Commission of the Customs Union, 6 October 2007.

secretary of EvrAzES since November 2008.[20] His deputy was Tat'yana Starchenko, formerly deputy economy minister of Belarus. The Commission's staff grew quite rapidly, from an authorized 135 in late 2009 to 180 by January 2011, including 25 senior staff appointed on a quota basis by member country (Russia – 11, Belarus and Kazakhstan – 7 each).[21] The Commission's budget rose from 268 billion roubles in 2010 to 463 billion roubles in 2011, the funding being shared according to the agreed proportions of Russia at 57 per cent and the other two countries at 21.5 per cent each.[22] The leadership of the Commission, three deputy prime ministers, was confirmed in November 2009, with Igor Shuvalov, first deputy prime minister of Russia, elected chair.

It was decided to declare the ECU formally in existence from 1 January 2010, but the new common Customs Code did not take effect until 1 July, and the creation of a real common customs area in the event took a year longer. The harmonization of customs duties was a time-consuming process but was facilitated by an understanding that the tariff rates of Russia would be adopted whenever possible. This decision was understandable given the expectation that Russia would be the first to gain membership of the WTO, obliging the other two countries to observe most of the agreed tariff rates. The elimination of border customs controls between countries was finally realized in July 2011 when controls between Kazakhstan and Russia were removed, followed twelve months later by those between Belarus and Russia.[23] An issue that had to be resolved before the ECU became active was the way in which the revenues derived from duties would be allocated between the three member countries. In May 2010 it was decided that trade volumes would

---

[20]   Glaz'ev, born in Zaporozh'e, Ukraine, in 1961, was elected Academician of the Russian Academy of Sciences in 2008. He was first deputy, then minister, for foreign economic relations in the Russian government of 1992–93 and then spent a number of years as deputy of the State Duma. In July 2012 he was appointed President Putin's adviser on Eurasian economic integration, with responsibility for securing the coordinated action of government agencies involved. See http://www.glazev.ru/about/107 and http://www.glazev.ru/sodr_evrazes/303 (accessed 22 January 2013).

[21]   Decision Nr 20 of Interstate Council of EvrAzES (Highest Organ of the Customs Union (HOCU)), 27 November 2009, Appendix 1; Decision Nr 499 of the Commission of the Customs Union, 8 December 2010.

[22]   Decision Nr 21 of the Interstate Council of EvrAzES (HOCU), 27 November 2009; Decision Nr 54 of the Interstate Council of EvrAzES (HOCU), 5 July 2010.

[23]   Vitalii Petrov, 'Tamozhnya ushla na peredovuyu', *Rossiiskaya Gazeta*, 1 July 2011.

serve as the basis, leading to a normative distribution of revenues of Belarus 4.70 per cent, Kazakhstan 7.33 per cent and Russia 87.97 per cent.[24]

The ECU Commission and Secretariat undertook a considerable volume of work to establish common rules of the game on many issues relating to external trade. There has been considerable progress in moving towards single systems of trade regulation, sanitary, veterinary and phytosanitary controls, technical regulation, and protective measures. By the beginning of 2012 it could be considered a functioning customs union, although much work remained to complete the process and ensure its fully effective operation.

During the establishment of the ECU one issue that preoccupied the member countries, in particular Russia, was its compatibility with the process of accession to the World Trade Organization. This issue is considered in detail by Connolly in Chapter 4 of this volume, so will be discussed here only briefly. When efforts to form the ECU started, Russia was the only country with a realistic prospect of early accession. It was agreed from the outset that the ECU would be based on WTO principles and Belarus and Kazakhstan understood that the terms of accession agreed for Russia would have a considerable impact on their own terms of entry.

As the ECU was being formed, there was for some time an attempt to gain accession to the WTO as a single entity rather than as three separate states. It is not clear where this initiative originated, but it was made public by a announcement by Putin in June 2009 following a meeting of the Interstate Council, which took a formal decision to this effect.[25] The WTO itself was taken totally by surprise. It soon became clear that there was no precedent of a customs union entering the WTO in this manner and that – unless reversed – the decision would inevitably greatly delay Russia's accession.[26] After some time, without any publicity, the ECU's policy stance shifted to one of coordinating negotiating positions to the maximum extent, but renewing separate negotiations and accepting that Russia would accede before Belarus and Kazakhstan. However, the latter stepped up its efforts to follow Russia as soon as possible. As of late

---

[24] Agreement on Establishment and Implementation within the Customs Union of a Procedure for Recording and Distributing Import Customs Duties, 20 May 2010.

[25] Decision Nr 10 of the Interstate Council of the EvrAzES (HOCU), 9 June 2009.

[26] Jonathan Lynn, 'WTO in Confusion after Russia Customs Union Plan', Reuters, 18 June 2009.

2012, Kazakhstan has a realistic prospect of accession in 2013 but will be preceded by the accession of another EvrAzES member (Tajikistan), which was agreed by the General Council of the WTO in December 2012 (see also Appendix 2).[27] Kyrgyzstan was the first CIS member to join, as early as 1998, but Belarus is still at an early stage of the accession process, though greater urgency has been shown more recently and the government is aiming to join by 2014.

5. TOWARDS A SINGLE ECONOMIC SPACE

The idea of forming a single economic space on the territory of all, or a set of, CIS member countries has a long history, dating back to the early 1990s. It began to move towards implementation in the late 1990s, with a landmark agreement in February 1999 by the Interstate Council of Belarus, Kazakhstan, Kyrgyzstan, Russia and Tajikistan, the forerunner of EvrAzES, to move towards, not only a customs union, but also a single economic space. In the early years of EvrAzES the development of the Customs Union had first priority, with the intention later to move towards the free movement of goods, services, labour and capital – the 'four freedoms'. However, in 2003 a new possibility arose: the formation of a common economic space with Ukraine. In February of that year the leaders of Belarus, Kazakhstan, Russia and Ukraine declared in favour of the principle of a common economic space; in September they signed a formal agreement at a summit in Astana and adopted an initial agenda for the preparation of legislation. However, developments in Ukraine began to slow the process and then set it into reverse. After the Orange Revolution of late 2004 and early 2005, Ukraine began to argue for the creation only of a free trade area, without the creation of any supranational agencies. By the end of 2005 the project was dead.

Within the framework of EvrAzES and the ECU, moves towards the creation of a SES accelerated after the Interstate Council approved a plan of action for its development in December 2009, requiring the drafting and approval of 20 basic documents setting out the enabling legislation.[28] Work proceeded much according to plan, with 17 documents being

---

[27] See http://www.wto.org/english/news_e/news12_acc_tjk_10dec12_e.htm (accessed 10 December 2012). On the same day the working party of the accession of Kazakhstan met for the 14th time and members expressed the hope that this would be achieved in 2013.
[28] Decision Nr 35 of the Interstate Council of EvrAzES (HOCU), 19 December 2009.

signed at the end of 2010, making it possible to declare the formal existence of the SES from 1 January 2012, even though not all provisions were then in place. According to a plan of measures for the period 2011–20 adopted by the Interstate Council in March 2011, some actions will not be completed until 2013 and beyond, especially those relating to the free movement of capital and the harmonization of economic policy. One measure that may prove very difficult to implement by the beginning of 2013, as planned, is the adoption of formal criteria for macroeconomic policy, the Eurasian equivalent of the EU's Maastricht criteria. According to the new rules, the state budget deficit should be no more than 3 per cent of GDP, the state debt no more than 50 per cent of GDP and the level of inflation no more than 5 per cent above that of the member country with the lowest rate.[29] The latter poses a particular challenge. However, it is not apparent that there will be sanctions for any breach of these criteria.

6. THE EURASIAN ECONOMIC COMMISSION

By late 2011, with the formation of the ECU and the SES soon to come into existence, it was decided to wind up the work of the Commission of the Customs Union and transfer all responsibility for economic integration to a new body, the Eurasian Economic Commission (EEC), approved by the presidents of the three ECU member countries on 18 November 2011.[30] The Commission has a two-level structure. The principal decision-making body is the Council of the EEC, consisting of three deputy prime ministers of the member countries: on foundation, Sergei Rumas of Belarus; chair in 2012, Kairat Kelimbetov of Kazakhstan, and Igor Shuvalov of Russia. Decisions are taken by consensus; the three members have an equal voice. The executive body of the Commission is its Collegium, consisting of nine members: the ministers of the EEC, three from each country. Viktor Khristenko, the Russian Minister of Industry and Trade, was appointed chair of the Collegium; at the same time eight more Collegium members (ministers) were appointed. A study of the backgrounds of department heads reveals that many have occupied senior posts in related ministries in their own countries or previously worked in the former ECU Commission. According to a decision of December 2012, the EEC was to have an initial staff of 600, rising to

---

[29] Ibid.
[30] Treaty on the Eurasian Economic Commission, 18 November 2011.

1071 by the beginning of 2013.[31] Most staff members have been
appointed on an open, competitive basis rather than by quota. It has been
claimed that 84 per cent of staff must be citizens of Russia, 10 per cent
of Kazakhstan and 6 per cent of Belarus, but no decision to this effect
has been traced.[32] The location of the EEC is in Moscow, although
Nazarbaev has on a number of occasions said that it should eventually
find a home in Kazakhstan. A new development at the beginning of 2013
was the decision to open representative offices of the EEC in Belarus and
Kazakhstan, tasked with liaising with local organs of state power.[33]

In its initial months the EEC undertook a considerable amount of work
to secure the effective functioning of the ECU and SES. With Russia's
accession to the WTO in August 2012 it became necessary to bring
customs duties in the ECU into line with the obligations Moscow signed
up to in the process of joining the organization. But much work is also
being undertaken on such issues as the improved administration of
customs, technical regulation, sanitary, veterinary and phytosanitary
regulation, and non-tariff measures, as well as on moving towards
harmonization in relation to competition and anti-monopoly policy,
industrial and agricultural policy, macroeconomic policy and financial
markets. The EEC in its early months was also active in establishing
international relations, recognizing that in time it will become the
principal institution for negotiating trade matters relating to the ECU
member countries, increasingly taking over responsibilities previously
vested in national governments. Some countries have been involved in
negotiations that predate the formation of the EEC to establish free trade
areas with the ECU. Most advanced are New Zealand, Vietnam and the
EFTA group of countries but also, with less publicity in recent times,
Syria.

From the outset one of the central issues facing the ECU has been
enlargement. The country that the existing members have been most
eager to engage is Ukraine, but notwithstanding the active pursuit, with
Russia at the fore, of a policy of carrots in the form of substantial

[31] Decision Nr 5 of the High Eurasian Economic Council, 19 December
2011. According to Khristenko, by December 2012 there were more than 650
staff in post, see http://www.evrazes-bc.ru/news/21283 (accessed 5 December
2012).
[32] See Margarita Lyutova et al., 'Novaya byurokratiya', *Vedomosti*, 6 February 2012. They claim that these proportions are found in the Rules (*Reglament*)
of the EEC, but they are not in the version published on the Commission's
website.
[33] 'Integratsiya', *Rossiiskaya Gazeta*, 24 January 2013, 1.

forecast economic benefits, and sticks in the form of threats of higher prices for gas with failure to accede, Ukraine has resisted the pressure. This is an important issue going beyond the present chapter, but is addressed by Delcour and Wolczuk in Chapter 10 of this volume.[34] Relations with Kyrgyzstan and Tajikistan have been much more positive. The Kyrgyz government wishes to join and in October 2011 the Interstate Council of the ECU established a working group for accession and a plan of measures which, if realized, could see the process near completion at the end of 2013.[35] In the recent period Tajikistan prioritized accession to the WTO and succeeded in joining it in March 2013. Interest has been expressed in joining the ECU but no official application has yet been submitted.

Two other institutions of the ECU merit consideration. The first is the EvrAzES Court located in Minsk, which now has the brief of handling disputes arising in the context of the ECU. This is still at a very early stage of development, as discussed by Dragneva in Chapter 3 of this volume. The second is the Inter-Parliamentary Assembly of EvrAzES, which also serves as an assembly for the ECU. With the possibility of the creation of a Eurasian Economic Union, discussed below, there is now debate on an appropriate form of parliamentary representation for this new structure. Some, like Nazarbaev and the speaker of the Russian Duma, Sergei Naryshkin, favour direct election of deputies; others favour an assembly as at present with deputies seconded from national parliaments.

7. TOWARDS A EURASIAN ECONOMIC UNION

As discussed above, it was in 1994 that President Nazarbaev of Kazakhstan first proposed the formation of a Eurasian Union. Almost 15 years later the idea resurfaced in a new form and with a much greater prospect of realization. Its first public mention was in December 2010, when the goal of creating a Eurasian Economic Union (EEU) appeared in a declaration adopted by the Interstate Council of EvrAzES at the presidential level. After the meeting, Lukashenko noted that it would not just be a Eurasian Economic Union, but it would also be concerned with

---

[34]   See also Rilka Dragneva and Kataryna Wolczuk, 'Russia, the Customs Union and the EU: Cooperation, Stagnation or Rivalry?', *Briefing Paper REP BP 2012/01* (Chatham House, August 2012).

[35]   Decision Nr 82 of the Council of the EEC, 12 October 2012.

other issues. Nazarbaev declared that this was the same Eurasian Union he had spoken of 16 years earlier at the Moscow State University.[36]

However, at this stage the nature of the Union had not been determined. This became a task for the Interstate Council of EvrAzES. A first draft declaration on the formation of the EEU was made public in May 2011 in the form of a draft decision of the Commission of the ECU.[37] This revealed some significant differences of opinion. In its preamble the declaration presented the formation of the EEU as a logical next step following the establishment of the ECU and the SES. The new Union would be founded on the generally recognized norms of international law, including respect for the sovereignty and equality of states. In their practical cooperation the member states would be guided by the norms and rules of the WTO. A number of basic directions of development were set out. The text reads, in part, as follows:

- securing the effective functioning of a common market of goods, services, capital and labour;
- forming a common industrial, transport and energy policy, deepening production cooperation, the creation of interstate financial-industrial groups, funds, and other structures comprising the material basis of integration;
- the further convergence and harmonization of national legislation;
- the development and realization of a common economic policy, transition to agreed parameters of basic macroeconomic indicators of member states, [movement towards a foreign currency union – *proposal of the Russian side, the Kazakh side opposed*];
- deepening cooperation in the sphere of [economic – *proposal of Kazakh side, Russian side against*] security, [including in sphere of energy – *proposal of Belarus side*] [including countering new challenges and threats – *proposal of Russian side, Kazakh side against*];
- [creation of a common integrated system of management of borders – *proposal of the Russian side, Kazakh side against*];
- [harmonization of immigration legislation in field of movement of labour resources – *proposal of Kazakh side, Russian side against*].[38]

It is clear from this draft declaration – which was intended for the next heads of state meeting to be held in Minsk in May but in the event was not on its agenda – that Kazakhstan had serious reservations. Russia, with Belarus following the Moscow line, envisaged a fully fledged

---

[36]   See http://www.kremlin.ru/transcripts/9764 (accessed 9 December 2010). Note the author has been unable to trace a copy of the declaration.
[37]   Decision Nr 636 of the Commission of the Customs Union, 19 May 2011.
[38]   Ibid.

Union, not just for economic integration but for securing cooperation in defence, border management and foreign policy. Kazakhstan, notwith-standing Nazarbaev's concept of 1994, wanted to form a Union for economic purposes only, but even so opposed the formation of a currency union.

Meanwhile, Vladimir Putin was actively promoting a future Eurasian Economic Union and putting forward an ambitious target for its form-ation. In May he declared that an agreement on the Union had to be reached by the beginning of 2013, adding that its basic task would be to create the basis for a common economic space with the European Union (EU). According to another report in July, Putin wanted to see the Union functioning by 2013, and he said that in the preceding year talks would be opened with the EU on developing a common free trade area.[39] Thus, in the summer of 2011 Putin was becoming impatient for progress with the next stage of integration.

That Kazakhstan has had major reservations was made absolutely clear when a new version of the draft declaration appeared in September, intended for the next EvrAzES summit in Almaty. Now, Kazakhstan no longer wanted to call the new entity a 'union', preferring to call it simply a 'single economic space'.[40] In the text all references to 'union' were challenged by the Kazakh side. What they wanted was made clear: a 'functioning' SES, not one that was only formally declared. This draft was dated 23 September 2011, the day before Putin took Russia and the wider world by surprise when he announced that he, not Dmitrii Medvedev, would be standing for a another term as president.

The next development made further Kazakh opposition difficult, if not impossible. On 3 October 2011, under the title 'A new integration project for Eurasia', Vladimir Putin – at this time candidate once again for the Russian presidency – set out his vision for a new Eurasian Economic Union.[41] He presented it as a purely economic project, a logical develop-ment of the ECU and SES, a 'link' between Europe and the dynamic Asia-Pacific region, an open endeavour not in any way conflicting with the development of the CIS, and not in any respect an attempt to restore the USSR. On this occasion Putin did not make reference to Nazarbaev as the original author of the idea of the Union, but has done so a number of times since. A fortnight later *Izvestiya* published the views of

---

[39] Maksim Tovkailo, 'Bol'she soyuzov', *Vedomosti*, 13 July 2011, 3.

[40] Appendix to Decision Nr 803 of the Commission of the Customs Union, 23 September 2011.

[41] Vladimir Putin, 'Novyi integratsionnyi proekt dlya Evrazii – budushchee, kotoroe rozhdaetsya segodnya', *Izvestiya*, 4 October 2011.

Lukashenko on Eurasian integration. He declared that the idea of the SES
was Putin's, who had first advanced it in 2003. Not surprisingly, he made
much of the Union states of Belarus and Russia, but made no mention at
all of the Eurasian Union.[42]

Finally on 26 October Nazarbaev set out his understanding, reminding
readers of the history of the idea and his first mention of the Eurasian
Union in March 1994. He made it clear that he viewed the SES as the
basis of the future Union and underlined that any integration has to be
completely voluntary. 'This is not and will not be any "restoration" or
"reincarnation" of the USSR', he declared, and concluded by arguing that
the executive organ of the Eurasian economic space should be located in
Astana.[43]

The declaration finally appeared in November, not at an EvrAzES
summit but at a meeting of the presidents of the ECU countries only. The
draft version had been approved by the Interstate Council at the level of
heads of government on 19 October.[44] It was now a 'Declaration on
Eurasian Economic Integration', clearly a concession to Kazakhstan, and
the reference to the future Union was brief: 'The parties will strive to
complete by 1st January 2015 the codification of international agreements comprising the normative and legal basis of the ECU and SES and
on this basis to create an Eurasian Economic Union'.[45]

From this it can be concluded that Kazakh reservations were taken into
account. The future Union was to be concerned with economic matters
only and, in effect, would represent little more than an effectively
functioning single economic space. It is likely that in the end Nazarbaev
became concerned that Russia's more ambitious intentions for a Eurasian
Union threatened to upset the delicate act of balancing between powerful
contending interests that has characterized the country's policy since
independence. It may take some time before the nature of the new Union
becomes clearer: in November 2012 the Collegium of the EEC approved
a draft decision that a treaty on the Eurasian Economic Union be
prepared by 1 May 2014.[46]

---

[42] Aleksandr Lukashenko, 'O sud'bakh nashei integratsii', *Izvestiya*, 18
October 2011, 1.
[43] Nursultan Nazarbaev, 'Evraziiskii Soyuz: ot idei k istorii budushchego',
Izvestiya, 26 October 2011, 1.
[44] Decision Nr 97 of the Interstate Council of EvrAzES (HOCU), 19 October
2011.
[45] Declaration on Eurasian Economic Integration, Interstate Council of
EvrAzES (HOCU), 18 November 2011.
[46] Decision Nr 233 of the Collegium of the EEC, 20 November 2012.

8. MEANWHILE, THE CIS EVOLVES

Over the past two decades the CIS has evolved steadily and the scope of its activities has broadened. It has become a more complex organization: an official presentation of the Commonwealth's organizations, commissions, councils and so on lists a total of 82 in a very wide range of fields.[47] It undertakes considerable activity of a practical character facilitating economic, social, educational and cultural cooperation between CIS member countries, going far beyond the simple continuation of links dating from Soviet times. In the author's view there has been a tendency for outside observers to underestimate the importance of the CIS. There has been an inadequate appreciation of the extent to which its activities over many years have helped to prepare the ground for economic integration.

The next step for the CIS is the creation of a genuine free trade area. A treaty to form a CIS FTA was signed in St Petersburg in October 2011 by eight member countries, including the EvrAzES five, Armenia, Moldova and Ukraine. Azerbaijan, Turkmenistan and Uzbekistan decided to take a decision by the end of the year.[48] In the event, in March 2012 Uzbekistan decided to join. In effect, this will be an updated version of the original April 1994 free trade treaty, but with account of economic and institutional changes since and of WTO requirements.[49] It has been estimated that the new FTA will replace some 100 multilateral and bilateral trade agreements.[50] In December 2012 Kazakhstan and Moldova ratified the agreement, following Ukraine, Russia, Belarus and Armenia.[51] Tajikistan and Kyrgyzstan will probably join in 2013. New Zealand and Vietnam, currently engaged in negotiations for the creation of free trade areas with the ECU, hope to begin similar talks in 2013 for equivalent relations with the CIS FTA.[52] This new FTA will simplify trading relations between CIS economies and bring them more into accord with WTO practice. For those countries still striving to join the WTO, this development may facilitate accession.

---

[47] See http://www.e-cis.info/page.php?id=2374 (accessed 20 November 2012).

[48] See http://www.1tv.ru/news/economic/189003 (accessed 23 October 2012).

[49] Treaty on the Free Trade Area, 18 October 2011.

[50] See http://www.e-cis.info/news.php?id=3884 (accessed 19 April 2012).

[51] See http://www.e-cis.info/news.php?id=4750 (accessed 9 December 2012).

[52] See http://www.e-cis.info/news.php?id=4453 (accessed 9 November 2012).

9. INTEGRATION, RE-INTEGRATION AND A FUNDAMENTAL ASYMMETRY

Before concluding this overview of the evolution of the ECU and SES it is worth considering briefly one significant factor that distinguishes this process from other experiences of regional economic integration. Unlike the development of the European Union, NAFTA, Mercosur or similar groupings, economic integration in the former Soviet space is more in the nature of re-integration. These were countries with a common past in the Soviet Union, with a shared economic system, common infrastructures in relation to energy, transport and communications, and the same educational, research and development systems. They also shared a common administrative language, Russian, and this is still to a large extent the case today. As noted above, many connections of the past have been kept alive or supplemented by the activities of the CIS. Thus, in principle, integration should be easier for these countries, and perhaps more rapid once initiated on an appropriate basis, than it was for the EU or Mercosur.[53] However, there is an important political difference. In the case of the CIS, we are speaking of new, young states, keen to preserve their new-found sovereignty.

Inevitably, Eurasian integration is asymmetric, Russia being the dominant party in terms of territory, population, economic strength and military might. This places particular obligations on the Russian leadership as any resort to pressure from a position of strength will have a negative impact on prospects for successful integration. As the dominant economy, there is also a danger that any negative developments in Russia will have spillover effects in the smaller economies of the region. In this respect, Mercosur in Latin America provides an instructive parallel. It is also an asymmetric grouping with Brazil as the dominant member. Research indicates that spillover effects from negative processes in the Brazilian economy have a direct impact on other member countries.[54]

---

[53] On this issue, see also Yevgeny Vinokurov and Alexander Libman, 'Post-Soviet Integration Breakthrough: Why the Customs Union Has More Chances than Its Predecessors', *Russia in Global Affairs*, 24 June 2012.

[54] Gustavo Adler and Sebastián Sosa, 'Intra-Regional Spillovers in South America: Is Brazil Systemic After All?', *Working Paper WP/12/145* (IMF, June 2012).

10. A PRELIMINARY ASSESSMENT

Since Russia and the other EvrAzES partner countries decided to embark on regional economic integration on a committed basis with account of WTO expectations, significant progress has been made in a relatively brief period of time. Clearly, there are many unresolved issues and uncertainties, including the soundness of the legal basis of the enterprise, discussed by Dragneva in Chapter 3 of this volume. There are also potential threats that could test the resilience of the new structures, not least the possibility that the security concerns of Russia or other member countries will prompt actions that run counter to the conditions for successful economic cooperation. Here the asymmetry of the project could prove to be decisive.

There is also the question of how other parties will respond, including the EU and the USA, and the way in which Russia implements its commitments to the WTO, issues explored elsewhere in the book. The next few years will make clear whether Russia and other CIS countries can make a success of their ambitious plans for Eurasian economic integration. Its evolution will merit attentive monitoring and research.

3. The legal and institutional dimensions of the Eurasian Customs Union

Rilka Dragneva

1. INTRODUCTION

The creation of the Customs Union within the Eurasian Economic Community (hereafter 'Eurasian Customs Union' or ECU) and the subsequent deepening of the integration agenda have been accompanied by important changes in the legal and institutional framework for structuring cooperation. An improved legal regime has been put in place: one which binds member states, provides for supranational delegation and binding dispute resolution, and incorporates best international norms and practices. Furthermore, the regime claims to operate in transparent ways consistent with Russia's undertakings on entering the World Trade Organization (WTO). In this sense, the ECU project is presented as a modern, rule-based common regime that is capable of delivering the benefits of advanced forms of economic integration.

This claim, which is central to understanding the ECU as a regional integration grouping, is worthy of close scrutiny for a number of reasons. Firstly, in contrast to previous initiatives, the design of the ECU signals a radical and comprehensive move towards legalized integration. Previous initiatives (see Appendix 1) within the Commonwealth of Independent States (CIS) have been consistently described as weak and fragmented, leaving the ordering of relationships to power politics and being unable to facilitate regional trade.[1] The Eurasian Economic Community

---

[1]   Lev Freinkman, Evgeny Polyakov and Carolina Revenco, 'Trade Perform-ance and Regional Integration of the CIS Countries', *Working Paper Series No. 38* (World Bank, 17 August 2004); Rilka Dragneva and Joop de Kort, 'The Legal Regime for Free Trade in the Commonwealth of Independent States' (2007) 56 *International and Comparative Law Quarterly* 233.

(EvrAzES) of 2000 was set up as a more robust international organization than the CIS; nonetheless, it failed to change the CIS institutional paradigm. While weakly legalized forms of cooperation are not necessarily without merit,[2] the operation of complex trade and customs regimes requires the predictability, credibility and transparency associated with legality. The question is whether the ECU's regime delivers on these benefits in regulating economic exchange. Secondly, this move to legality in regional relations also links to one of the key issues in the post-Soviet world, namely Russia's dominant position. Comparative research shows that hegemonic powers rarely engage in binding, legalized forms of integration.[3] Russia's record over the past two decades of ultimately preferring bilateral, 'soft' arrangements in trade relations with its post-Soviet partners was consistent with this proposition.[4] The question, then, is about the extent to which the rules of the ECU represent a break with this pattern and are likely to bind Russia to a multilateral framework. Thirdly, as noted elsewhere in this volume, the ECU has emerged as a part of a fast-moving political agenda for economic integration. In this sense, the development of its legal and institutional framework can be described as a 'big bang' reform process. It is important, then, to consider the effect of this dynamic on the quality and nature of the legal regime, and its resulting ability to deliver the benefits promised to economic actors.

Therefore, this chapter will examine the legal regime of the ECU by focusing on the extent of its legalization relative to previous regional initiatives. Special attention will be given to the overall approach to reform and institutional design over time and the importance of institutional learning. While the chapter provides a detailed overview of the legal regime, it also seeks to evaluate its nature and limitations in a theoretically informed manner. It draws on the international law and comparative regional integration literature examining the importance of law and legality for international cooperation. A range of studies have examined the variations in international regimes in terms of the extent to which states rely on legalized or rule-based as opposed to political

[2]   Kenneth W. Abbott and Duncan Snidal, 'Hard and Soft in International Governance' (2000) 3 *International Organization* 421; Rilka Dragneva, 'Is "Soft" Beautiful? Another Perspective on Law, Institutions, and Integration in the CIS' (2004) 29(3) *Review of Central and East European Law* 279.
[3]   James McCall Smith, 'The Politics of Dispute Settlement Design: Explaining Legalism in Regional Trade Pacts' (2000) 1 *International Organization* 137.
[4]   Dragneva and de Kort, above note 1.

mechanisms for structuring cooperation.[5] Legalized forms of cooperation take place through legally binding and legally enforceable, precise undertakings, extensive delegation to developed international bureaucracies, and binding, third-party dispute resolution. Political cooperation, on the other hand, is associated with soft, political pledges of a general nature and loose frameworks for negotiation and consultation. The design features of different international regimes can be examined along a continuum between two extremes.[6] Thus, this literature provides a suitable framework for capturing the role and the limits of legal coordination in a region with complex socio-legal and historical legacies, such as Eurasia, and to reflect the dynamics of its development.

The chapter starts by providing an overview of the legal genesis of the ECU regime in response to the developing agenda for economic integration. The emphasis here is on clarifying the legal nature of the ECU and the approach to its institutional design. The discussion then turns to examine in detail three key design features identified in the comparative literature: (i) the extent of legally binding effect of the regime; (ii) delegation of decision-making and implementation to common bodies; and (iii) dispute resolution. In doing so, the state of legalization of the ECU regime relative to previous initiatives is assessed. In view of the dearth of existing research on the subject, the overview of the legal framework undertaken here is extensive, though not exhaustive. Importantly, while the role of domestic law in giving effect to the common framework is touched upon, its detailed analysis remains beyond the scope of this work.

---

[5] See Special Issue 'Legalization and World Politics' (2000) 54(3) *International Organization*, in particular Kenneth W. Abbott et al., 'The Concept of Legalization' (2000) 54(3) *International Organization* 401; McCall Smith, above note 3; Kal Raustiala, 'Form and Substance in International Agreements' (2005) 99 *American Journal of International Law* 581.

[6] According to Abbott et al., ibid., the state of pure legalization of international relations would resemble a constitutional regime in a federal state and, while comparable to some areas of decision-making within the European Union, is arguably an extreme state, as rare as a state of pure power politics or anarchy. In practice, it is the intermediate states between complete legalization and complete anarchy that prevail in real life. Raustiala, ibid., differs in exempting 'obligation' (or the extent of the legally binding effect) from this continuum of intermediary states, arguing that it is a binary concept reflecting a clear-cut choice between legal and non-legal undertakings. We have found the approach of Abbott et al. to be a more helpful one in relation to the CIS (see Dragneva, above note 2) and, in view of the continuities, will retain this perspective.

The chapter concludes by presenting its findings and identifying the features and factors that pose limitations on the effectiveness of the legal regime. Ultimately, it will be argued that there has been a sustained effort to improve the framework for cooperation. In terms of the substance of the customs regime, there is evidence of alignment with international norms and best practice, strengthened by Russia's entry into the WTO. Furthermore, the common customs regime is embedded in what, by comparative and historical terms, can be described as a highly legalized institutional framework. A more careful examination, however, shows that there are several features and factors that put in question the benefits that can be derived from these achievements. While some of the problems are transitional, others reveal more serious institutional fault lines with important implications for the integration project.

2. THE GENESIS OF THE ECU

The ECU was inaugurated with the signing of its founding agreements in October 2007. It was set up not as a new international organization but as a treaty-based regime *within* the existing EvrAzES. This origin is critical to understanding its legal nature and institutional boundaries.

The EvrAzES grew out of a set of agreements signed in January 1995 between Russia, Belarus and Kazakhstan with the aim of forming a customs union (CU-95).[7] The CU-95 regime started as very loosely institutionalized, yet it gradually deepened its agenda and provided for a set of common bodies in 1999.[8] The EvrAzES itself was set up in October 2000 as a fully fledged international organization. Its founding treaty explicitly endowed it with a separate legal personality and the ability to sign international agreements, acquire property, as well as sue and be sued.[9] It provided for its own set of bodies: the Interstate Council, Integration Committee, Inter-Parliamentary Assembly, and a Court (see

---

[7] Agreement on the Customs Union between the Russian Federation and Belarus, 6 January 1995; Agreement on the Customs Union, 20 January 1995. As discussed in Chapter 2, the grouping soon attracted additional members: Kyrgyzstan in 1996 and Tajikistan in 1997.

[8] The Agreement between Russia and Belarus did not envisage any coordination bodies. Powers to represent the Customs Union were to be vested with one of the contracting parties. In an interesting twist, the agreement with Kazakhstan, signed two weeks later, envisaged the formation of an executive body on the basis of a subsequent agreement.

[9] Treaty on the Foundation of EvrAzES, 10 October 2000 (hereafter 'EvrAzES Treaty'), Art. 11.

Table 3.1). EvrAzES pursued its agenda predominantly through providing a forum where its members could sign agreements on specific matters of economic integration. Thus, the formation of EvrAzES was an act of political significance, which represented also an institutional upgrade in response to the weakness of the previous arrangements.

Upon its formation the ECU was embedded into the framework of EvrAzES. First, it 'inherited' the agreements concluded within EvrAzES. Indeed, the 'treaty basis' (*dogovornno-pravovaia baza*) of the ECU is defined as consisting of two parts – the agreements adopted within EvrAzES and those adopted within the framework of the ECU.[10] Interestingly, Part One of the treaty basis also includes agreements signed within the CU-95. Second, the ECU's organizational structure (see Table 3.1) developed as a spin-off from the EvrAzES structure on the basis of amendments to the EvrAzES Treaty. The amendments referred to two bodies. The first was the Interstate Council of the ECU, which was the Interstate Council of EvrAzES in a diminished format.[11] Indeed, the formal name of this body was Interstate Council of EvrAzES (Highest Organ of the Customs Union). The Highest Organ of the Customs Union (HOCU) was intended to operate under its own rules of procedure, which were adopted a year later by amending the EvrAzES Council Rules.[12] The second body was the Court of EvrAzES, whose competence was extended to customs union matters.[13] In such cases, the Court was to be composed of judges only from the member states of the ECU. The organizational 'fit' between the ECU and the EvrAzES was selective in that no specific reference was made to the Inter-Parliamentary Assembly of EvrAzES, leaving existing arrangements in place and attributing to it no particular function with regard to the new project.

A new body, the Commission of the Customs Union, was envisaged as the permanent regulatory and executive body of the grouping, which was set up by a separate agreement of the three member states.[14] The powers

---

[10]   Protocol on the Procedure for Entry into Force of the International Agreements Directed to Forming the Treaty Basis of the Customs Union, 6 October 2007 (hereafter '2007 Protocol'), Art. 1.

[11]   EvrAzES Treaty as amended on 6 October 2007, Art. 5.

[12]   Regulation of the Interstate Council of EvrAzES approved by Decision Nr 3 of the Interstate Council of EvrAzES, 31 May 2001, as amended by Decision Nr 378 of the Interstate Council of EvrAzES, 10 October 2008.

[13]   EvrAzES Treaty as amended on 6 October 2007, Art. 8. The Court of the EvrAzES existed only on paper until 2012. From 2004 until then the Economic Court of the CIS performed its functions, as is discussed below.

[14]   Treaty on the Commission of the Customs Union, 6 October 2007.

of this body were only gradually clarified with the adoption of its rules of procedure in November 2009,[15] but have also expanded with competences being granted to it in successive international agreements.

Table 3.1   Eurasian integration initiatives and their organs[16]

Organs	Plenary policy-making	Non-plenary policy-making (permanent executive)	Parliamentary	Judicial
CU (1999)	Interstate Council	Integration Committee	Inter-Parliamentary Committee	No
EvrAzES (2000)	Interstate Council	Integration Committee	Inter-Parliamentary Assembly	Court of EvrAzES
ECU (2007–2011)	Interstate Council of EvrAzES (High Organ of the Customs Union)	Commission of the Customs Union	Same – no designated role	Court of EvrAzES (reduced format)
ECU and SES (2012)	High Eurasian Economic Council	Eurasian Economic Commission	Same – no designated role	Court of EvrAzES (reduced format)

The history of the evolution of the ECU suggests that while there was a strong political will driving the achievement of its economic objectives, there was real pragmatism in the approach to its design. On the one hand, the use of the EvrAzES framework and its selective and incremental upgrading in line with the emerging agenda was institutionally economical. On the other hand, this approach has led to complex overlaps between the various generations of agreements, as discussed below. Importantly, it has also resulted in 'gaps' or 'grey areas' in the new regime and raised questions which remain unanswered.

---

[15]   Rules of Procedure of the Commission of the Customs Union, approved by Decision Nr 15 of the Interstate Council of EvrAzES (HOCU), 27 November 2009 (hereafter 'Decision Nr 15').

[16]   The classification of organs follows Henry G. Schermers and Niels M. Blokker, *International Institutional Law* (3rd edn, Martinus Nijhoff, 2001).

For example, Article 9 of the EvrAzES founding treaty states that:

> membership to EvrAzES is open to all countries who will assume the
> obligations stemming from the EvrAzES Treaty and other international
> agreements listed by the Intergovernmental Council and who, according to the
> existing EvrAzES members, are able and intend to fulfil those obligations.

Membership of the ECU, however, is not addressed separately in a
comprehensive manner; nor is clear how membership of the ECU relates
to membership of EvrAzES. The only relevant rule is that countries may
accede to the ECU as long as they accede to all agreements in Part Two
of the treaty basis.[17] Currently we see that some of the members
preparing for accession to the ECU, such as the Kyrgyz Republic, are
EvrAzES members. Ukraine, which, as is elaborated elsewhere, has been
the explicit target for attracting to the ECU, is not. However, even in the
case of the Kyrgyz Republic, membership is one of the issues that the
Eurasian Economic Commission has been called on to clarify and, if
necessary, propose amendments to existing agreements.[18]

In sum, the ECU was not set up with a separate legal personality in
international law.[19] The institutional boundaries between EvrAzES and
ECU can be described as flexible, with the ECU regime emanating from
that of EvrAzES. Yet there has been a process of growing differentiation
between EvrAzES and the ECU, which has accelerated with the launch
of the Single Economic Space (SES) and the planned formation of the
Eurasian Economic Union (EEU). There has been an expansion of the
treaty basis between the ECU signatories while redesigning some of its
bodies (see Table 3.1). The Interstate Council (Highest Organ of the
Customs Union) has been renamed the High Eurasian Economic Council
(HEEC) with no change of powers.[20] Yet the transition from the
Commission of the Customs Union to a Eurasian Economic Commission
(EEC) is a much more ambitious and substantive change. The expansion
of its powers, including through the delegated power to negotiate and

---

[17]   2007 Protocol, above note 10, Art. 4.

[18]   Plan of Activities on the Accession of the Kyrgyz Republic to the Customs
Union, approved by Decision Nr 82 of the Council of the EEC, 12 October 2012.

[19]   This is recognized as an issue within EvrAzES too: see S.A. Dyatlov and
P.B. Zverev, 'Sovershenstvovanie organizatsionno-pravovogo mekhanizma formi-
rovaniya Edinogo ekonomicheskogo prostranstva' (2012) 11 *Evraziiskaya Integratsiya: Ekonomika, Pravo, Politika* 61, 63.

[20]   Treaty on the Eurasian Economic Commission, 18 November 2011
(hereafter 'Treaty on the EEC'), Art 38.

conclude international agreements on behalf of the grouping,[21] arguably has the potential to strengthen the standing of the ECU as an international actor.

The expanding agenda of the ECU founders has in turn highlighted the issue of the reform, or indeed the possible liquidation, of EvrAzES itself.[22] At the moment it is not clear whether the organization will survive and, if so, how it will relate to the proposed Eurasian Economic Union. The drafts currently in circulation refer to setting up the Union as a new organization with strong federative features, as well as a new set of bodies – the High Eurasian Economic Council, the Eurasian Economic Commission, the Eurasian Court, and the Eurasian Parliament.[23] Yet, as is noted in Chapter 2, no real clarity on the design is expected for some time.

Thus, the ECU shares some similarities with the CU-95 in that it is a treaty regime. It differs from it, however, in that the ECU has been embedded in an organizational structure of common bodies from its inception. Yet this institutional arrangement is characterized by frequent changes in response to the rapidly changing political agenda, as well as selective continuity and incremental innovation, rather than adherence to a comprehensive design. Against this general background the following three sections examine in detail the features of institutional design identified at the beginning of the chapter.

3. THE BINDING EFFECT OF THE ECU REGIME

Following from the overview of the legal standing of the ECU, this section will now examine its legal basis – namely the international agreements concluded within it and the decisions of its coordinating bodies. As will be seen, while it is clear that the ECU's institutional design exhibits an explicit move towards 'hard law' characteristics,

---

[21] Sections 39–41 of the Rules (*Reglament*) of the Work of the Eurasian Economic Commission, approved by Decision Nr 1 of HEEC, 18 November 2011 (hereafter, 'Rules of the EEC'); Decision Nr 120 of the Council of EEC, 18 December 2012.

[22] Decision Nr 30 of the Council of the EEC, 25 April 2012. It is also clear that the ECU rather than EvrAzES as a whole is at the core of such reorganization initiatives.

[23] M.T. Alimbekov, 'K voprosu o politico-pravovom statuse budushchego Evraziiskogo ekonomicheskogo soyuza', and T.N. Neshataeva, 'Evraziiskii Sud: nazad v budushchee', both at http://sudevrazes.org/main.aspx?guide=2371 (accessed 20 December 2012).

particularly in comparison with previous initiatives, there are design flaws which are likely to reduce the benefits of legality.

3.1 International Agreements

The practice of structuring cooperation through the conclusion of international agreements has a long pedigree in the post-Soviet world – from the CIS, to the CU-95 regime, to EvrAzES itself. Their use, it can be argued, was not so much in contrast with the softer, political forms of cooperation, emphasized in comparative analysis, but to the centralized decision-making and the *diktat* that characterized the Soviet Union. Adhering to international law in the post-USSR world was a statement of sovereignty rather than necessarily a reflection of a commitment to being bound beyond the realm of political pledges. In this sense, it is not surprising that a variety of devices were used within the CIS to soften or negate the binding effect of agreements.[24] For example, many agreements were signed, and much was made of this in terms of political symbolism, but were not ratified. For the CIS countries, which follow the doctrine of monism, transformation into national law (which requires ratification for most agreements)[25] is necessary for international agreements to assume an obligatory role within the country. The absence of ratification, or delayed ratification, were deemed to be a key obstacle to the path of integration in the CIS. The problem was exacerbated by the formula of signing hundreds of international agreements to deal with different aspects of cooperation (rather than the negotiation of comprehensive accords) as well as the explicit provision that a member state may choose not to participate in a decision or enter into an agreement in which it is not interested without this affecting the validity of the agreement vis-à-vis its other signatories or the status of that member state (the so-called 'interested party principle').[26] The result was that there was no identifiable legal framework binding on all members, but a confusing 'spaghetti bowl', which made it difficult to establish the applicable law, let alone to implement it. Certainly in the area of trade, the 'pick and mix' approach to cooperation ultimately limited the effect of multilateral engagement and favoured bilateral relations.[27]

---

[24] Dragneva, above note 2.
[25] William Butler, *The Law of Treaties of Russia and the CIS* (Cambridge University Press, 2002).
[26] Charter of the CIS, 22 January 1993, Art. 23.
[27] Dragneva and de Kort, above note 1.

The CU-95 did little to improve the situation: it added international agreements while continuing to refer to selected CIS multilateral and bilateral trade accords, although the reduced number of signatories facilitated coordination. EvrAzES produced a modest but important institutional upgrade by abandoning the 'interested party' principle and encouraging ratification through parliamentary cooperation. Nonetheless, it incorporated the pre-existing international agreements,[28] to which it added new ones.

As noted, the ECU continued the general approach of proliferation of agreements. Yet it was more ambitious in improving on past problems by seeking to identify the agreements which govern cooperation and ensure their simultaneous legal effect throughout all member states. Importantly, it also sought to provide comprehensive regulation of the substance of customs cooperation through the adoption of the Customs Code of the Customs Union.[29]

3.1.1. The treaty basis

The founding agreements of the ECU sought to clarify the treaty basis of the initiative and identify the agreements that are part of it. This was achieved by empowering the Interstate Council to determine the list of such agreements.[30] So far two such lists have been issued, the latest of which refers to Part One, consisting of 13 EvrAzES agreements, and Part Two, consisting of 38 agreements 'dedicated to the completion of the legal basis of the Customs Union'.[31] Part One does not contain all EvrAzES agreements but only those that, presumably, were deemed relevant. Part Two has not been updated despite the fact that the number of ECU agreements has more than doubled since the last list in November 2009. The website of the Eurasian Economic Commission currently refers also to 43 'other international agreements'.[32]

---

[28] Art. 2 of the EvrAzES Treaty (above note 9) provided that they retain validity to the extent to which they do not contradict the treaty.

[29] Treaty on the Customs Code of the Customs Union, 27 November 2009, entered into force with regard to Russia and Kazakhstan on 1 July 2010 and Belarus on 6 July 2010.

[30] 2007 Protocol, above note 10, Art. 1.

[31] The first list adopted according to Decision Nr 1 of the Interstate Council of EvrAzES (HOCU), 6 October 2007, referred to 10 EvrAzES agreements and 12 ECU agreements, some of which were at the time in draft form. The second list was adopted by Decision Nr 14 of the Interstate Council of EvrAzES (HOCU), Appendix 4, 27 November 2009.

[32] See   http://www.tsouz.ru/Docs/IntAgrmnts/Pages/Perechen_MDTS.aspx (accessed 28 February 2013).

It is significant that the agreements in Part Two enter into force simultaneously across the territory of the ECU. This takes place following a decision of the Interstate Council after all member states have completed ratification (or similar required domestic procedure).[33] This 'block' adoption of agreements within the ECU seeks to ensure that all members subscribe to the same set of agreements which become simultaneously applicable across the common customs territory.

An international agreement which has entered into force becomes part of the domestic legal systems of the ECU member states. Some agreements require domestic implementing acts. Those which do not require such acts are deemed to have direct effect.[34] In addition, the binding effect of international agreements is ensured through the provision that norms of international treaties prevail over inconsistent norms of domestic law. This domestic effect depends crucially on the strength of domestic institutions (courts as well as administrative agencies) and their ability to establish the applicable law.

The ECU approach to its treaty basis signals a clear intent to introduce order in place of the previous body of contradictory and overlapping 'spaghetti bowl' of agreements. Yet, the resulting regime remains problematic. For example, the status of the so-called 'other agreements' is questionable. Furthermore, key agreements relating to EvrAzES institutions, such as the agreements for the EvrAzES Court, are not included in the list at all. It is not clear whether such agreements form an explicit part of the 'treaty basis' of the ECU or not. These are not trivial points as the 'treaty basis' serves as a benchmark for the single undertaking for accession to the ECU or withdrawal from it. It also delineates the competence of the EvrAzES Court in examining the conformity of the acts of the bodies of the ECU to that basis, as will be discussed below. To this it needs to be added that the number of signed agreements continues to rise with the launch of the SES.[35]

It may look as if this problem will be resolved when the Part Two list is updated. However, given the discretion of the Council in determining

---

[33] 2007 Protocol, above note 10, Art. 2.
[34] For example, Russian Law of 27 November 2010, Nr 311-FZ 'On the customs regulation in the Russian Federation', Art. 4 provides that the officially published international agreements comprising the treaty basis of the Customs Union are directly applicable in the territory of the country if they do not require the adoption of domestic acts for their application.
[35] Seventeen framework agreements in relation to the SES have been adopted to date. Many of them require the adoption of further measures, so the 'sprawl' of legislation is likely to grow.

the treaty basis, it is uncertain whether some agreements will be omitted from a future update. This clearly was also a matter of concern for the members of the Working Party on the Accession of Russia to the WTO, which sought clarification of the criteria for inclusion of treaties in the lists. The response of the representative of the Russian Federation was not necessarily reassuring: 'neither of these lists were exhaustive ... and [t]here were no special criteria for identifying the treaties to be included in these lists'.[36]

The real possibility for improvement lies in the planned codification of the legal regime of the Customs Union and the SES in preparation for the launch of the Eurasian Economic Union in 2015.[37] Given the voluminous and fragmented treaty basis, this is an important but complex task. Thus, the scope, format and quality of this codification remain to be seen, especially in view of the tight politically driven deadlines.

3.1.2. The substantive scope of agreements

The question here is about the degree to which the ECU regime departs from the established CIS method of drafting a multiplicity of general and specific issue agreements and resorting extensively to cross-referencing. This approach increases the chances of substantive conflict or plain mistakes. It also poses significant challenges in establishing the applicable law and applying it in a consistent and effective manner.

On the one hand, the ECU members succeeded in adopting a Customs Code of the Customs Union ('the Code'), which is a voluminous document containing the bulk of the common customs regime. Following its entry into force, it replaced the respective domestic legislation in the ECU member states. The Code was hailed as a piece of modern customs legislation – one which simplifies customs requirements and implements the provisions of the revised Kyoto Convention on the Simplification and Harmonization of Customs Procedures of 1999.[38]

On the other hand, the Code regulates customs issues in conjunction with a number of specific issue agreements. It also requires the adoption

---

[36] Working Party on the Accession of the Russian Federation to the WTO, Report, WT/ACC/RUS/70, 17 November 2011 (hereafter 'Accession Report'), section 19, http://www.wto.org/english/thewto_e/acc_e/a1_russie_e.htm (accessed 20 December 2012).

[37] Decision Nr 73 of the Interstate Council of EvrAzES (HOCU), 15 March 2011; Decision Nr 104 of the Council of the EEC, 26 November 2012.

[38] Kazakhstan acceded to the Convention as of 19 June 2009, Belarus 19 January 2011, and Russia 4 April 2011.

of further international agreements as well as decisions of the Commission of the Customs Union.[39] In addition, the Code contains numerous references to the application of domestic law in certain matters. In fact, the extensive cross-referencing to domestic law has been one of the main criticisms of the Code.[40]

Thus, the various customs issues are subject to complex, multilevel regulation. For example, customs valuation is dealt with in Chapter 8 of the Code. In addition, the Agreement on the Determination of the Customs Value of Goods of 25 January 2008 and four other agreements deal with procedural aspects, the exchange of information and control over the accuracy of customs valuation.[41] These are supplemented by a range of decisions of the Commission of the ECU.[42] It is not surprising then that business actors have described the state of the legal basis as highly problematic, noting that 'regulation has become more complicated. It is harder to get a handle on the numerous regulatory acts'.[43]

A comprehensive revision of the Code has been under way since the summer of 2011, following a process that purports to have been widely inclusive.[44] How significant the break with the past will be remains to be seen. It is also unclear how the process of codifying the legislation of the Customs Union and the SES, as already mentioned, will affect this process.

---

[39]   The Plan on the Activities Needed for the Entry into Force of the Customs Code, approved by Decision Nr 17 of the Interstate Council of EvrAzES (HOCU), 27 November 2009, lists the 16 international agreements and 17 decisions of the Commission of the Customs Union to be adopted.

[40]   Vadim Visloguzov, 'Kodeks Razdora', *Kommersant*, Nr 108/P, 21 June 2010; Mikhail Nesterov, 'Poteri I priobreteniya: Biznes vyskazal svoi pretenzii k organizatsii Tamozhennogo soyuza', *Rossiiskaya Gazeta*, 5 October 2010.

[41]   See list at http://www.tsouz.ru/Docs/IntAgrmnts/Pages/Perechen_MDTS.aspx (accessed 15 January 2013).

[42]   There are six decisions of the Commission of the Customs Union and two decisions of the Collegium of the EEC applicable to customs valuation: see http://www.customs-union.com (accessed 12 January 2013). For more on the complexity of the valuation rules, see Alexander Kosov, 'Valuation Rules of the Customs Union', *The Moscow Times*, 30 November 2010.

[43]   Galina Dontsova, 'Assessment of How the Customs Union is Working', *The Moscow Times*, 29 November 2011, reporting on an Ernst & Young survey of major foreign investors.

[44]   Federal Customs Service of the Russian Federation, News Update, 23 July 2012, http://master-www.customs.ru/index.php?option=com_newsfts&view=fresh&id=57&Itemid=1948 (accessed 23 December 2012). According to this information, the drafting group has approved 370 changes in 222 articles of the Code.

Thus, it can be argued that, as far as the substance of customs regulation is concerned, the ECU regime has contributed to a legislative reform along the lines of international law. Yet, the drafting approach leaves open the potential problems of overlap between scores of agreements. This is exacerbated by the practice of carrying forward old agreements, such as the 1995 CU agreements, which were clearly adopted in a very different political and regulatory context. While this is best described as a token of politically significant continuity, it does not amount to a simplified, business-friendly legal regime.

3.1.3. The ECU treaty basis and the WTO

As discussed by Connolly in Chapter 4 of this volume, during the accession of the Russian Federation to the WTO there was particular concern about the interaction between the ECU and WTO regimes, especially in terms of avoiding conflict between rules and ensuring the implementation of WTO obligations.[45] The interaction between the two regimes was addressed in the Treaty on the Functioning of the Customs Union in the Multilateral System, which entered into force in November 2011. It ensures that the provisions of the WTO agreement, as set out in the Accession Protocol of a state which is a member of the ECU, become an integral part of its legal framework as of the date of accession of that state. In addition, member states are obliged to ensure that existing, as well as future, ECU international agreements and decisions comply with the WTO regime, even in the case of non-WTO members. WTO law will prevail over any conflicting ECU provisions, thus introducing a dimension to the ECU regime that distinguishes it sharply from any previous initiatives.

3.2. Decisions of Bodies

The decisions of the cooperation bodies are another key source of the common regime. Their legal status is of principal importance in describing the regime in view of the ambitious supranational delegation within the ECU. Given the differences in the institutional design of the Interstate Council and the permanent regulatory body of the ECU already mentioned, their acts are examined in turn. The focus here is on the binding effect of these acts and the degree to which they can be deemed to be part of the treaty basis of the ECU.

---

[45] Accession Report, above note 36, section 43.

3.2.1. Decisions of the Interstate Council

The decisions of the Interstate Councils of post-Soviet integration regimes have typically been defined as 'binding'. Yet there have been important variations in terms of the meaning attributed to the binding effect and the domestic effect of Council decisions. For example, the decisions of the CIS Council of Heads of State and Government were defined as 'binding',[46] where the term was interpreted as 'binding in the manner of international law'. This meant that decisions had the status of international agreements, and were thus subject to ratification or other procedure for transformation into domestic law, unless they were of a political, declaratory nature.[47] In contrast, the CU-95 project sought to adopt EU-style supranationalism by granting direct effect to certain decisions. Making strong reference to the EU terminology, the 1999 Treaty on the Customs Union and the Single Economic Space provided that the Council may adopt (i) decisions (*resheniya*), which are binding in their entirety and subject to direct implementation (*neposredstvennoe primenenie*) by the member states; (ii) resolutions (*rezolyutsii*), which are binding as to the result to be achieved leaving the member state to choose the form and method of implementation; and (iii) non-binding recommendations *(rekomendatsii)*.[48] Yet the similarity between decisions and their EU template remained semantic. A few months later, in another agreement 'direct implementation' was defined as 'through transformation into the national legislation of member states', thus reverting to the view that decisions are binding as international agreements.[49] The EvrAzES Treaty of 2000 emphasized the continuity with the previously existing organs of the Customs Union and the agreements concluded within it.[50] It addressed the issue of the binding effect, reaffirming the

---

[46]   Art. 12 of the Agreement on the Temporary Rules of the Council of 15 May 1992 and Art. 20 of the Procedural Rules of the Council adopted by a Decision of 17 May 1996 also envisaged the possibility for issuing directly applicable acts.

[47]   Dragneva, above note 2. As discussed there, the distinction between 'normative' and 'political' decisions was not necessarily easy.

[48]   Art. 58. Art. 24 of the Agreement on Deepening Integration in the Economic and Humanitarian Area of 29 March 1996 also envisaged acts subject to direct implementation.

[49]   Agreement on the Legal Guarantees for the Formation of the Customs Union and the Single Economic Space of 26 October 1999, Art. 8. Similarly, the agreement refers to the introduction (*vvedeniya*) by national parliaments and governments of the decisions and the resolutions of the Councils.

[50]   EvrAzES Treaty, above note 9, Preamble and Art. 3; also Decision Nr 2 of the Interstate Council, 31 May 2001.

'international law' position by stating that decisions are implemented 'through the adoption of the necessary domestic normative acts in accordance with national legislation'.[51]

The twists and turns described illustrate the problems of incremental and fragmented institutional design, and the challenges to interpretation resulting from it even with regard to key constitutional issues such the status of Council decisions. All of this matters to the analysis of the ECU as the issue of the legal status of the decisions of the Interstate Council, functioning as the 'highest organ of the Customs Union', was not revised in the key documents regulating the Council – that is, the amendments to the EvrAzES Treaty or the amended Rules of Procedure of the Council.[52]

Looking at the functioning of the ECU, there has been a swing away from the EvrAzES formula in that Council decisions are treated as directly binding without ratification. The issue has not led to practical problems; yet it is of more than doctrinal importance. Some decisions of the Council are of a declaratory nature, but others embody substantive undertakings – of an economic as well as an institutional nature.[53] A critical institutional issue, for example, relating to the domestic legal force of the decisions of the Commission of the Customs Union was dealt with not in an international agreement but in a Council decision.[54] Apart from the domestic constitutional questions this raises (and which are not discussed here), the issue is that such decisions are not an explicit part of the treaty basis of the ECU. This is even more confusing in view of the contrast with the decisions of the Eurasian Economic Commission which, as discussed below, are defined as belonging to the treaty basis of the Customs Union and Single Economic Space and subject to direct application in the territories of the member states. This lack of legal clarity is symptomatic of the casual, 'make and mend' approach to the institutional design.

---

[51] EvrAzES Treaty, ibid., Art. 14. This view was upheld in Consultative Resolution Nr 01-1/3-05 of the Economic Court of the CIS (sitting as a Court of EvrAzES), 10 March 2006. It concluded that none of the constitutions of the EvrAzES member states provided for an act of an international body to have direct effect (i.e. without domestic transformation) as a source of law in these countries.

[52] Equally confusingly the 1999 Treaty on the Customs Union and SES and the 2000 EvrAzES Treaty are included in Part One of the treaty basis of the ECU, whereas the Agreement on the Legal Guarantees for the Formation of the CU and the SES of 26 October 1999 is not.

[53] The powers of the HOCU are defined in the Regulation of the Interstate Council as amended by Decision Nr 378 of 10 October 2008.

[54] Decision Nr 15, above note 15.

3.2.2. Decisions of the permanent regulatory body

The Commission of the Customs Union, the permanently functioning regulatory organ of the ECU, was the only new body established in 2007. Given the importance of this body in running the integration project, its very effectiveness was associated with the need to ensure that the Commission's decisions are made binding on the member states of the ECU. Thus, for the first time in the post-Soviet period, provision was made for decisions to formally enter into force within a month of their official publication[55] and, as of that date, to become 'binding' on the member states.[56] Such acts do not have to be transformed into national law – they automatically become part of it. A Decision of the Interstate Council provides further that 'such decisions are subject to direct application in the member states of the customs union' and have legal force equivalent to that of the acts issued by these state organs and officials of the member states competent to regulate the issues transferred to the Commission of the Customs Union.[57] Their legal force and rank then depend on which national body regulated it prior to the transfer of competence to the Commission. If this was a government agency – for example, the Federal Customs Service in Russia – then the Commission's act will have a status equivalent to the acts of that agency. This is a practical design solution but, yet again, not necessarily an easy one for economic actors to decipher.

The same approach was followed in the design of the Eurasian Economic Commission that was set up in 2011 as the 'single permanently functioning regulatory body of the Customs Union and the Single Economic Space'.[58] The EEC may issue two types of act within its competence: (i) decisions, which are binding on the member states, and (ii) recommendations, which are non-binding on the member states. The decisions are published officially on the Commission website. They enter into force 30 calendar days after the date of the official publication, unless anything to the contrary is provided in an international agreement.

---

[55] The rules on official publication were dealt with in the Rules of Procedure, approved by Decision Nr 15 (above note 15), and Art. 2 of the Protocol amending and supplementing the Treaty on the Commission of the Customs Union of 6 October 2007, 9 December 2010.

[56] Treaty on the Commission of the Customs Union, 6 October 2007, Arts 7 and 8. Section 29 of the Rules of Procedure of the Commission of the Customs Union, adopted by Decision Nr 15 (above note 15) also refers to recommendations, which are of non-binding nature.

[57] Decision Nr 15, above note 15, section 4.

[58] Treaty on the EEC, above note 20, Art. 1.

In extraordinary circumstances this period can be shorter, but not less than ten days following official publication.[59]

Thus, the permanent regulator of the ECU may issue binding decisions, which are also publicly available. Importantly, decisions become part of the treaty basis of the ECU and SES, thus adding clarity to the scope of the legal regime.[60]

4. SUPRANATIONAL DELEGATION

Chapter 2 of this volume devotes considerable attention to the origin and development of the coordination bodies of Eurasian economic integration. The discussion shows that the setting up of the permanent executive – the Integration Committee of EvrAzES as well as the Commission of the Customs Union and its successor, the Eurasian Economic Commission – was subject to significant negotiation. Nonetheless, there has been a clear move towards extensive delegation to a developed supranational bureaucracy which purports to overcome the asymmetry in its decision-making.

Table 3.2   The evolution of the permanent executive organ in Eurasian integration

	Member states' representation level	Mode of decision-making	Vote distribution
Integration Committee	Deputy head of government	Two-thirds majority	Weighted: Russia – 40, Belarus and Kazakhstan – 20 each, Kyrgyz Republic and Tajikistan – 10 each
Commission of the Customs Union	Deputy head or member of government	Two-thirds majority or consensus	Weighted: Russia – 57, Belarus and Kazakhstan – 21.5 each
Eurasian Economic Commission			
Council	Deputy heads of government	Consensus	Equal votes
Collegium	Independent professionals	Two-thirds majority or consensus	Equal votes

---

[59]   Ibid., Art. 5(3).
[60]   Ibid., Art. 5(1).

The Integration Committee of EvrAzES was not granted extensive competences, although these could be extended by the Interstate Council. Its main powers relate to facilitating the decision-making of the Council of heads of state and government as the primary decision-making forum by preparing drafts and monitoring the implementation of its decisions.[61] Further, the diversity between member states, and Russia's dominant position in particular, was clearly reflected in the decision-making rules of the Integration Committee. It operated on the basis of weighted voting affording 40 votes to Russia, 20 votes each to Belarus and Kazakhstan, and 10 votes each to the Kyrgyz Republic and Tajikistan.[62] The 2000 Treaty made the politically significant gesture of empowering the Committee to decide by a two-thirds majority. Yet the distribution of votes meant that no decision may be taken without Russia's consent. In such cases it was provided that if four member states have voted but no overall majority has been achieved, the decision is referred to the Interstate Council to be decided by consensus. In effect, Russia has a guaranteed veto within the organization. At the same time, it is also clear that for a decision to be passed, Russia always has to secure the cooperation of at least two, and sometimes three, other countries. Similarly, the effectiveness of majority voting was reduced by the limited competence of the permanent executive.

Although there was little change in the competence of the Interstate Council as the Highest Organ of the Customs Union,[63] the Commission of the Customs Union was clearly designed as a more important body than the Integration Committee. Its powers were defined in its founding Treaty and could be expanded by a decision or subsequent delegation (if provided by an international agreement) of the Interstate Council. The Commission prepared drafts for the Council and implemented its decisions.[64] It also had the power to monitor the overall implementation of the international agreements concluded within the ECU and assist member states in resolving disputes prior to turning to the EvrAzES Court. Given the proliferation of international agreements within the Customs Union, however, the powers of the Commission with regard to

---

[61]   EvrAzES Treaty, above note 9, Art. 6. Also Regulation of the Integration Committee of EvrAzES, approved by Decision Nr 6 of the Interstate Council of EvrAzES, 31 May 2001.

[62]   EvrAzES Treaty, ibid., Art. 13.

[63]   Regulation of the Interstate Council of EvrAzES as amended by Decision Nr 378 of the Intergovernmental Council of EvrAzES, 10 October 2008.

[64]   Treaty on the Commission of the Customs Union, 6 October 2007, Art. 6.

customs regulation accumulated rather incrementally. Given the fragmented nature of the treaty basis of the ECU discussed above, it could be
argued that these powers were not clearly outlined.

The Commission of the Customs Union continued the practice of the
EvrAzES when it came to voting power and decision-making. Member
states' votes were weighted (57 votes for Russia and 21.5 votes each for
Belarus and Kazakhstan) and decisions required a two-thirds majority.
Similarly, Russia's dominant position was guaranteed: the votes of the
other two member states could never amount to a two-thirds majority.[65]
In addition, if one member state disagreed with the decision, it was to be
referred to the Interstate Council. At the same time, Russia could not pass
a decision on its own. In fact, every country had a veto in the
Commission with the effect that any issue could be referred for a
decision by the highest decision-making body by consensus, thus negating the idea of supranational delegation. At any rate, the scope of the
Commission's majority decision-making was limited, with the requirement for consensus on 'sensitive' decisions.[66]

By comparison, the design of the Eurasian Economic Commission
represents a more radical step towards the formation of a developed
supranational bureaucracy entrusted with extensive functions. The upper
tier of the Commission (the Council) is defined as the body providing
'the general regulation of integration processes ... as well as the general
management of the activities of the Commission'.[67] It is responsible for
taking the key decisions of the common customs policy, such as tariff and
non-tariff regulation, licensing, and technical standards, but also decisions in relation to the main areas of cooperation and harmonization
within the SES.[68] Importantly, the opportunity was taken to summarize
the competences transferred to the common permanent body in the
various international agreements. While the powers of the High Eurasian
Economic Council, as the principal policy-making body of integration,
remain unchanged, as previously noted, it can be observed that it is not

---

[65]   Ibid., Art. 7.

[66]   For example, in relation to maintaining the tariffs of 'sensitive goods',
which are those identified in lists approved by the Interstate Council: Agreement
on Common Customs and Tariff Regulation, 21 January 2008, Art. 8(3).

[67]   Treaty on the EEC, above note 20, Art. 8.

[68]   Rules of the EEC, Appendix 'Functions and competences of the Council'.

the HEEC but the Council of the EEC that has been the most active decision-making body in substantive terms since its inception.[69]

The Collegium is defined as the 'executive organ' of the Commission and is seen as a professional body independent of the member states.[70] Collegium members are nominated by, and should be, citizens of the member states. Their appointment and distribution of portfolios is approved by the HEEC. In EU-style, however, it is provided that in carrying out their duties they should remain independent of those states and cannot request or receive directions from state organs or officials of member states.[71]

A further important development represents the enhanced enforcement power of the Commission in relation to the implementation of the international agreements forming the treaty basis of the Customs Union and the Single Economic Space and the decisions of the Commission. If there are grounds to believe that a member state is not implementing these, the Collegium may by a two-thirds majority issue a notification informing the member state of the need for mandatory compliance within a reasonable period of time.[72] If the member state fails to comply, the Collegium brings the matter before the Council of the EEC. Ultimately, the Collegium may lodge a complaint with the Court of EvrAzES.

Another significant change relates to the composition of the Eurasian Economic Commission, which signals a departure from the principle of weighted voting. The Council's three members each have one vote. Thus, for the first time, the decision-making rules make it possible for Russia to be outvoted. Similarly, in the Collegium each of its nine members – three from each country – carries one vote. Importantly, the Collegium may take decisions by a two-thirds majority or consensus.[73] The distribution of votes means that, again, any country can be overridden.

---

[69] For example, in 2012 the Council of the EEC held 13 sessions adopting 125 decisions, whereas the HEEC met twice adopting 12 decisions: see http://www.tsouz.ru/eek/Pages/default.aspx (accessed 25 January 2013).

[70] Treaty on the EEC, above note 20, Art. 14.

[71] Ibid., Art. 15. They must have a suitable professional qualification with not less than seven years of relevant experience, with at least one year in government.

[72] Ibid., Art. 20.

[73] In order to take a decision the Collegium needs to be quorate – i.e. at least two-thirds of its members (i.e. 6) need to be present and there should be at least one member from each member state present: Rules of the EEC, above note 21, section 58.

Yet, the effect of this equal basis is that supranational delegation is mitigated in several important ways. Firstly, the consensus requirement for decisions of the Council of the EEC preserves the veto right of every country, including Russia. If no consensus can be reached at the level of the Council of the Commission, then the matter is brought before the HEEC. Secondly, the range of issues which the Collegium may decide by a two-thirds majority is restricted. These issues are specifically determined by the international agreements of the Customs Union and SES, and the decisions of the HEEC that relate to such matters not falling within the explicit powers of the Council.[74] Accordingly, potentially contentious decisions have been placed with the Council and not the Collegium. Thirdly, any member state or member of the Council of the EEC can query any decision of the Collegium,[75] and can propose amendments or request its revocation within ten days of the adoption of the decision. The matter is then examined by the Council of the Commission. If the member state is still dissatisfied with the decision of the Council, it can be brought before the HEEC. In any event, a head of government may bring before the HEEC any decision of the EEC (Council or Collegium) which has not entered into force. This provision aims to set up a clear schedule for the possibility of amending or revoking decisions.

Thus, potentially all issues are subject to veto and negotiation at the highest level of political decision-making.

5. DISPUTE RESOLUTION: THE COURT OF EVRAZES

The availability of a third party, permanent dispute resolution body is typically associated with a high degree of juridicization of international relations.[76] The CIS has been quite unusual in comparative terms in providing for such a body through the Economic Court of the CIS. Yet, there have been a number of factors that mitigate its importance as a dispute resolution mechanism within the CIS. As discussed at length elsewhere, the mandate of the Economic Court in relation to both the type of dispute that can be brought before it and the scope of the subjects who may lodge them has been found lacking.[77] Most importantly, the

---

[74] Rules of the EEC, ibid., Appendix.
[75] Treaty on the EEC, above note 20, Art. 13.
[76] McCall Smith, above note 3.
[77] G. Danilenko, 'The Economic Court of the CIS' (1999) 4 *NYU Journal of International Law and Politics* 893–918; Dragneva, above note 2.

decisions of the Court have no binding force, but are recommended for adoption by the country found to be in violation.[78] In any event, the Economic Court has been underused as a dispute resolution body and there have been a very small number of disputes brought before it. Most of its rulings relate to the interpretation of acts of the CIS.[79] This can be attributed to the preference for diplomatic solutions, but also to the negative perception of the Court. In the words of none other than the Kazakh President Nazarbaev, 'nobody … pays any attention to the decisions adopted by the Court'.[80]

As noted, the EvrAzES Treaty provided for a special judicial body of the organization. Yet there seemed to be no rush in actually setting it up, nor was there any great ambition in departing from the CIS design. The Statute of the Court of EvrAzES was ultimately adopted in April 2003.[81] Like the Economic Court of the CIS, the EvrAzES Court was empowered to resolve interstate economic disputes arising from the application (*primenenie*) of EvrAzES international agreements and the decisions of its bodies and the implementation of the obligations (*ispolnenii obiazatel'stva*) arising from such agreements and decisions. The decisions of the Court are not explicitly defined as binding. The Statute provides that every state undertakes to fulfil the decisions of the Court and that implementation takes place according to domestic legislation.[82] Further, the decision was taken in the autumn of 2003 for the Economic Court of the CIS to fulfil the functions of the EvrAzES Court.[83] This was the position inherited on the founding of the ECU in 2007. In fact, until the formation of the EvrAzES Court in 2012, the CIS Court's engagement as an EvrAzES Court was minimal.[84]

---

[78] Agreement on the Status of the Economic Court, 6 July 1992, Art. 3(4).

[79] In the period from 1994 to December 2012, only about 10 per cent of rulings relate to inter-state disputes: see http://sudsng.org/database/sudobzor (accessed 18 December 2012). The information includes cases where the Economic Court acted as the Court of the EvrAzES.

[80] Statement at the Council of Heads of State summit in Astana, *Rossiiskaya Gazeta*, 17 September 2004.

[81] Statute of the Court of EvrAzES, approved by Decision Nr 122 of the Interstate Council of EvrAzES, 27 April 2003 (hereafter '2003 Statute').

[82] 2003 Statute, ibid., Art. 6.

[83] Decision of the Council of Heads of Government of the CIS, 19 September 2003; Agreement between EvrAzES and the CIS, 3 March 2004.

[84] The Court sat twice: (i) to interpret the 2000 EvrAzES Treaty: Consultative Resolution Nr 01-1/3-05, 10 March 2006, and (ii) to resolve the dispute brought by Belarus against Russia in levying export tariffs on oil and petrochemicals: Ruling Nr 01-1-E/2-10, 20 April 2011. The latter, as discussed by

Strengthening the dispute resolution mechanism was important for the ECU. A new Statute of the Court was adopted in July 2010 to coincide with the launch of the Customs Union.[85] There were several improvements. Firstly, the substantive competence of the Court was extended to include: (i) examining the conformity of the decisions of the ECU bodies with the treaty basis of the Customs Union; (ii) disputes arising out of acts or omissions of the bodies; and (iii) disputes between the Commission and the member states, as well as between the member states, in relation to the implementation of duties undertaken within the Customs Union.[86] This competence may be expanded with relation to disputes envisaged in separate international agreements.

Secondly, in addition to member states and the bodies of the Customs Union, commercial actors were allowed to lodge an appeal with the Court. This right was envisaged in the 2010 Statute and further regulated in a special Agreement of December 2010.[87] In principle, this right was seen as essential for the effective functioning of the ECU and could be pivotal in ensuring the rule-based functioning of the ECU as it gives a useful remedy to private parties. It is worth noting that in the year since the EvrAzES Court started to function, there have been two such private appeals, both resulting in the claim against the Commission of the Customs Union being upheld.[88]

Thirdly, the decisions of the Court are defined as binding on the parties to a dispute. Certainly the first case before the Court shows that the EEC has complied with the ruling of the Court finding against it.[89] The domestic constitutional meaning of this binding effect and its implications for compliance, however, requires further investigation. Article 20(2) of the 2010 Statute provides that if decisions are not implemented within the given time period, the party can turn to the Interstate Council of EvrAzES for a decision on the matter. Thus, it is high-level political decision-making that remains the ultimate measure of legally binding obligation.

Frear in Chapter 7 of this volume, was ultimately resolved through a bilateral agreement.

[85]   Statute of the Court of EvrAzES, approved by Decision Nr 502 of the Interstate Council of EvrAzES, 5 July 2010 (hereafter '2010 Statute').

[86]   2010 Statute, ibid., Art. 13(4).

[87]   Treaty on the Application of Commercial Subjects to the Court of the EvrAzES in relation to Disputes within the Customs Union, 9 December 2010.

[88]   Decisions of the Collegium of the EvrAzES Court, 5 September 2012 and 15 November 2012, and of the Appeals Chamber, 29 November 2012.

[89]   Decision Nr 7 of the Collegium of the EEC, 23 January 2013.

Finally, there have been particular concerns about the extent to which the Court will remain independent from political interference and pressure from vested interests. Certainly, at the level of legal regulation, the Statute makes a number of provisions with regard to the independence of judges from political and commercial interests. However, it remains to be seen what kind of reputation the Court will develop.

6. CONCLUSIONS

The examination of the legal and institutional framework for Eurasian integration strongly supports the view that tangible steps have been taken to ensure that the ECU is a highly legalized regime. This move suggests a break with the past in a number of ways. First, the preference for relations to be governed by a legally binding framework of international agreements and decisions is explicit. Second, there is extensive delegation to a common coordination body, the Eurasian Economic Commission, which has become a developed international bureaucracy. The effectiveness of the Commission as a regulator has yet to be evidenced, although it has shown promise in its short life. There is much greater transparency in publishing decisions and other acts than was the case under the EvrAzES or CIS regimes. Third, there exists a mechanism for third-party dispute resolution to which private parties may resort. The very early practice of the Court, to the extent that it can be judged, suggests that it is able to process cases rapidly and is pro-business.

Thus, in terms of the institutional set-up of the regime, developments reflect extensive institutional learning from the integration experience over the last two decades. In terms of the substance of the regime, a common customs regime has been adopted and a significant reform of domestic customs regulation has followed. The improvements also reflect alignment with international norms and best practices.

At the same time, it is important to stress that this detailed analysis has also revealed a number of critical institutional fault lines, which constrain the move to legality and reduce the benefits to business as well as soften the extent to which member states are bound by the common regime. In sum, these fault lines are rooted in what can be described as a fragmented, incrementally developing, and frequently changing legal and institutional regime.

The fragmentation that results from relying on multiple agreements and decisions creates a complex, voluminous and potentially incoherent regime, which presents significant challenges. While there was an effort to delineate the treaty basis of the project, this has proved to be difficult with the accumulation of agreements. It is true that the preference for multiple agreements as opposed to comprehensive accords is not unique in international practice. Arguably, such an approach reduces the negotiating costs of integration. Yet, the sheer complexity of the regime and the extensive reliance on cross-referencing is likely to result in mistakes, gaps and conflicting interpretations. It puts pressure on domestic institutions – administrative as well as judicial bodies – which, in the post-Soviet context, are already challenged in terms of capacity, as is also pointed out by Connolly in Chapter 4 of this volume.

Importantly, the problems of fragmentation are exacerbated by their combination with the pattern of incremental change. As noted, institutional changes have been introduced in pragmatic ways with an eye to achieving results. Despite the institutional learning, this pragmatism has tended to be quite 'relaxed'. As demonstrated, the outcome has meant significant legal uncertainties. While the resulting regime may be relished by commercial lawyers and bureaucrats, it is very doubtful that it will deliver the simplification and predictability desired by economic actors.

This problem can be viewed as transitional in view of the pending revisions of the Code and the planned codification of the legislation of the Customs Union and SES. Yet, the fate of this promise is as yet unclear. Its fulfilment may be hindered by the tradition of fragmented and incremental design evident throughout the post-Soviet period. Comprehensive improvement may also be sacrificed in a rush to meet the targets of a fast-developing political agenda. At the same time, the context of continuous institutional reform (with yet another round looming in the context of the preparation for the Eurasian Economic Union) makes long-term planning and business development costly and uncertain.

This chapter also explored the question of the degree to which the move to legality is likely to bind Russia as the regional hegemon to a multilateral rule-based regime. The set-up of the ECU suggests that many of the sovereignty sensitivities of the past have been overcome, resulting in extensive delegation to common regulatory bodies. The Commission of the Customs Union and especially the Eurasian Economic Commission have been endowed with extensive powers accompanied by a corresponding loss in unilateral policy-making. Importantly, in terms of formal institutional design, Russia has opted to be bound by a framework of decision-making where it is an equal amongst equals. In combination with the strengthened enforcement through the Court of EvrAzES, this suggests a break with the past.

Yet, it is clear that high-level politics and diplomatic resolution remain critical both in relation to the decisions of the EEC and the ultimate enforcement of the rulings of the Court. Even more importantly, the binding commitment of member states has been tempered by the nature of the institutional design described above. Given the complex legal regime and the challenges to its implementation, practical integration critically depends on supplementary coordination mechanisms – political as well as relational – to ensure its sustainability. Similarly, the frequent revisions of the Eurasian project's bodies and rules signal that no commitment is non-negotiable.

Thus, while the achievements in developing the legal regime of Eurasian integration to date are noteworthy, they also show the primacy of an ambitious political agenda for cooperation. Whether this agenda will be conducive to eliminating the institutional deficiencies of the common regime and facilitating economic growth remains to be seen. The broader implications of these findings are explored in the concluding chapter of this volume.

4. Russia, the Eurasian Customs Union and the WTO

Richard Connolly

1. INTRODUCTION

On 10 July 2012 the Russian parliament voted to ratify Russia's accession to the World Trade Organization (WTO). This ended the rather anomalous absence of the world's largest country from the regime governing global trade. Before accession, Russia was the only member of the G20 that was not a WTO member, and it possessed the largest economy in the world that was not a member. By joining the WTO, Russia committed to bringing its trade laws and practices into compliance with WTO rules. These commitments include: non-discriminatory treatment of imports of goods and services, binding tariff levels, ensuring transparency when implementing trade measures, limiting agriculture subsidies, enforcing intellectual property rights for foreign holders of such rights, and forgoing the use of local content requirements and other trade-related investment measures. In the future, Russia will, through WTO dispute settlement procedures, be accountable to other members for fulfilling its WTO commitments. Russia will also be in a position to hold other WTO partners accountable for adhering to WTO rules, thus minimizing discrimination against Russian producers on world markets. Russia will also have the opportunity to play an important role in shaping the development of the international trade regime.

Russia's road to accession, however, became complicated in October 2007 when Russia announced the formation of the Eurasian Customs Union (ECU) with Belarus and Kazakhstan, both of whom were, and remain, outside the WTO. As a result, Russia's accession was held up by the need to ensure that ECU rules were consistent with WTO rules. In addition, Russia's initial proposal – subsequently rejected – that the three countries enter the WTO as a group, and not as individual countries, also contributed to the delay in Russia's accession. Ultimately, Russia was able to join the WTO on the condition that the terms agreed for Russia's

accession would not be contradicted by the rules and commitments
governing the ECU and the wider process of the creation of a Eurasian
Economic Union (EEU). Therefore, the simultaneous implementation of
two international policy commitments – the creation of the ECU, itself
part of a wider move towards regional integration under the aegis of the
Eurasian Economic Community (EvrAzES), and the Russian accession to
the WTO – both have important implications for the ECU and regional
integration more generally. In very simple terms, the trade-related aspects
of regional integration within EvrAzES are and will continue to be
shaped by the terms of Russia's agreement to join the WTO. In effect, the
formal WTO institutional framework (being trade-related commitments,
such as tariff levels and rules on market access) will function as the basis
for the development of the ECU. This was necessary as failure to ensure
that ECU rules complied with WTO commitments would have precluded
accession for all ECU countries.

This chapter will examine how Russia's terms of accession to the
WTO are likely to affect the evolution of the ECU and Eurasian
integration more widely, with an emphasis on the prospects for economic
reform and the likelihood of successful implementation of the ECU and
the WTO rules. The first section explores the extent to which the WTO
(and the goal of accession to it) has been a driving force in the formation
of the ECU, arguing that the multilateral trading regime has, to this point,
served as a reference point for the functioning of the ECU, at least as far
as trade-related rules are concerned, and is likely to continue to do so for
the foreseeable future. The second section describes how Russia's
membership of the WTO will be likely to affect the three members of the
ECU, both in terms of the effects on economic activity and on the
prospects for economic reform. Section 3 outlines some of the potential
obstacles to implementation of the commitments to both the ECU and the
WTO made by the three countries, which may diminish any potential
gains that might come from increased regional and global integration.

Overall, the chapter will argue that the WTO has played, and will
continue to play, a key role in shaping trade-related opportunities and
constraints for the ECU (as has been the case with other regional
agreements such as NAFTA, Mercosur and the European Union). However, we should be wary of the distinction between *de jure* commitments
made by countries under multilateral agreements – such as the WTO and
the ECU – and the capacity of states to adhere *de facto* to these
commitments. In countries characterized by relatively low levels of state
administrative capacity, as is the case with all three ECU countries, the
effects of accession to multilateral agreements are likely to be muted. As
such, neither WTO accession nor the creation of the ECU are likely to

result in significant gains – whether in the form of improved governance or in increased economic output – for Russia, Belarus or Kazakhstan. Instead, domestic processes will remain the most important factors in shaping the potential for positive economic and political change across the region.

2. THE WTO AND THE ECU: PARALLEL PROCESSES OF DEVELOPMENT

Negotiations over the terms of accession to the WTO for all three countries have been taking place since 1993.[1] Only Russia has so far been successful, joining on 22 August 2012. As the three countries have negotiated with the WTO, efforts have been under way, in one form or another, since 1995 to create a customs union in the former Soviet space. First, in January 1995, the same three countries created a customs union. Despite subsequent enlargement to incorporate Tajikistan (1996) and Kyrgyzstan (1997), the first attempt at customs union was largely a failure. In the event that it had been implemented, Russia would have benefited disproportionately from transfers from Central Asian countries, which had to buy either lower quality or higher priced Russian manufactured goods under the tariff umbrella.[2] In addition, the legal framework was fragmented and weak.

After the initial failure of moves towards a functioning customs union, negotiations were restarted in 2006. By October 2007, Belarus, Kazakhstan and Russia agreed to establish the Eurasian Customs Union with the hope that it would help to forge closer economic ties between the three countries. On 1 January 2010 the import tariffs of the three countries were harmonized into a single common external tariff for third countries. With very few exceptions, the initial common external tariff schedule was the Russian tariff schedule. As such, for Russia relatively few tariff lines changed, but for Kazakhstan approximately 60 per cent of items were affected, despite having negotiated exceptions from the common external

---

[1]   Russia was the first country to lodge an official application to join the WTO in June 1993. Soon after, Belarus applied on 23 September 1993. Kazakhstan applied later, on 29 January 1996. See also Appendix 2.

[2]   David Tarr, 'The Eurasian Customs Union among Russia, Belarus and Kazakhstan: Can It Succeed Where Its Predecessor Failed?', *FREE Policy Brief Series* (Stockholm Institute of Transition Economics, 11 May 2012).

tariff for just over 400 tariff lines.[3] In July 2010, the three countries ratified a Customs Code and other documents forming the regulatory base of the union, which began by harmonizing not only tariffs, but also procedures and non-tariff regulations. Internal border controls were removed too. Import tariff revenues are now pooled and disbursed to national budgets according to predetermined levels that are subject to periodic review.[4]

The formation of the reinvigorated ECU did not occur without reference to the respective WTO accession processes of the three countries. Indeed, at first the creation of the ECU caused further delay in Russia's protracted accession to the WTO as in June 2009 Russia's then Prime Minister, Vladimir Putin, floated the idea of entering the WTO not as a single entity but alongside Belarus and Kazakhstan as a single customs union bloc.[5] Later, erstwhile President Medvedev stated that joint accession was, in fact, not necessary and, after it was made clear to Russia that WTO accession would be held up if it insisted on bloc entry, Russia reverted to individual accession negotiations, completing them in December 2011.[6] To assuage any fears of the WTO that the ECU would compromise the application of WTO regulations in Russia or elsewhere, Russian negotiators made a commitment to ensure that the ECU would be complementary to its WTO obligations.[7]

The formal relationship between the ECU and the WTO was outlined in the Treaty on the Functioning of the Customs Union in the Multilateral System, which entered into force in November 2011, immediately before Russia concluded its accession negotiations with the WTO. The Treaty provides that the provisions of the WTO agreement, as set out in the Accession Protocol of a Customs Union state, become an integral part of the legal framework of the Customs Union as of the date of the accession of that member state (Article 1). At the time, this opened the door to the

---

[3]   And in most cases tariffs increased because Kazakhstan possessed the more liberal trade regime upon the creation of the ECU. Those tariff lines where Kazakhstan negotiated exceptions were to be phased out over a period of five years.

[4]   Russia receives 88 per cent of all revenues; Belarus, 5 per cent; and Kazakhstan, 7 per cent.

[5]   A. Shapovalov, 'Bargaining at Triple the Stakes', *Kommersant*, 10 June 2009, 3.

[6]   P. Netreba and D. Butrin, 'Three's a Crowd: Russia Is Returning to Unilateral Negotiations with the WTO', *Kommersant*, 11 July 2009, 1.

[7]   Richard Connolly and Philip Hanson, 'Russia's Accession to the World Trade Organization: Commitments, Processes, and Prospects' (2012) 53(4) *Eurasian Geography and Economics* 479.

conclusion of Russian accession negotiations, but it also laid out a clear framework for any subsequent entry to the WTO by Belarus or Kazakhstan, with the Treaty stating that member states of the Customs Union are obliged to ensure that trade-related aspects of the ECU framework – both existing and in the future – comply with the WTO regime.

Using the trade-related WTO rules as the basis for the evolution of the ECU is significant for economic reasons. Belarus and Kazakhstan have agreed that the common external tariff of the Customs Union will change to accommodate Russia's WTO commitments. As a result, the applied unweighted average tariff will fall in stages from 10.9 per cent in 2012 to 7.9 per cent by the year 2020.[8] The new ECU, like the previous attempt at customs union, employs the Russian tariff, which is higher than that of Kazakhstan. However, because of Russia's recent accession to the WTO, the tariff of the Customs Union will fall by around half, rendering the ECU a more open customs union. This will significantly reduce transfers from Kazakhstan to Russia and, according to Tarr, 'thereby reduce the pressures from producers and consumers in Kazakhstan on their government to depart from enforcement of the tariffs of the Customs Union'.[9]

In addition, it was also agreed that the common tariff would serve as a goods schedule for any subsequent entry to the WTO by Belarus and Kazakhstan, although the two countries would still be required to negotiate their own separate schedules for services and non-tariff measures. This means that Belarus and Kazakhstan will be obliged to meet WTO commitments similar to those undertaken by Russia, despite not yet being members of the organization themselves.

In principle, the existence of a preferential trade regime on the territory of the ECU member states is not inconsistent with either established international practice or WTO regulations. Indeed, many members of the WTO are engaged in regional trade agreements (RTAs) or, more accurately, preferential trade agreements.[10] The number of such trade agreements increased from approximately 70 in 1990 to almost 300 in

---

[8] Oleksandr Shepotylo and David Tarr, 'Impact of WTO Accession and the Customs Union on the Bound and Applied Tariff Rates of the Russian Federation', *Policy Research Working Paper No. 6161* (World Bank, August 2012).

[9] Tarr, above note 2, 6.

[10] The trade agreements called 'preferential' by the WTO are also known as 'regional', despite not necessarily being concluded by countries within a certain region.

2010.[11] What is different about the ECU case is the fact that both Belarus and Kazakhstan are not yet members of the WTO, yet will be obliged to share a common external tariff with a member, Russia. This means that industries within the two countries will, in principle, be exposed to greater competition (that is, non-ECU) from imports from third countries that are members of the WTO. However, without WTO membership, exporters from Belarus and Kazakhstan will not enjoy greater access to foreign markets. Finally, in the event that the three ECU countries all become members of the WTO, it is possible that they will act as a bloc within the WTO and attempt to shape the evolution of the global trade regime, perhaps in conjunction with any future entrants to the ECU that are also members of the WTO (Kyrgyzstan or Ukraine, for example).[12]

However, beyond the fact that only Russia is currently a member, several other factors weigh against any future assertion of Eurasian influence within the WTO. First, the combined weight of the three countries, in terms of collective gross domestic product (GDP), is extremely modest.[13] Second, all three countries possess markedly different export profiles. Although Russia and Kazakhstan are both major exporters of natural resources, they occupy different segments of global trade in manufacturing.[14] Belarus, on the other hand, has little in the way of raw materials; it has instead so far relied on the imported and underpriced Russian crude oil, which is then refined in Belarus and exported, as well as some medium-technology products, such as tractors and heavy trucks, to sustain its export industry.[15] Consequently, it is more

---

[11]   Data taken from the World Trade Organization's website, http://www.wto.org/english/tratop_e/region_e/region_e.htm (accessed 6 November 2012).

[12]   At the time of writing, Kazakhstan appeared to be closer to accession than Belarus.

[13]   The ECU countries together account for 2.5 per cent of world merchandise trade, compared to 15 per cent for NAFTA, 2 per cent for Mercosur, 6.6 per cent for the ASEAN trade bloc, and 12.5 per cent for the EU's extra-EU trade, or 35.9 per cent for the EU if intra-EU trade is included: author's calculations based on WTO data, http://www.wto.org/english/tratop_e/region_e/region_e.htm (accessed 6 November 2012).

[14]   Richard Connolly, 'The Structure of Russian Industrial Exports in Comparative Perspective' (2008) 49(5) *Eurasian Geography and Economics* 586; Martin Myant and Jan Drahokoupil, 'International Integration and the Structure of Exports in Central Asian Republics' (2008) 49(5) *Eurasian Geography and Economics* 604.

[15]   Richard Connolly, *Economic Structure and Social Order Development in Post-Socialist Eastern Europe* (Routledge, 2012) Chapter 4; World Bank, *Innovation Performance Review: Belarus* (UNECE, 2011).

likely that the three countries will find allies from elsewhere in the organization with whose interests they are aligned. For example, some sub-sectors of the Russian agricultural industry may see their interests aligned more with other members of the Cairns Group than with other ECU members.[16] The practice of countries organizing along sectoral lines is more common within the WTO, and has certainly been in evidence in, for example, countries from other RTAs across the world, such as Mercosur.[17] It is also plausible that ECU members might join the 'recently acceded members' (RAMs) group of countries, which currently includes a large number of ex-socialist countries such as China and Ukraine. The RAMs group seeks reduced commitments to liberalization on the basis that the members have already undertaken significant changes as part of the accession process.

In the short term, the ECU requires formal recognition from the WTO, especially if the Eurasian Economic Commission (EEC) – the executive body of the ECU – is to build a reputation as an important actor, both within the ECU and beyond.[18] Consequently, full membership of the WTO for both Belarus and Kazakhstan will be a requirement and therefore a major goal of the ECU in the coming years. This presents the EEC with an opportunity to gain credibility by ensuring full implementation of WTO commitments throughout the ECU. Without accession, though, Belarus and Kazakhstan will be exposed to increased competition from imports without enjoying the benefits of increased market access

---

[16]   Agricultural issues represent perhaps the most complicated, and apparently intractable, negotiations in the WTO. Indeed, disagreements over agricultural trade continue to block progress in the Doha Round of trade negotiations. Developing countries demand a substantial reduction in, and ultimately elimination of, farm subsidies in developed countries. In comparative terms, Russia does not allocate large subsidies to its agricultural producers, and this is likely to diminish upon implementation of the accession agreement. Consequently, Russia is likely to press for a reduction of farm subsidies in developed economies. On this narrow issue, one might expect Russia to side with the Cairns Group (including Canada, Australia, New Zealand, Brazil) where there is little or no subsidization of agricultural production. It should, however, be noted that in some agricultural sub-sectors (e.g., livestock farming or dairy production) Russia is not competitive. As such, it is unclear just how well aligned the interests of Russia and the Cairns Group are.

[17]   Sam Laird, 'Mercosur: Objectives and Achievements', *Staff Working Paper TPRD-97-02* (WTO, February 1997).

[18]   Olga Shumylo-Tapiola, 'The Eurasian Customs Union: Friend or Foe of the EU?', *The Carnegie Papers* (Carnegie Endowment for International Peace, October 2012) 8.

that is conferred upon WTO members. This might increase the pressure from lobbies within the two countries to opt out of ECU decisions, whether formally or through non-implementation. However, in the event that all three ECU members are part of the WTO, it is by no means clear that they will wish to, and/or be able to, operate effectively within the WTO as a cohesive advocate of any putative Eurasian economic interests.

3. RUSSIA'S ACCESSION TO THE WTO: POTENTIAL EFFECTS ON THE ECU AND ITS MEMBERS

It is difficult at this early stage to know what the combined effects of the creation of the ECU and Russia's accession to the WTO are likely to be. However, if we assume that Belarus and Kazakhstan have 'imported' tariff-related rules as a direct consequence of Russia's accession to the WTO, then we might expect to see those generic consequences of increased trade liberalization that economic theory suggests should be enjoyed by countries that liberalize trade regimes. This section outlines some of the theoretical benefits of trade liberalization, followed by a brief discussion of how this might affect the prospects for economic reform (broadly conceived and henceforth referred to as 'institutional reform') and reducing barriers to foreign direct investment (FDI) in the three countries.

3.1. The Economic Benefits of Trade Liberalization for ECU Countries

The first benefit of trade liberalisation is that lower tariffs should increase trade and enhance consumer choice. According to the European Bank for Reconstruction and Development (EBRD), the immediate 'trade creation' effects of the ECU would mainly reflect the elimination of administrative barriers as customs checks are removed from internal borders.[19] In addition, as a result of Russia's accession to the WTO, consumers in Belarus and Kazakhstan would, like their Russian counterparts, have access to a greater array of goods at more competitive prices.

Second, producers within the ECU might benefit from increased market size, while consumers will also benefit from greater competition in product markets. These effects crucially depend not just on the creation of a single customs area, but also on the elimination of non-tariff

---

[19]   EBRD, *Transition Report 2012* (EBRD, 2012) Chapter 4.

barriers to market access. However, the gains on the producer side are likely to be considerably less than those for consumers since Belarusian and Kazakh producers will gain access to Russia's market, but not to the markets of other WTO members.

A third benefit could emerge from participation in international production networks (or cross-border value-added chains), where producers gain greater access to international supply chains. This has, for example, been a key area of success in other RTAs, such as NAFTA, ASEAN and Mercosur. However, the gains to producers in ECU countries in this area appear to be limited for two reasons. First, as the EBRD notes, 'the structure of exports [within the ECU] suggests that regional production chains with vertical specialisation have yet to evolve'.[20] This is largely a function of the low levels of FDI flows between the three countries. Second, while trade costs for firms within the ECU have declined with the removal of customs posts, measures associated with Russian concerns about trans-shipment have caused the cost of trade with countries outside the ECU to *rise*. This acts as a disincentive for third-country multinational firms to invest in ECU countries.[21]

Thus, for as long as Belarus and Kazakhstan remain outside the WTO, the benefits from the ECU are likely to come from (i) increased access to ECU markets; and (ii) increased consumer choice and competition from imports. Producers in Belarus and Kazakhstan, however, are unlikely to benefit directly (that is, through increased access to foreign markets) although they may benefit indirectly through measures taken to increase competitiveness in response to the threat of greater competition from imports. In other trade-related areas that are not as yet under the purview of the ECU – such as foreign investment regulations and government procurement policies – WTO accession is unlikely to affect either Belarus or Kazakhstan too much, at least in the short term. However, unless progress is made in reducing barriers to FDI, such as those noted above relating to trans-shipment, the prospects for integration with international production networks will remain relatively muted.

---

[20]   Ibid., 62.
[21]   See Tarr, above note 2, 4. Because of concerns relating to trans-shipment of goods from China through Kazakhstan, and from the European Union through Belarus, Russia negotiated and achieved agreement within the ECU on the imposition of stricter controls on the origin of imports from countries outside the Customs Union.

3.2. WTO Accession: Implications for Economic Reform in the ECU Countries

The increased level of international integration achieved through both the creation of an ECU shaped by WTO principles, and also through Russia's accession to the WTO itself, might be expected to help to improve the prospects for economic reform, leading to positive institutional change. This, at least, is a view associated with those who view international regimes as performing a positive role as an 'external anchor' to domestic reform.[22] The three ECU member states undertook varying levels of economic reform in the 1990s; this ranged from wide-scale liberalization and mass privatization in Russia – which was in some areas reversed over the past decade – to more limited reform in Kazakhstan and the absence of any serious economic reform in Belarus, described by one observer as a 'command economy without central planning'.[23] Indeed, for all three countries, their standing on numerous international indicators of economic freedom and institutional development are comparatively low and, in many cases, has deteriorated over the last decade (see Table 4.1). It is perhaps then not surprising that the increased international liberalization and integration that is part of both ECU membership and the WTO accession process offers the prospect of greater domestic economic reform.

There is, however, very little evidence to suggest that joining the WTO will help to improve institutional quality in either Russia, or Belarus and Kazakhstan should they join at a later point. If WTO accession is to exert a positive effect on institutional quality in a country, an observable change in a country's rating for institutional quality might be expected to occur either before the date of accession, as a country liberalizes to achieve accession, or immediately after accession, as the reforms undertaken as part of the accession negotiations take effect. Figure 4.1 shows the experience of five ex-communist economies and the relationship between WTO accession and a simple average of the six World Bank Governance Indicators (voice and accountability, political stability and absence of violence, regulatory quality, rule of law, and control of corruption). The data cover the four years immediately before and after accession.

---

[22]   See, for example, Marc Bacchetta and Zdenek Drabek, 'Effects of WTO Accession on Policy-Making in Sovereign States: Preliminary Lessons from the Recent Experience of Transition Countries', *Staff Working Paper DERD-2002-02* (WTO, April 2002).

[23]   Mario Nuti, 'Belarus: A Command Economy without Central Planning', in Mario I. Bléjer and Marko Škreb (eds), *Transition: The First Decade* (MIT Press, 2001).

Table 4.1   *ECU countries: World Bank Governance Indicators (2000 and 2010) (percentile rank, 0–100)*

	Belarus		Kazakhstan		Russia	
	2000	2010	2000	2010	2000	2010
Voice and accountability	10.6	7.1	20.7	14.2	37.0	21.8
Political stability	48.6	40.1	45.7	61.8	10.6	18.9
Government effectiveness	28.3	12.0	25.9	44.5	23.4	41.6
Regulatory quality	5.4	10.5	27.0	40.7	27.9	39.7
Rule of law	17.7	15.2	15.8	31.8	13.4	26.1
Control of corruption	37.1	25.4	8.3	15.8	16.6	12.4

Source: Compiled by the author using the WB Governance Indicators data basis, http://info.worldbank.org/governance/wgi/sc_country.asp (accessed 17 February 2013).

In these cases, neither negotiations to join the WTO nor actual accession appears to have exerted a significant influence, in either direction, on institutional quality. Only in Georgia did institutional quality improve both before and after accession. The reverse is true of China, where institutional quality decreased before and after accession. In Vietnam, institutional quality fluctuated around roughly the same level for the four years both before and after accession, while in Armenia and Ukraine institutional quality rose before accession and dropped thereafter.[24] This evidence suggests that it is highly likely that any progress or otherwise in domestic institutional reform is driven primarily by domestic political factors, and that there is no discernible 'external anchor' effect. Therefore, if the experience of these countries means anything for ECU

---

[24]   We are aware of the methodological limitations associated with such measures. For example, subjective survey data used to measure countries' performance – sometimes collated from sources unfamiliar with the country being measured – often reflect perceptions more than reality. In addition, because the World Bank's Governance Indicators are composite measures, the final component scores reflect the average of a large number of different measures, concealing what can often be large variation between those individual measures which form each composite indicator.

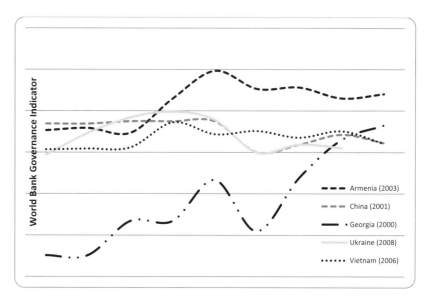

Source: Compiled by the author using the WB Governance Indicators data basis, http://
info.worldbank.org/governance/wgi/sc_country.asp (accessed 17 February 2013). Higher
values correspond with better institutions.

Figure 4.1   *Trends in institutional quality before and after WTO accession
in selected ex-communist countries*

members, then it is probably that WTO accession – or at least in the case
of Belarus and Kazakhstan, the importation of some WTO trade-related
rules – will, by itself, be unlikely to act as the catalyst for a surge in
domestic economic reform.

The evidence that membership of RTAs can help to push economic
reform forward is also equally unconvincing. In an analysis of trends in
institutional change in regional trade blocs, the EBRD finds only that
there are no clear trends.[25] Again, using a simple average of the six
World Bank Governance Indicators, it is argued that institutional quality
has declined in Mercosur and ASEAN countries, and exhibited no
discernible course in the Caribbean Community (CARICOM). Only in
the EU has the trend over time been positive for institutional change – a
fact, the authors surmise, that may be attributable to 'the deeper
institutional integration and the special role of supranational governance

---

[25]   EBRD, above note 19.

structures within the Union'.[26] If this is true, the more limited aims of the ECU, at least in the early stage of its life, would suggest that positive institutional change is unlikely to be generated by the formation of the Customs Union on its own.

There is, however, some evidence from the same EBRD report that deeper regional economic integration has led to some degree of convergence in institutional quality within regional trade blocs. Unfortunately, the scope for convergence within the ECU group is limited by the fact that the range of institutional quality – again, as measured by the World Bank Governance Indicators, and notwithstanding some recent modest improvements in some cases – is narrower in the ECU than in any other regional trade bloc from their sample. Put simply, the three countries of the ECU are, in terms of institutional quality, equally poor. The absence of a single country with institutions that are strong enough to act as the natural leader with the potential to drag the other countries upwards – as, it might be argued, was the case with EU enlargement – does not augur well for the ECU performing as a driver of institutional change in the future.

3.3.   The Challenge of Using the ECU and the WTO to Attract Higher Inflows of FDI

If the prospects for leveraging membership of international trade agreements to secure positive institutional reform appear relatively bleak, then the primary mechanism for securing economic gains appears to come from the gains associated with increased flows of inward FDI. This is at least the view expressed by several *ex ante* studies on the potential impact of WTO accession on growth, incomes and welfare in Russia.[27] The gains envisaged by these studies can be grouped into three categories: (1) gains from *imports* – from greater competition and improved resource allocation as a result of Russian tariff reduction; (2) gains from

---

[26]   Ibid., 76.

[27]   Thomas Rutherford and David Tarr, 'Poverty Effects of Russia's WTO Accession: Modelling Real Households and Endogenous Productivity Effects' (2008) 75(1) *Journal of International Economics* 131; Thomas Rutherford, David Tarr and Oleksandr Shepotylo, *Poverty Effects of Russia's WTO Accession: Modelling 'Real' Households and Endogenous Productivity Effects* (World Bank, 2004); Thomas Rutherford, David Tarr and Oleksandr Shepotylo, 'The Impact on Russia of WTO Accession and the Doha Agenda: The Importance of Liberalization of Barriers against Foreign Direct Investment in Services for Growth and Poverty Reduction', in Thomas Hertel and L. Alan Winters (eds), *Poverty and the WTO: Impacts of the Doha Development Agenda* (World Bank, 2005) 467–96.

exports – as a result of improved market access for Russian producers from more favourable treatment of Russian exporters in anti-dumping cases; and (3) gains from foreign direct investment – from the liberalization of barriers to FDI, both in the services sectors and (as the investment climate improves) in industry. The studies found that the overwhelming majority (72 per cent) of the estimated welfare gains from Russia's accession to the WTO would be likely to come from liberalization of the barriers to FDI in business services.

While the studies focused only on Russia, it is reasonable to assume that the effects would be broadly similar, if not greater, in Belarus and Kazakhstan because of the lower levels of FDI penetration in those two countries. If this assumption has some validity, then it is possible that the countries of the ECU could stand to make significant gains from increased FDI flows, both from other ECU countries and from third countries. Attracting higher levels of FDI inflows does not necessarily require wholesale institutional reform of the sort measured by the World Bank Governance Indicators mentioned above. They do require, however, some reduction in barriers to FDI (the existence of favourable infrastructure and beneficial tax regimes, for example) as well as some other favourable non-institutional factors (such as geographical proximity to markets and a large domestic market).

However, according to OECD data, barriers to FDI are comparatively high in Russia and Kazakhstan, comparing unfavourably with most other post-communist countries, as well as with most other OECD countries.[28] OECD data for Belarus is not available, but given that the stock of FDI as a proportion of GDP in Belarus is among the lowest in the post-communist region – less than 10 per cent of GDP according to UNCTAD data – it is reasonable to assume that barriers to FDI in Belarus are also high.[29] Indeed, since the early 1990s, the reluctance on the part of the leadership to engage in significant privatization – and its distrust of private property more generally – caused it shun FDI to a large degree.[30]

---

[28] EBRD, above note 19.
[29] UNCTAD, 'Statistics on Foreign Direct Investment', http://stats. unctad.org/fdi/ReportFolders/ ReportFolders.aspx (accessed 12 May 2012).
[30] Leonid Zlotnikov, 'Possibilities for the Development of a Private Economic Sector and a Middle Class as a Source of Political Change in Belarus', in Margarita Balmaceda, James Clem and Lisbeth Tarlow (eds), *Independent Belarus: Domestic Determinants, Regional Dynamics, and the Implications for the West* (Harvard University Press, 2002).

Foreign ownership was met with enthusiasm by neither the state, which controlled most of the economy anyway, nor the general population.[31]

In Russia and Kazakhstan, FDI flows have been much higher. Indeed, at around 40 per cent of GDP, both countries have relatively high stocks of FDI given their income levels. However, the bulk of FDI flows to these two countries are concentrated in extractive industries, especially energy extraction and production. Given that the gains from WTO accession – and also from increased integration through the ECU – are projected to come primarily from a higher volume of FDI in business services (such as finance, insurance, transport, communications) the relatively low level of FDI flows outside extractive sectors could well hamper economic development in the two countries.

In light of the high barriers to FDI that exist in all three ECU countries, it is difficult to see how they can realize the full potential gains from increased international integration and liberalization, both through actual (Russia) and prospective (Belarus and Kazakhstan) WTO accession, and also through involvement in the ECU. Working towards improving the business environment, especially that for foreign investors, is thus an important challenge for all three countries. Indeed, it is an obvious area where the EEC might be able to build up its reputational capital, if it is able to coordinate an effective response to the challenges associated with improving the business environment and reducing the regulatory restrictiveness of existing FDI regimes. However, reducing barriers to FDI, improving the business environment, and successfully implementing the laws to which the three countries have agreed to adhere (both as part of the WTO and the ECU) require states to have a robust administrative capacity. This is the subject of the next and final section.

4. IMPLEMENTATION OF MULTILATERAL AGREEMENTS: THE IMPORTANCE OF STATE CAPACITY

The three countries of the ECU have agreed to adhere to a common set of rules, based on WTO principles, regarding trade-related activities. As outlined in the previous section, simply joining multilateral groups is unlikely by itself to generate positive institutional change. However, there are still significant economic gains to be made from involvement in

---

[31] Timothy Colton, 'Belarusian Public Opinion and the Union with Russia', in Balmaceda, Clem and Tarlow, ibid.

multilateral economic agreements, but only if countries are able to ensure that behaviour within their respective territories corresponds with the new formal rules to which they have committed. If states can guarantee that economic agents operating from within their territory will adhere to the new rules generated by membership of the WTO or the ECU, then it is more likely that those states will enjoy the benefits offered by increased trade liberalization and integration. If, however, states are not able to ensure the implementation of policies agreed at the multilateral level, the prospects for successful economic change are significantly reduced.

The successful implementation of trade-related rules – or any rules for that matter – requires effective state capacity, or what Michael Mann describes as infrastructural power, the 'institutional capacity of a central state, despotic or not, to penetrate its territories and logistically implement decisions'.[32] In simple terms, state capacity refers to the ability of a state to 'get things done'. Measuring the extent to which a state has infrastructural power is not easy, but the World Bank's Government Effectiveness indicator – a composite measure that attempts to capture perceptions of the quality of public services, the quality of the civil service and the degree of its independence from political pressures, the quality of policy formulation and implementation, and the credibility of the government's commitment to such policies – provides a useful starting point.

Unfortunately, the ECU states are characterized by comparatively low levels of government effectiveness. All three states occupy positions towards the lower end of a sample of post-communist states and also when compared with several other so-called emerging economies.[33] Government effectiveness has increased in Russia and Kazakhstan and appears to be greater than in some other Central Asian and Caucasian states. Yet it remains much lower than the countries of Central and Eastern Europe. Belarus exhibits the second lowest score in the post-communist sample, suggesting that implementation of government policy is a particular weakness.

It is, therefore, by no means clear that the commitments made as part of either the WTO accession process or the ECU can be implemented consistently in any of the three states. In those areas where rules are clearer and administrative capacity is stronger, the ECU countries are

---

[32] Michael Mann, *The Sources of Social Power: The Rise of Classes and Nation-States, 1970–1914* (Cambridge University Press, 1993) 59.

[33] World Band Governance Indicators data basis, http://info.worldbank.org/governance/wgi/sc_country.asp (accessed 17 February 2013).

likely to be more successful in carrying out their commitments. However, in areas where higher levels of state administrative capacity are required, either as a result of WTO commitments or a deepening of economic integration among the ECU countries – for example, in terms of sanitary and phytosanitary standards or intellectual property rights – the three countries may encounter more difficulty in fulfilling their commitments, even if the central governments are, at least on a formal level, willing. This is of crucial importance because the success of the ECU and the SES will be dependent upon the capacity of domestic institutions to implement decisions taken at the supranational level.

5. CONCLUSION

It has been argued in this chapter that the WTO has played, and will continue to play, an important role in shaping the opportunities and constraints for the future development of the ECU. Initially, this may prove problematic for Belarus and Kazakhstan who have agreed to import *de facto* Russia's tariff-related WTO obligations. However, the fact that the ECU will be based on the principles of the WTO confers certain advantages upon its members. For example, it gives the ECU greater institutional clarity and legitimacy, and has the potential to make the ECU more attractive to prospective members. However, whether membership of the ECU or the WTO will exert a positive effect on the bloc's institutional development is unclear. Evidence from most other regional trade blocs suggests that membership does not tend to shape institutional development in either direction.

The economic benefits of trade liberalization through membership of both the ECU and the WTO will require strict adherence to the commitments made by all three countries as part of their respective accession processes to the ECU and the WTO. In particular, efforts will need to be stepped up to improve the business environment, especially for foreign investors. Moreover, we should be wary of the distinction between *de jure* commitments made by countries under multilateral agreements – such as the WTO and the ECU – and the capacity of states to adhere *de facto* to these commitments. In countries characterized by relatively low levels of state administrative capacity, as is the case with all three ECU countries, the effects of committing to multilateral agreements are likely to be muted. As such, neither WTO accession nor the creation of the ECU is likely to result in significant economic or institutional gains for Russia, Belarus or Kazakhstan. Instead, it is likely that domestic processes will remain the most important factors in shaping the potential for positive economic and political change across the region.

PART II

The ECU as viewed from the member states

5. Russia and the Eurasian Customs Union

Julian Cooper

---

1. INTRODUCTION

Because of the scale of the Russian Federation in terms of territory, population, resources and military might, any economic integration within the Commonwealth of Independent States (CIS) must inevitably have a highly asymmetric character. This fact, coupled with Russia's own sense of being, if no longer a superpower, then at least a great power, makes any process of integration a sensitive one for the partner countries. But during the 1990s, for Russia and the other new nations of the ex-Soviet Union, the principal concerns were post-communist economic transformation and state-building. In these circumstances it is not surprising that it took over 15 years after the collapse of the USSR before meaningful economic integration began to become a reality. In this chapter the evolution of Russia's economic engagement with other CIS countries is first explored and consideration is then given to the role of domestic actors, the political dimension and public opinion. There is also discussion of an issue that tends to be overlooked in examining Russia's economic relations with its CIS partners: the role of the defence industry. The chapter closes with some conclusions about the prospects for Russia of Eurasian economic integrations, costs, benefits and possible dangers.

2. THE OVERALL EVOLUTION OF RUSSIA'S APPROACH TO CIS ECONOMIC INTEGRATION

Russia's approach to economic integration within the CIS has been shaped by a number of general factors, including the influence of domestic reform priorities, changing drivers of economic growth, the personal inclinations and ideas of leaders, external shocks and the stance, actual or perceived, of other ex-USSR nations. The role of these factors has changed over time in such a manner as to strengthen the commitment of Russia's leadership to deepening and widening integration.

In the early 1990s, for Boris Eltsin, President of the newly independent Russia, and his government there were three overriding priorities: (i) the consolidation of the structures and institutions of a new state; (ii) the development of a market economy on the basis of the ruins of the Soviet planned economy that was in deep crisis by the end of 1991; and (iii) management of the processes of the disintegration and breakup of the USSR, not least securing the safe transfer of the nuclear capability of the Soviet state to Russian control. In these circumstances, domestic issues had understandable priority and Moscow tended to view the CIS as a mechanism for implementing a 'civilized divorce' rather than a structure for managing economic integration. Here, an additional factor may also have played a role: the Russia-first policy stance of Eltsin himself. In the telling assessment of the well-known 'political technologist', Gleb Pavlovskii, 'I think Yeltsin was autistic in geopolitical terms. He loved grandiose, grand-style politics, summits and so on. But as far as he was concerned all that mattered happened in Moscow'.[1] In the initial post-Soviet years there were also strong centrifugal forces at work. The leaders of most of the other newly independent nations were also preoccupied with state-building and market transformation. Separate development paths were being pursued, a fact underlined by the emergence in each country of new units of currency as the ruble zone disintegrated.[2]

In the case of Russia another factor influenced policy. Eltsin, his government, and much of the new political elite had a liberal orientation. This was especially true of the approach to the economy, where efforts focused on a rapid transition to the market and privatization. In this, and many other aspects of policy, they were anxious to distance the new Russia from the practices and attitudes of the Soviet past. Thus, the initial orientation was to the West rather than the former communist world. At the same time, there was a desire to maintain effective working relations with CIS neighbours and to support constructive cooperation in forms that did not run counter to Russia's own market transformation. From this

---

[1]   Ivan Krastev et al., 'The Politics of No Alternatives. How Power Works in Russia: An Interview with Gleb Pavlovsky', *Eurozine*, 9 June 2011, 14, http://www.eurozine.com/articles/2011-06-09-pavlovsky-en.html (accessed 15 February 2013).

[2]   On trends of development within the CIS at this time, see Richard Sakwa and Mark Webber, 'The Commonwealth of Independent States, 1991–1998: Stagnation and Survival' (1999) 51(3) *Europe-Asia Studies* 379.

perspective it is understandable that Moscow was willing to support in principle initiatives to promote free trade and prospects for future economic integration, but then draw back from early implementation. So, in September 1993 Russia signed an agreement on establishing an economic union, but this was more a declaration of intent than a measure requiring action in the immediate future. Similarly, in April 1994 Russia signed up to the creation of a CIS free trade area, but then failed to ratify the agreement.

By 1998 the trade flows and economic relations more generally of Russia and other CIS countries had diversified to quite a significant degree.[3] It was becoming increasingly clear that the CIS states had diverse orientations and goals, and this fact was given organizational expression in 1997 with the creation of GUAM, linking Georgia, Ukraine, Azerbaijan and Moldova, countries with a general orientation to Europe. In response to these developments, the Russian leadership appears to have drawn the conclusion that any efforts to promote economic integration should focus on those CIS members that share similar perspectives on the merits of integration – in the first instance, Belarus and Kazakhstan. In the case of Belarus, it is likely that another influence was at work. As discussed below, enterprises in Belarus play an important role in supplying the Russian defence industry.

In Russia, the turbulent and costly process of post-communist economic transformation was beginning to bring some positive outcomes, with modest GDP growth achieved in 1997.[4] But in the following year there was a major setback that had a significant impact on thinking in Russia about economic security and the need for closer integration. This was the 1998 financial-economic crisis, which had a major impact on Russia and other CIS member countries. It showed the vulnerability of these immature market economies with inexperienced leaderships to powerful external forces and organizations beyond the control of single nation states. Aided by a sharp devaluation of the ruble, Russia rapidly recovered from the crisis and resumed growth, without any resort to external economic assistance. This experience led to some distrust of international economic agencies and prompted a new interest in regional economic integration. This increased steadily and, with the election of

---

[3]   See Julian Cooper, 'Russia's Trade Relations within the Commonwealth of Independent States', in Elana Wilson Rowe and Stina Torjesen (eds), *The Multilateral Dimension in Russian Foreign Policy* (Routledge, 2009) 167–70.

[4]   On the process of the post-communist economic development of Russia, see Anders Aslund, *Russia's Capitalist Revolution. Why Market Reform Succeeded and Democracy Failed* (Peterson Institute, 2007).

Vladimir Putin as President in early 2000, started to be expressed in new initiatives, above all the transformation in October that year of the formal 'customs union' into EvrAzES, the evolution of which is discussed in Chapter 2.

During the years of Putin's first two terms as President, Russia changed in a number of important respects. Fuelled by oil and gas exports, plus institutional reforms initiated by the Economy Minister, German Gref, that improved the functioning of the market, the economy grew rapidly. Living standards improved and the country entered a new phase of stability in contrast to the turbulence of the 1990s. In international terms, Russia became more self-confident and assertive. Security concerns also mounted, especially after the events of 11 September 2001, which heightened Moscow's interest in Central Asia and the Caucasus as potential sources of instability. This has undoubtedly been a factor as is evident in the keen interest in rebuilding links with partners.

Another stimulus to the acceleration of the pace of economic integration was undoubtedly the impact on Russia and its CIS neighbours of the global financial-economic crisis of 2008–09. This was a rerun of the events of 1998. For the Russian leadership the conclusion was clear: disruptive global economic forces would not have such a serious effect on the domestic economy (GDP fell in 2009 by almost 8 per cent) if it were embedded in a larger, more diverse, economic community. This view appears to have been shared by the leaders of Belarus and Kazakhstan and this may help to explain why the formation of the Eurasian Customs Union (ECU) and the development of the Single Economic Space (SES) occurred so rapidly from early 2009. In addition, unlike Eltsin, Vladimir Putin exhibited a keen interest in CIS economic integration almost from the outset, and maintained his commitment while serving as Prime Minister. While he has at times shown some nostalgia for the USSR – notably when he declared in his state of the nation address to parliament in 2005 that 'the collapse of the Soviet Union was the greatest geopolitical tragedy of the century' – Putin has on a number of occasions explicitly disavowed claims that moves towards greater integration are linked to any attempt to restore the former Union.[5] In December 2012, for example, after the US Secretary of State, Hillary Clinton, charged Russia with seeking to restore the USSR by developing the ECU, he characterized such claims as 'nonsense', adding that 'the

---

5 Vladimir Putin, 'Poslanie Federal'nomu Sobraniyu Rosiiskoi Federatsii', 25 April 2005, http://archive.kremlin.ru/appears/2005/04/25/1223_type63372 type63374type82634_87049.shtml (accessed 11 December 2012).

entire world is taking the path of integration'.[6] However, unlike Eltsin, Putin appears to have a keen appreciation of the geopolitical importance of Russia, the largest country in the world, serving as the centre of a wider community of nations, and one senses that he perceives this as a key factor in his future historical legacy. No-one could charge Vladimir Putin with geopolitical 'autism'.

Before considering the domestic institutions and drivers of economic integration in Russia, within the CIS two other regional groupings merit attention. Military and security issues have been handled for a number of years within the framework of the Collective Security Treaty Organization (CSTO). In terms of members, the CSTO, founded in October 2002, is a military alliance of the EvrAzES countries, plus Armenia. Uzbekistan was a member between 2006 and June 2012.[7] The organization replaced a CIS collective security treaty structure dating back to 1992. It is worth noting that Ukraine has never joined a CIS security organization. Defence industry cooperation and arms transfers between member countries are handled within the framework of the CSTO, leaving EvrAzES with all issues of civilian economic cooperation. Russia is also a founding member of the Shanghai Cooperation Organization (SOC), established in June 2001. The original membership also included China, Kazakhstan, Kyrgyzstan, Tajikistan and Uzbekistan. A number of countries have observer status and future full membership cannot be ruled out: these are India, Iran, Mongolia, Pakistan and, since June 2012, Afghanistan. Within the SCO, Russia in the early years prioritized cooperation relating to security issues and tended to resist pressure from China to give the organization a larger role in economic affairs. However, since the global financial-economic crisis, Russia has been more supportive of economic cooperation and in time the SCO could become a forum for broader Eurasian economic cooperation.[8]

---

[6] Andrei Rezchikov, 'Posadki dolzhny byt' obyazatel'no', *Vzglyad*, 10 December 2012.

[7] Prompting speculation that Uzbekistan was seeking closer relations with the US in advance of the withdrawal of Western troops and armaments from Afghanistan in 2014, perhaps in expectation of aid and arms supply: James Kilner, 'Uzbekistan Withdraws from Russia-led Military Alliance', *The Telegraph*, 2 July 2012.

[8] Russia's interest in the economic role of the SCO was underlined by its representative, Kirill Barskii, at the time of the organization's summit in Bishkek, December 2012, including backing for the creation of a SCO development bank, http://www.infoshos.ru/ru/?idn=10817 (accessed 4 December 2012).

3. THE INSTITUTIONS AND DRIVERS OF EURASIAN ECONOMIC INTEGRATION

The process of Eurasian integration has quite substantial support in Russia, across the political spectrum, but it is not easy to identify specific institutions that can be considered powerful and energetic drivers of the project and initiators of policy. It is possible, however, to identify some key people and structures of government that are most directly involved. The commitment of Putin is clear, but the extent to which he draws on high-level expertise within the presidential administration is not entirely clear. Socio-economic relations with CIS countries are the responsibility of a dedicated division of the administration but its head, Yurii Voronin, is not a prominent figure.[9] Much more prominent is Sergei Glaz'ev, appointed Putin's adviser on Eurasian economic integration in the summer of 2012, a long-time advocate of the process, and a central actor in the shaping of policy. Academician Glaz'ev also remains active as an economic analyst and has led research into the economic outcomes of integration, at times offering very ambitious forecasts of likely gains in terms of GDP growth, not only for Russia, Belarus and Kazakhstan, but also for Ukraine in the event that Kiev decided to join the ECU.[10] Glaz'ev, born in Zaporozh'e, is a tireless advocate of the Ukrainian membership of the Customs Union. At a meeting in Putin's presence in December 2012, he declared with confidence that by 2015 this would be realized.[11]

In the government, overall leadership of economic relations within the CIS is exercised by the First Deputy Prime Minister, Igor Shuvalov, who is also a member of the Council of the Eurasian Economic Commission (EEC). There is no doubt that Shuvalov has been a key driver of the integration process. There is a division of labour in the government: security issues of the CIS and the work of the CSTO are overseen by Deputy Prime Minister, Dmitrii Rogozin, who also chairs the Military-Industrial Commission. Rogozin is also a strong advocate of integration and at one time was a leading figure in the Rodina Party, together with Sergei Glaz'ev. The apparatus of the government has a department

---

[9] See http://state.kremlin.ru/administration/division (accessed 10 December 2012). Voronin was appointed in early June 2012 and was previously Deputy Health Minister.
[10] See Sergei Glaz'ev, 'Real'noe yadro postsovetskom ekonomicheskoi integratsii: itogi sozdaniya i perspektivy razvitiya Tomozhennogo soyuza Belorussii, Kazakhstana i Rossii' (2011) 6 *Rossiiskii Ekonomicheskii Zhurnal*.
[11] http://www.evrazes-bc.ru/news/21402 (accessed 10 December 2012).

concerned with international cooperation, including CIS relations. It was led from 1999 by Tat'yana Valovaya, now Minister of the EEC for overall integration policy.[12]

Within the government, the body most centrally concerned with policy for Eurasian economic integration is the Ministry for Economic Development, which has a department of economic cooperation and integration with the countries of the CIS, headed by Sergei Chernyshev, who has a strong trade background. This department works closely with the department for trade negotiations, headed by Maksim Medvedkov, who for many years fronted Russia's bid to join the World Trade Organization (WTO) and in that connection had the task of convincing the accession Working Party of the compatibility of the ECU with WTO requirements. It is probably not surprising that the economics ministry has been the source of a number of senior staff appointees to the Eurasian Economic Commission, including the Trade Minister, Andrei Slepnev. It is worth noting that the Ministry of Foreign Affairs, responsible for relations with CIS countries, appears to have only modest engagement in economic matters.

Energetic promotion of economic integration has been an activity of members of the Committee for CIS Affairs and Relations with Compatriots of the State Duma. Its chair, Leonid Slutskii, has been a visitor to such countries as Azerbaijan, Armenia and Moldova, setting out the potential benefits of ECU membership.[13] One of his particular concerns has been Ukrainian accession. Slutskii and his colleagues have also helped to secure the ratification of legislation relating to economic integration. Also active has been the Duma Speaker, Sergei Naryshkin, who has been exploring options for a future Eurasian parliamentary assembly with leading political figures in Kazakhstan and Belarus.

Another constituency with interests in Eurasian economic integration is the business community. To the fore has been the Russian Union of Industrialists and Entrepreneurs led since 2005 by Aleksandr Shokhin. The Union has a Committee for Integration Policy, Trade-Customs Policy and the WTO, chaired by a leading industrialist, Aleksei Mordashov, general director of the Severstal metallurgical company. Similarly, the Russian Chamber of Trade and Industry has a Committee for Questions

---

[12] She was replaced by her former deputy, El'mir Tagirov, who for a number of years worked in the Ministry of Foreign Affairs, http://ria.ru/politics/20120209/561118862.html (accessed 10 December 2012).

[13] See http://www.duma.gov.ru/structure/deputies/131318 (accessed 10 December 2012). Slutskii is an economist and member of the Liberal Democratic Party of Russia.

of Economic Integration of the Countries of the Shanghai Cooperation Organization and the CIS, headed by Vladimir Salamatov, general director of the Moscow 'Centre for International Trade', a firm advocate of the ECU and related developments.[14] It is likely that there are close links between Russian business groups and the Eurasian Business Council, based in Moscow, which is committed to promoting economic integration throughout EvrAzES. The Council is headed by Oleg Soskovets, a prominent figure in the government and metals industry of Kazakhstan, but from 1993 to 1996 First Deputy Prime Minister of Russia. In this capacity he will have worked with such figures as Shokhin and Glaz'ev, both government ministers in the early 1990s.

This overview of centres of expertise and influence in the Russian executive and legislature is far from comprehensive, but it serves to indicate that there is a somewhat dispersed network rather than any coherent centralized agency with the authority to pursue economic integration in a vigorous manner. What is perhaps surprising is the relatively small number of government officials with expertise in the issues. However, Russia's dispersed network with a relatively small number of actors may have the merit of flexibility and it is likely that informal contacts play a role, not only within Russia, but also with the equivalent key actors in other countries of EvrAzES. This brings us to another related issue: CIS economic integration and political forces in Russia.

4. THE POLITICS OF EURASIAN ECONOMIC INTEGRATION

According to Tat'yana Valovaya, Minister of the EEC, in Russia there is support for the Eurasian economic integration project across the entire political spectrum.[15] This is an overstatement, but the observation undoubtedly has a core of truth. United Russia, the 'party of power' – linked closely during his first two terms of office to Vladimir Putin and during his third to Dmitrii Medvedev – has always backed new initiatives for integration, but this is also true of other parties close to power such as Just Russia and the Liberal Democratic Party of Russia. On the left, the

---

[14]   See, for example, his presentation at the Gaidar Forum, Moscow, 16 January 2013, http://www.wtcmoscow.ru/about/news.aspx?id=8722 (accessed 20 January 2013).

[15]   Interview with Tat'yana Valovaya, 'Integratsiya ob'edinyaet vsekh – ot kommunistov do "Edinoi Rossii" i pravykh', *Izvestiya*, 10 July 2012.

Communist Party of the Russian Federation (CPRF) is also supportive, not so much because it favours market-based integration based on WTO principles – it has consistently opposed Russia's WTO accession – but because it approves of any measures perceived to bring closer the countries of the ex-USSR. For the Communists, the reconstitution of the Soviet Union has been a goal since 1992. The same applies to the many political groupings on the left which rival the CPRF. The stance of the political parties represented in the State Duma is such that any measures for advancing Eurasian economic integration encounter no robust, informed opposition.

More problematic is the stance of those of a more liberal political orientation, generally supportive of the West and wary of initiatives that could be interpreted as efforts to form something resembling a Russia-dominated 'empire' in the former Soviet territory. One response is silence. Thus the 2012 programme of the Yabloko Party, 'Democratic Manifesto', makes no mention of the ECU, Eurasian integration or even the CIS, but simply declares in favour of a 'European path for Russia'.[16] This is also the position of other liberal, democratic parties and group-ings and their leaders: it is rare to find any reference to this important policy issue. In practice, given the weakness of such parties and their lack of representation in parliament, they have no influence on policy for economic integration. However, there have been exceptions, a notable case being the well-known figure of Anatolii Chubais, leader of privat-ization in the early 1990s, a close colleague of the liberally orientated Yegor Gaidar, and in recent years head of the Rosnano state corporation for the development of nanotechnology. There was much surprise within Russia and abroad when, in 2003, Chubais declared in favour of the development of what he termed a 'liberal empire'.[17] In his view there is no question that Russia is the leading nation of the former Soviet Union and as such he considered it a 'mission' to gather the other countries into an 'empire' founded on the market, democracy and human freedoms. Chubais has been silent on this issue in recent times.[18]

The relative silence of liberally minded political figures is matched by the stance of economists. It is notable that in Russia research and expertise on Eurasian economic integration tends to be the preserve of

---

[16]   See http://www.yabloko.ru/content/programma_demokraticheskij_manifest (accessed 10 December 2012).

[17]   Anatolii Chubais, 'Missiya Rossii', St Petersburg, 25 September 2003, http://www.sps.ru/?id=120083 (accessed 10 December 2012).

[18]   There is now no reference to 'liberal empire' on the personal website of Chubais: see http://www.chubais.ru (accessed 12 December 2012).

older generation economists, often members of institutes of the Academy of Sciences, some nostalgic for the Soviet past, others simply of a 'statist' rather than liberal orientation – the above-mentioned Glaz'ev being an excellent example. In such centres as the High School of Economics, or the Gaidar Institute of Economic Policy, there appears to be little expertise or interest in the topic. It is indicative that the comprehensive review of the socio-economic strategy to 2020 – undertaken by many academic economists in 2010–11 under the leadership of Vladimir Mau (director of the Academy of the National Economy, but also with a long association with the Gaidar Institute) and Yaroslav Kuz'minov (Rector, High School of Economics) – had only a brief section at the end on the ECU and related developments; furthermore its main author was not an academic economist, as for most other sections, but a government official, namely Tat'yana Valovaya, who served as co-leader of the expert group involved.[19] This can probably be explained by the lack of a suitably qualified academic specialist in the community of economists of liberal orientation.

Before leaving the role of Eurasian economic integration in Russian politics, one short-lived initiative deserves a mention. For a time in the 2000s there was a political party which styled itself the Eurasian Party – Union of Patriots of Russia. This was part of a political coalition, 'Great Russia – Eurasian Union', led by Pavel Borodin, who was at the time State Secretary of the Union State of Belarus and Russia. It was formed to contest the State Duma elections of December 2003 and had the goal of creating a Eurasian Union. Inspired by the Eurasianist ideas discussed in the next section, the party gained the backing of a number of leading figures from those republics of Russia which had large Islamic populations and built links with Kazakhstan.[20] It received few votes in the elections, 0.3 per cent, in part because another patriotic but integrationist political coalition emerged, namely 'Rodina', led by Glaz'ev and Rogozin, which managed to capture over 9 per cent of the total vote. After a troubled existence, what was left of the Rodina Party joined Just Russia

---

[19]   *Strategiya-2020: Novaya model' rosta – novaya sotsial'naya politika. Itogovyi doklad rezeul'tatakh ekspertnoi raboty po aktual'nym problemam sotsial'no-ekonomicheskoi strategii Rossii na period do 2020 g.*, http:// 2020strategy.ru/documents/32710234.html (accessed 10 January 2013). The 14-page section on CIS economic integration was the final group report of this 864-page document.

[20]   Nikolai Anisimov, 'Novaya sila novoi Rossii', *Rossiiskaya Gazeta*, 24 July 2003; Valerii Korneshov, 'Evraziiskaya liniya v partiinom inter'ere', *Rossiiskaya Gazeta*, 26 August 2003.

in 2006, but without its two well-known leaders.[21] Glaz'ev went on the become secretary of the ECU and Rogozin between 2008 and 2011 was Russia's representative at NATO; thus they remained close to power notwithstanding their excursion into nationalist politics. However, the episode probably served to increase the prominence of the idea of a possible Eurasian Union. Given the current direction of development, it is likely that economic integration will come to occupy a larger place in the politics of Russia and new party initiatives in this spirit cannot be ruled out.

This brings us to a related issue: Russian public opinion. A number of polls have explored the attitudes of citizens towards their CIS neighbours and the prospect of closer integration. In assessing the options, nostalgia for the USSR is still a factor, but a declining one. This is shown by regular polls of the Levada Centre. Asked whether they regretted the collapse of the USSR, 49 per cent of those asked in December 2012 said 'yes', but this was the lowest figure yet; in 2000 the share had been 75 per cent. When asked what form of relations between republics of the ex-USSR they would favour, 16 per cent declared in favour of the restoration of the Soviet Union in its previous form (30 per cent in 2001), 24 per cent backed the formation of a closer union of those states wishing to do so, 17 per cent favoured integration of all the former republics to form something resembling the European Union (EU), 20 per cent favoured the retention of the existing CIS, and 11 per cent the completely independent existence of all countries.[22] This suggests that Eurasian integration enjoys support in principle but not on a very substantial scale. Unfortunately, no poll asking questions on the ECU has been traced; the author would not be surprised if a quite sizeable proportion of the population were found to have little or no knowledge of its existence.[23]

---

[21]   In September 2012 the Rodina Party was reborn under the leadership of Aleksei Zhuravlev, formerly of United Russia; its programme makes no reference to CIS economic integration: see http://www.rodina.ru/documents/programma-partii (accessed 12 December 2012).

[22]   See http://www.levada.ru/11-01-2013/rossiyane-o-raspade-sssr (accessed 11 January 2013). Note that 12 per cent were unable to answer.

[23]   This was the case for 40 per cent of those asked whether they had heard of the Single Economic Space in November 2011: see http://fom.ru/globe/10267 (accessed 11 January 2013).

5. EURASIANIST IDEOLOGY IN RUSSIA

Eurasianism has been a current of thought in Russia over a long period although it has never had a large following. Leading exponents have been Nikolai Trubetskoi and Petr Savitskii in the early twentieth century and, in more modern times, Lev Gumilev, who has a large following in Kazakhstan and other Central Asian countries. In post-communist Russia, what is probably better termed 'neo-Eurasianism' has been tirelessly promoted by Aleksandr Dugin, philosopher, political thinker, professor of Moscow State University and prolific author. This is not the place for a detailed discussion of Eurasianist ideology but it merits brief consideration as its influence has undoubtedly grown as Eurasian economic integration has become more of a reality.[24] Eurasianists in Russia today emphasize a strong cultural affinity with Asia, often accompanied by a belief in the historical task of creating a 'Greater Russia' – restoring, in effect, the pre-1917 Russian Empire. For Dugin and his followers there is also a deep antagonism towards the United States, with a hope that a Europe–Asia alliance, with Russia playing a prominent role, has the potential to challenge, and even roll back, Atlanticism. It is a school of thought that tends to bring together adherents of both Orthodoxy and Islam.

The available evidence provides no support for the view that Eurasianist ideology has promoted economic integration; on the contrary, it is the development of the ECU and the prospect of a future 'union' that has generated some new interest in Eurasianist ideas in Russia. An expression of this was the formation in 2012 of a new organization, the Izborskii Club – a self-styled think tank named after the location of its first meeting, a historic town near Pskov. Leading figures in this initiative are Aleksandr Dugin and the editor of the left nationalist weekly, *Zavtra*, Aleksandr Prokhanov.[25] Meetings of the club have been attended by some prominent members of the Orthodox and Islamic communities of Russia. There have been claims that the presidential administration has been supportive of the club's formation, providing as it does an alternative source of ideas from such liberally orientated think tanks as the Institute of Contemporary Development led by Igor' Yurgens, often linked with Dmitrii Medvedev. It may be significant that the second

---

[24] For an overview of Eurasianism and neo-Eurasianism, see Mark Bassin, 'Eurasianism "Classical" and "Neo": The Lines of Continuity', in Tetsuo Mochizuki (ed.), *Beyond the Empire: Images of Russia in the Eurasian Cultural Context* (Slavic Research Centre, 2008) 279–94; Marlène Laruelle, *Russian Eurasianism: Ideology of Empire* (John Hopkins University Press, 2012).

[25] Aleksandr Prokhanov, 'Izborskii klub', *Zavtra*, 12 September 2012.

gathering of the Izborskii Club was attended by Sergei Glaz'ev.[26] Those active in the Izborskii Club are often critical of Putin, regarding him as too supportive of liberal market principles and not sufficiently anti-American, but they are strongly supportive of any moves to strengthen relations with CIS neighbours, especially Ukraine and the countries of Central Asia. They clearly hope to convert Putin into a more resolute Eurasianist and may have been encouraged by the fact that he made reference to Gumilev in his state of the nation speech in December 2012.[27] It remains to be seen whether the Izborskii Club will become more prominent as a source of an ideology supportive of Eurasian economic integration (see also Malle, Chapter 6 of this volume).

6. THE DEFENCE AND SECURITY FACTOR

As discussed in Chapter 2, when the idea of a Eurasian Union was first considered in practical terms in early 2010, Russia expressed the view that it should be concerned not only with economics, but also defence and security. This stance was not shared by Kazakhstan and was not reflected in the final agreed declaration in the future evolution of integration. In these circumstances, it is likely that defence issues will remain the concern of a separate organization, the Collective Security Cooperation Organisation. However, there is a dimension that cannot be ignored in exploring Russia's commitment to economic integration, namely the defence industry. To some extent the requirements of military production have helped to drive the process of Eurasian economic cooperation, and the defence industry can be regarded as an interest group favouring integration.

With the collapse of the USSR at the end of 1991 the vast defence industry of the country fragmented into 15 components, which left each of the newly independent states with an inheritance which lacked coherence and economic logic, providing even Russia with a far from comprehensive defence industrial base. A number of countries became significant suppliers of arms, systems, components and materials. In particular, this applied to Belarus and Ukraine. The former remains a major supplier of microelectronic components essential for Russia's arms manufacture, heavy duty missile transporters, optical equipment and many other systems. Ukraine has a near monopoly as a supplier of

---

26 'Izborskii klub. Votoroe zasedanie', *Zavtra*, 3 October 2012.
27 Vladimir Putin, 'Poslanie Prezidenta Federal'nomu Sobraniyu', http://www.kremlin.ru/news/17118 (accessed 12 December 2012).

engines for helicopters, power units for ships, Antonov heavy transport aircraft, some types of air-launched missile, and many systems and components. The country also has shipyards capable of building very large naval surface ships, a capability to a large extent absent in Russia. Over recent years Russia has sought to reduce dependence on Ukraine, but with limited success.

Kazakhstan is less important as a supplier but many traditional links remain, and the same applies to Kyrgyzstan. A peculiarity of the Soviet defence industry was that the manufacture of some naval arms, including torpedoes, was located in Central Asian states.[28] Kazakhstan also has the Baikonur space launch centre which is leased to Russia until 2050, but this is now less important than it was and there has been speculation that the arrangement may end earlier than previously envisaged.[29] Tashkent in Uzbekistan is the location of a major production facility building Ilyushin transport aircraft, but in recent years militarily sensitive production has been switched to Russia.

Finally, one cannot ignore the significance of the defence industry within Russia itself, in particular the fact that there are major facilities located in the Far East. Not least of these is the vast aviation plant in Komsomol'sk-na-Amur, building Sukhoi combat aircraft, including the T-50 fifth generation plane now under development, and the Sukhoi Superjet-100, the first really new passenger aircraft developed since the end of the USSR. Other important factories include the Arsen'ev Progress works building Kamov helicopters for the military, the Amur shipyard building both naval and civil vessels, and a major shipyard at Bolshoi Kamen' supporting the nuclear submarine fleet. The maintenance and development of these facilities, vital to the Russian military, is a factor that cannot be ignored in consideration of the developmental priority of the Far East and its compatibility with Eurasian economic integration, as discussed by Malle in this volume.

The fact that Belarus was the first country with which Russia undertook practical initiatives for economic integration from the mid-1990s is not at all surprising if account is taken of the importance of maintaining a stable and coherent defence industrial base. For Russia, Belarus is regarded to a large extent as a domestic supplier, not a foreign country.

---

[28]   For an overview of the defence industry inheritance of ex-USSR countries, see Julian Cooper, 'The Soviet Union and the Successor Republics: Defence Industries Coming to Terms with Disunion', in Herbert Wulf (ed.), *Arms Industry Limited* (SIPRI/Oxford University Press, 1993) 87–108.

[29]   See   http://www.rbc.ru/politics/16/12/2012/836803.shtml   (accessed   16 December 2012).

While there are many reasons why Moscow wishes Ukraine to join the ECU, the military production factor is clearly significant. Whenever Russia seeks to persuade Ukraine to participate more fully in Eurasian economic integration, the potential of cooperation in high technology spheres is invariably emphasized, above all joint activity in aviation, shipbuilding and space technology. Given that Ukraine wishes to develop its own domestic defence industry but is underdeveloped in many sectors and has a small domestic market for its products, such cooperation undoubtedly has a strong economic rationale. Defence industry cooperation also features when possible membership of the ECU is raised with other countries, notably Kyrgyzstan, Armenia and Moldova. Now that the Russian defence industry has an energetic leader in Dmitrii Rogozin, chair of the Military-Industrial Commission and a strong supporter of Eurasian integration, this factor may play a more decisive role in the future.

7. THE COSTS AND BENEFITS TO RUSSIA OF THE ECU AND CIS ECONOMIC INTEGRATION MORE GENERALLY

It is beyond the scope of this chapter to analyse in detail the costs and benefits of Eurasian economic integration.[30] However, a number of key potential benefits can be identified. Given the common Soviet past of the economies of the region, there are evident complementarities and still-existing supply chains, the functioning of which should be improved and made economically more effective, for example, in the defence industry and the engineering industry more generally. In Russia there is a belief that Eurasian integration will support efforts to diversify the economy away from a one-sided focus on hydrocarbons and resource-intensive activities in general. The development of more competitive consumer-orientated manufacturing will probably be part of the process and this could be assisted by the creation of a larger market for goods and services without border customs. There are also potential benefits if a more business-friendly environment for FDI can be created, again boosted by the development of a larger market, freedom of movement of capital and labour, and the likely improvement over time of transport links. The development of a CIS free trade area may also be supportive.

---

[30] European Bank for Reconstruction and Development, *Transition Report 2012* (EBRD, 2012), Chapter 4.

The economic benefits from these new arrangements are likely to be superior to those derived from the complex network of bilateral relations that has hitherto characterized Russia's relations with CIS partners.

But Eurasian economic integration may also have serious costs. If firms focus on the less competitive and demanding regional market of the ECU rather than the EU and other more developed economies, there must be a danger of trade diversion. Without Ukraine, the ECU will still be a common market of relatively modest scale. The likely addition within the next few years of Kyrgyzstan and Tajikistan, two countries of a relatively modest level of economic development with populations of fewer than 10 million will not have a significant impact and may indeed increase the danger of reducing competitive pressures on Russian firms. The past experience of British industry may be relevant here. It is generally accepted that its performance in the early post-war years was held back by the existence of the Commonwealth preference system, providing access to less developed markets on favourable terms. For Russia there may also be opportunity costs, in particular the possibly competing priority of the development of the Russian Far East and the pursuit of a broader pan-Asian economic orientation (see Malle, Chapter 6 in this volume).

While economic integration in the ex-Soviet region is the primary concern, for Russia the benefits are clearly not viewed solely from an economic point of view. The country's leadership, with Putin to the fore, sees the world today in the early twenty-first century as no longer one with a single predominant power, the USA, but as a multi-polar system with competing centres of power, in particular the rapidly emerging nations of Asia. For Moscow it is a matter of crucial importance that Russia not only retains its status as a major power, but enhances further the country's influence and standing in the world. Being the centre and principal driving force of a regional integration project is clearly seen as contributing to the achievement of this national goal. In the author's view it is a mistake to characterize this policy as one of seeking to restore the Soviet Union: that would be a futile and backward-looking policy in today's world, as most in Russia now recognize. Instead, the project could be considered forward-looking, a response to a rapidly changing world. That some other powers may perceive this as an unwelcome development is hardly a surprise, but policy responses need to be based on sound analysis.[31]

---

[31] The assessment of the US Secretary of State, Hillary Clinton, that in creating the Customs Union Russia is seeking to 're-Sovietize' the region is

8. RUSSIA'S CAPACITY TO IMPLEMENT THE OBLIGATIONS OF INTEGRATION

In assessing the viability of the ECU and more developed forms of integration in the future an important consideration is the capacity of Russia to meet the challenge of new economic arrangements with a supranational authority. This is not a trivial matter. To date, Russia has not always found it easy to operate within a multilateral framework, perhaps in part because of residual superpower attitudes and behavioural characteristics, with a tendency to view small countries as inferior actors on the international stage.[32] Now Russia has to adapt to new circumstances, not only within the framework of the ECU and the SES, but also the WTO and, shortly, the OECD. A learning process is under way. The fundamental asymmetry of the ECU, with Russia as the unambiguously dominant power, clearly gives plenty of scope for inappropriate behaviour. But heavy-handed actions or domineering attitudes within the ECU will threaten its viability. At the time of writing, the end of 2012, the record is reasonably encouraging. Within the ECU and the EEC, Russia's approach so far has been pragmatic and flexible and this applies also to relations with potential members, Kyrgyzstan and Tajikistan. However, Moscow's attempts to induce Ukraine to join the ECU have not been free from heavy pressure, with a tendency to confront Kiev with a simple either/or – Brussels, or the ECU – choice of the latter being tempted by the promise of significant gas price discounts.

On a more mundane level, there is a further significant issue: Russia's administrative capacity to meet the new demands posed by the ECU and associated developments. As the EEC develops, it will take on many responsibilities. Yet the changes required to adapt the customs service to the demands posed by new technical regulations and measures for the harmonization of policies in many spheres will be challenging. It is not clear how Russia will be able to meet the demand for many administrative personnel with new skills. This is already a problem with respect to

---

indicative but US economic interests may not be well served if the ECU, and Eurasian economic integration in general, is understood in such limited terms: see http://www.rferl.org/content/clinton-calls-eurasian-integration-effort-to-resov ietize/24791921.html (accessed 7 December 2012).

[32] On Russia and multilateralism, see Wilson Rowe and Torjesen, above note 3, especially Chapters 1 and 2.

the WTO, as the lead negotiator Medvedkov has frankly acknowledged.[33] Indeed, several months after accession, Moscow had yet to appoint an ambassador to the WTO in Geneva.

Another issue is the preparation and ratification of an extremely large volume of new legislation. On economic matters, a heavy burden falls on the Ministry of Economic Development. The State Duma has a demanding legislative agenda focused on domestic matters but is now having to deal with many new issues arising from the ECU and the SES, with the need to ratify treaties and other agreements. It is not clear, with limited time available and tight deadlines, that this is being done with any real rigour. There is a danger that many potentially important decisions will be taken in simply a formal manner with the possibility of negative consequences in the future. It is striking, for example, that there was no public debate in Russia on the establishment of a supranational agency, the EEC, and the fact that it may take decisions that run counter to vested interests within the country. The Speaker of the Russian Duma, Sergei Naryshkin, is a keen supporter of the creation of a parliamentary assembly for the ECU and the SES, plus the future Eurasian Union, elected by direct franchise. In promoting this option he may be seeking to reduce to some extent the legislative burden of Eurasian economic integration on the Russian parliament. As he notes, there are already *'Evrazooptimisty'* and *'Evrazoskeptiki'* ('Euro-optimists' and 'Euro-sceptics') with regard to the politics of Eurasian integration.[34]

9. CONCLUSION

Since the late 1990s, driven by considerations of economic advantage and an urge to obtain some insulation from global shocks, coupled with security concerns and the geopolitical interests of the country as perceived by Vladimir Putin and his colleagues in the political elite, Russia has moved ever more decisively in the direction of Eurasian economic integration. There is no doubt that the Russian leadership now has a major commitment to the success of the ECU and the phased programme of deepening and widening integration. However, in many respects this is

[33] Maksim Medvedkov, 'Spetsialistov ekstra-klass po voprosam VTO Rossiya vyrastit cherez 20 let', http://www1prime.ru/news/interviews (accessed 13 November 2012).
[34] Sergei Naryshkin, 'Evraziiskaya integratsiya: parlamentskii vektor', *Izvestiya*, 4 October 2012.

a new and challenging project that requires skilful and sensitive management. Potentially, Russia and the partner countries have much to gain from Eurasian economic integration, but it will require a focus on the economic dimension, with Moscow reigning in 'imperial' ambitions, and learning to behave as a more equal actor in a multilateral environment. Within EvrAzES, the record to date has been relatively favourable, but less so in relations with Ukraine, the country that Russia is most eager to draw into the ECU and SES. The Russian government will also have to learn to manage its relationship with a new supranational organization, the EEC, which is already gaining authority and confidence and to some extent is becoming an independent driver, within Russia, of the entire project of integration. What is being established is not, of course, the 'liberal empire' championed by Chubais. Yes, it is based on the market, but the three current members of the ECU are far from being vibrant democracies fully respecting human rights. There are many potential factors that could drive the process off course; not least of these are security considerations, which could lead Russia to resort to 'harder' power positions generating friction with partner countries. An interesting learning process is under way with the potential to change both Russia's economic standing and the country's role in international relations.

6. Russia, the Eurasian Customs Union and the Asian dimension

Silvana Malle

1. INTRODUCTION

Russia's engagement in Eurasian integration highlights, and stems from, the challenges that Russia faces in Asia. The deepening of Eurasian integration together with the opening of the initiatives to participation from other countries of the Commonwealth of Independent States (CIS) was at the core of Putin's first Presidential Decree on foreign policy in 2012.[1] The contemporaneous Decree on long-term economic policy focused on accelerating social and economic development in Siberia and the Far East, including transport to remote areas.[2] Yet these two facets of Russia's strategy are by no means identical in vision, means and policies, though there are important linkages between them that one cannot ignore.

This chapter examines Russia's economic integration policy in relation to Central Asia and beyond, towards Asia as a continent. It is argued in this chapter that even if Russia coveted the restoration of the Soviet Union – a frequent yet unsubstantiated claim – it would have neither the economic nor military capacity to do so. Rather, integration prospects are better examined in a global context in which Russia – as recognized by the authorities themselves – is one of the players, and not even a major one.

Pursuing integration strategies vis-à-vis the emerging markets of the Asia-Pacific region primarily requires a reorientation of the domestic

---

[1] Decree of the President of the Russian Federation Nr 605 'On the Measures for Realizing the Foreign Policy Direction of the RF', 7 May 2012, http://graph.document.kremlin.ru/page.aspx?1610881 (accessed 31 January 2013).

[2] Decree of the President of the Russian Federation Nr 596 'On the Long-term State Economic Policy', 7 May 2012, http://graph.document.kremlin.ru/page.aspx?1610833 (accessed 31 January 2013).

priorities in favour of the Russian territories beyond the Urals. These are geographically part of Asia while still rather impermeable to trade and joint ventures with China, the most attractive economy of the Asia-Pacific region. Such a reorientation entails Russian intragovernmental discussion, agreement and implementation. Looking eastwards, Russia's authorities hope that within a few years trade in the Asia Pacific region will reach at least 50 per cent of the total Russian foreign trade, which is about the current volume of trade with Europe.[3] Such projections look extremely ambitious and may need, *ceteris paribus*, more than a generation to materialize. Nonetheless, what really matters – and could become a concern for outsiders in the future – is that such goals are at present framing Russia's roadmap for medium to long-term development. That is why the development of Siberia and the Far East – the regions most exposed to Central Asia and China – has become important for Russia.

However, to maintain her eastward-focused integration drive, it is imperative for Russia to re-establish political and economic influence in Central Asia, despite the high costs involved.[4] Relations with Central Asia are marred by a number of complications arising from competing interests with respect to oil and gas supplies, as well as enormous differences in wealth and security problems. Except for Kazakhstan, most countries are poor, suggesting that they will represent an economic liability for Russia within the Eurasian Customs Union (ECU). Moreover, in some countries the rule of law is particularly weak while the strength of indigenous customs may hinder exchange between multinational businesses. Yet such liabilities may be perceived by Russia as the price worth paying for the pursuit of geopolitical goals, which include building a south-eastwards bridge to China and Pacific Asia. From an economic point of view, however, this price could be too high. Russian geopolitical

---

[3]   Igor Shuvalov in Singapore on 25 September 2012, 'Rossia planiruet uvelichit' doliu tovaroborota s Aziatskim regionam', http://www.1prime.ru/News/20120925/757268678.html (accessed 13 February 2013).

[4]   In November 2012, the President of the Russian Council for Foreign Affairs, Igor Ivanov, recalled that 'the Central Asian region has been one of the most difficult regions in the world from the security point of view'. Adding that the United States and the European Union have their own interests in this region, he stressed that 'today the Central Asian region is an object and a subject of the global policy in all its major aspects and its development impacts on the region and beyond': see http://www.eurasianet.org/node/66271 (accessed 8 December 2012).

interests in Central Asia and the efforts to integrate these countries into the ECU give them possibly an excessive negotiating power.

In this context, the cooperative nature of Russian policies is the *conditio sine qua non* for the planned establishment of the Eurasian Economic Union (EEU) in 2015 and its sustainable development. There has been progress in this respect since the 2000s, but much work needs to be done in a difficult environment. Central Asia's economic and social geography, as well as its history and culture, are not particularly favourable. Post-Soviet nation states have their own reasons for resentment, worries, temptation and ambitions.[5] Moreover, conflicting interests between major powers will continue to intersect in the region, making it even more difficult for substantive integration.[6]

No fewer problems stem from Russia's far-reaching integration prospects towards Asia-Pacific economies. Russia's neglected 'backyard' territory from Siberia to the borders of the Far East represents two-thirds of the country. If the Northern Chinese provinces, South Korea and Japan are to be linked with European Russia to effectively reach the European market, massive investment will be necessary. The modernization of the Far East's infrastructure is costly, as it would demand easier flows of commodities eastwards, mainly towards China, and westwards towards Europe. Massive investments in derelict transport infrastructure and missing logistics are needed to facilitate the transit of goods and commodities in both directions. This chapter examines why Russia is engaging in such an ambitious programme for the Far East and assesses how compatible this is with the expansion of the ECU to Central Asia.

At the same time, the pre-eminence of the Asian continent – especially China – for Russia's sustainable growth and reduced dependence on major Western economies is indisputable. The problem is that economic interests and political concerns do not always overlap. Russia will need to watch both aspects in weaving external relations.[7] This very fact may represent a tremendous challenge to Russia's ambitious integration

---

[5] Marlène Laruelle, 'When the "Near Abroad" Looks at Russia: The Eurasian Union Project as Seen from Southern Republics', *Russian Analytical Digest* No. 112 (Center for Security Studies, 20 April 2012) 8–11.

[6] Hillary Clinton's dismissal of Eurasian integration as 'a move to re-Sovietize the region' is reported at http://www.rferl.org/content/clinton-calls-eurasian-integration-effort-to-resovietize/24791921.html (accessed 7 December 2012).

[7] Vladimir Putin, 'Vladimir Putin on Foreign Policy: Russia and a Changing World', *Valdai Discussion Club*, 27 February 2012, http://valdaiclub.com/politics/39300.html (accessed 13 February 2013).

policies. While robust intra-ECU trade would suggest, in principle, that further enlargement of the ECU may help to isolate a larger internal market from the negative effects of world imbalances, the very nature of the economically poor and institutionally problematic Central Asian countries is unhelpful in achieving that aim. The region itself, moreover, is far from homogeneous, with Kazakhstan clearly emerging as competitor to Russia, as outlined below. Meanwhile, geographic proximity with China and militant powers in the region pose strong challenges to all parties.

2. RUSSIA, CENTRAL ASIA AND THE ECU

Central Asia – mainly owing to Kazakhstan's membership of the ECU and the Single Economic Space (SES) – acquired an importance of its own for the immediate prospects of the ECU's enlargement to other countries in the region.

Russia's foreign relations with Central Asia were complicated by the effects of war in Afghanistan and social unrest in some countries, which remained subdued until 2011. But recent developments – including the planned withdrawal of Western forces in Afghanistan and widespread concerns about ensuing instability – suggest that Russia will need to engage in a major reshaping of its policy towards Central Asia as a whole. Although security problems may be prevalent in a short time, how they are tackled may make a difference for the future prospects of economic integration. Political engineering based on mutually supportive goals will be needed. Through this approach, Russia may try to make a virtue of necessity.

Kazakhstan is the wealthiest of the Central Asian countries (with a GDP per capita at the level of two-thirds of that of Russia) and one of the most independent and forward-looking in shaping policies, advancing proposals, and keeping a multi-vector policy of alliances that may or may not include Russia.[8] Its negotiating power within the ECU and the SES is based on its relative economic strength, as analysed by Kassenova in Chapter 8 of this volume. It is worth emphasizing here that given Kazakhstan's size and relative wealth, second only to Russia in the region, the country may well be seen as a forerunner by the other four Central Asian countries in many fields, as well as a strong partner worthy of consideration vis-à-vis Russia. As such, this chapter includes more

---

[8] Evgeny Vinokurov and Alexander Libman, *Eurasian Integration: Challenges of Transcontinental Regionalism* (Palgrave Macmillan, 2012).

than one reference to Kazakhstan. Kazakhstan's trade with China is booming (about $24 billion in 2011) and is expected to reach $40 billion in 2015. It is also noteworthy that China has become Kazakhstan's second largest trade partner after the European Union (EU) and the top import partner since 2010.[9]

However, other countries in Central Asia have a very different economic profile and significance in comparison with Kazakhstan. Kyrgyzstan and Tajikistan have a GDP per capita of $2,400 and $2,100 respectively. Workers' remittances – an indicator of a country's low level of development – count for 47 per cent of Tajikistan's and 29 per cent of Kyrgyzstan's GDP.[10] Both Kyrgyzstan and Tajikistan are set for accession to the ECU in the near future, but integration with such poor countries is causing strains in Russia that are unlikely to abate. Despite their economic dependence on Russia, their negotiating power is high, as they both exploit Russia's security concerns.

As argued below, in comparison with Central Asia, integration policies beyond this area are more likely to reap the benefits of trade with the booming Asia-Pacific region, and China in particular. In this context, the Chinese borders, rather than the current state of the economy of Kyrgyzstan and Tajikistan (in addition to Kazakhstan) may be more important to Russia when it comes to expansion of the ECU to Central Asia. While enlarging the ECU market would facilitate trade, it would also help to stem the Chinese shuttle trade that is becoming a common concern in the region. With the accession of Kyrgyzstan (expected in 2014) and Tajikistan (soon after) to the ECU, alternative routes to China could also help Russian companies to compete with Kazakhstan's successful companies. It is worth noting that Russia's interests in attracting Kyrgyzstan and Tajikistan into an integration area (and common set of rules) arise also from social unrest and turmoil that could easily spread beyond their borders.

---

[9] 'Win-win for China and Kazakhstan', *China.org.cn*, 27 February 2012, http://www.china.org.cn/opinion/2012-02/27/content_24743753.htm; See also http://trade.ec.europa.eu/doclib/docs/2006/september/tradoc_113406.pdf (accessed 1 December 2012).

[10] David Trilling, 'Putin to Central Asia: Join Customs Union, Nudge Nudge, Wink Wink', *EurasiaNet.org*, 12 December 2012, http://www.eurasianet.org/print/66290 (accessed 12 December 2012).

2.1. The ECU's Expansion to Central Asia: What Credibility of Commitment?

However, Central Asian countries are not easy partners for Russia. Russia's efforts to draw 'Westward-orientated' countries into the ECU have been comparatively less demanding (with the exception of Belarus), although still time-consuming, than luring Central Asian countries to back her continent-wide strategic plans. Foreign trade agreements have taken time to materialize and ratification by parliament may turn out to be problematic. The pursuit of a free trade area (FTA) among CIS countries is a second best option where Russia seems to have some success, possibly because agreements signed so far are at the stage of memoranda of intent. Finally, ratification by some signatories should not be taken for granted. As pointed in by Cooper (in Chapter 2 of this volume), agreements on the CIS FTA have been signed so far by Russia, Armenia, Belarus, Kazakhstan, Kyrgyzstan, Moldova, Tajikistan and Ukraine. Uzbekistan, Turkmenistan and Azerbaijan remain sceptical, albeit to different degrees.[11] CIS FTA agreements should take on board any commitments to the World Trade Organization (WTO). Ironically, while Kyrgyzstan's WTO membership since 1998 should, in principle, facilitate accession to the existing ECU, in practice it may turn out to be an obstacle since existing WTO-agreed tariffs would have to be increased to the higher ECU levels.[12]

Interest in a CIS-wide FTA is understandably stronger in smaller and/or poorer countries, as shown by the apparent eagerness of Kyrgyzstan and Tajikistan to become members of the ECU (see also Cooper's Chapter 2). Russia welcomed this interest with stabilization grants and loans,[13] aware that bilateral negotiations for membership will entail mutual, but not always evenly matching, concessions and challenges from foreign powers competing for geopolitical influence.[14] In

---

[11] A. Akhundov, 'Azerbajian Not to Join the Eurasian Customs Union', *Trend*, 16 July 2012, http://en.trend.az/capital/business/2046965.html (accessed 13 February 2013).

[12] 'Ukraina, Belorussia i Rossiia stali zonoi svobodnoi torgovli', *RBK*, 20 September 2012, http://top.rbc.ru/economics/20/09/2012/670586.shtml (accessed 20 September 2012); Tatyana Valovaya, 'Integratsiia ob'ediniaet vsekh – ot kommunistov do 'Edinoi Rossii', *Izvestiya*, 9 June 2012.

[13] Jim Nichol, *Central Asia: Regional Developments and Implications for US Interests* (Congressional Research Service, 18 May 2012), http://fpc.state.gov/documents/organization/191601.pdf (accessed 18 September 2012).

[14] For example, Tajikistan secured the partial writing off of its debt to Russia, the supply of oil products at a discounted price, the building of a hydropower

fact, *do ut des* agreements often consist of economic aid from Russia for military concessions by partner countries.

Even after the signing of treaties and agreements, implementation will need *ex-post* scrutiny. A mature approach to contractual agreements will take time to develop in the existing cultural and political context regardless of the penalties attached to breaching contracts and how independent the supranational Court will be. Russia, as peer in the proposed EEU, will need to adapt to persuasion rather than threat while pressing for the terms of implementation. It is likely that the roadmap to integration will entail an accommodative stance towards certain countries, which is new to Russia. As mentioned above, while from an economic point of view Russia has little to gain from associating with Kyrgyzstan and Tajikistan – accounting for only 0.2 and 0.1 per cent respectively of her volume of trade[15] – regional security has a price that Russia will need to consider.

More relevant to Russia, at the stage of incipient integration, could be security concerns.[16] With regard to imperialist ambitions, often evoked, one should note that while Russia never concealed her own interest in maintaining or restoring the economic ties with the former Soviet countries, the country does not have the military, economic and financial means to control the region. Thus, a cooperative approach becomes inevitable.

The current prospect for post-Soviet integration policies is carefully framed in a rather novel, more or less friendly and open attitude to policy dialogue with any country sharing – but not forced to share – Russia's interests in strengthening and deepening economic integration in Eurasia.

---

plant in exchange for the deployment of a Russian Air Force base: see Natalia Maqsimchook, 'Chronicle of Eurasian Regional Integration 2010', in Eurasian Development Bank, *Eurasian Integration Yearbook 2011* (EDB, 2011) 247. Kyrgyzstan secured a 20 per cent write off of its $500m debt to Russia in exchange for the extension to the lease of a Russian military facility: see Chris Rickleton, 'Kyrgyzstan and Russia Warily Eye Dotted Line in Raft of Agreements', *EurasiaNet.org*, 4 September 2012, http://www.eurasianet.org/print/65861 (accessed 13 February 2013).

[15] See http://trade.ec.europa.eu/doclib/docs/2006/september/tradoc_113440.pdf (accessed 13 February 2013).

[16] Jeffrey Mankoff, 'What an Eurasian Union Means for Washington', *The National Interest*, 19 April 2012, http://nationalinterest.org/commentary/what-eurasian-union-means-washington-6821 (accessed 13 February 2013); Leonid Ivashov, 'Nado uskoriat sozdanie Evraziinskovo Soyuza', *Voennoe Obozrenie*, 14 July 2012, http://topwar.ru/16431-leonid-ivashov-nado-uskoryat-sozdanie-evraziy skogo-soyuza.html (accessed 13 February 2013).

This vision was highlighted in Prime Minister Putin's October 2011 manifesto on Eurasian integration.[17]

This agenda focused on the potential for a growing Russian sphere of influence in the Asian continent compared with major powers including (but not limited to) the EU and United States, whose image and appeal in the eyes of the authorities and nationalist circles in the region had been severely damaged by the global economic crisis. It is worth noting that among the big powers Putin may have had in mind China was to play a major role, and for good reasons. China has become in less than two decades a major competitor with Russia in Central Asia. Investment doubled during the period 2000–10 and trade turnover in the region (including Kazakhstan) grew from $1 billion in 2000 to $26 billion in 2009. The next steps by China involve investments in transport infrastructure,[18] more than one-third that of Russia.

Integration strategies, according to Putin, should be forward-looking, based on market institutions, endowed with supranational bodies capable of fostering integration processes in the CIS region and beyond, and organizationally capable of representing a powerful (collective) partner for dialogue with the EU.

With regard to the prerequisites for an effective Eurasian Economic Union to enter into force in 2015, the idea is that the Single Economic Space will provide for coordination of macroeconomic policy, competition rules, technical regulations, agricultural subsidies, transport, and tariffs on natural monopolies, while also facilitating single visa and migration procedures. Only in the long term would Eurasian structures provide for the creation of a FTA from the Atlantic to the Pacific, working on a polycentric mechanism of management. Putin's manifesto sounds optimistic in the light of past and current developments punctuated by ongoing strains between the tripartite ECU as well as the precarious state of international relations. One can also question whether in dealing with Central Asian countries, where other powers with their own economic and/or political interests continue to play an important

---

[17]   Vladimir Putin, 'Novyi integratsionnyi proekt dlia Evrazii – budushchee, kotoroe pozhdaetsia sevodnia', *Izvestiya*, 3 October 2011.

[18]   Paul Globe, 'China Replacing Russia as "Elder Brother" in Central Asia', *Window on Eurasia*, 12 December 2012, http://windowoneurasia2.blog spot.co.uk/2012/12/window-on-eurasia-china-replacing.html (accessed on 13 February 2013).

role, Russia will be able to employ the stick-and-carrot approach often used with other countries in the past.[19]

2.2. The Economics of Stability and Control over Energy

Maintaining and enhancing the supply of oil and gas throughout the continent is crucial for Russia, but also a concern for other Central Asian producing countries. Interestingly, intraregional competition on gas supply eastwards towards the Asian-Pacific region may force random inter-governmental agreements, despite each separate country's interest in raising fences around its own supply channels. Integration policies may help to build mutually supportive projects in pipeline extensions and connections. China's market for energy is enormous and is more easily reachable from Central Asia than from Northern Russia. It would be in Russia's interest to establish her own access from the South.

Bilateral or multilateral agreements have proven difficult to negotiate and implement given the intricacy of the pipeline network in the region and the temptation to outmanoeuvre negotiating partners. Cheating on the agreed supply share by each country is also common among OPEC countries. Tensions in this area have already occurred. Kassenova (in Chapter 8 of this volume) refers to some issues related to Kazakhstan's oil and gas delivery to China. After Russia discontinued the purchase of Turkmen gas delivery to China in 2010, the country tried to diversify further its outlets. Having completed the gas pipeline to China in 2009, Turkmenistan moved to build another East-West gas pipeline bypassing Russia with an annual capacity of 30 billion cubic metres (bcm) at a cost of $1 billion. Uzbekistan started to export gas to China from August 2012, planning to reach 25 bcm in 2016 from 11 bcm in 2012. There are plans to supply natural gas to China along the extended Central Asia–China pipeline, which runs from Turkmenistan through Uzbekistan and Kazakhstan to China. Its current annual capacity is 30 bcm, and will reach 55 bcm annually in 2014–15.[20] Russia is cut off from this project.

---

[19]   On the USA, see Mankoff, above note 16. On China, see Zabikulla S. Saipov, 'China's Economic Strategies for Uzbekistan and Central Asia: Building Roads to Afghan Strategic Resources and Beyond', *Eurasia Daily Monitor*, 21 September 2012, http://www.jamestown.org/single/?no_cache=1&tx_ttnews%5Btt_news%5D=39873 (accessed 13 February 2013).

[20]   Uzbekistan is the largest producer and consumer of natural gas in Central Asia: see Aleksandra Jarosiewicz, 'Uzbekistan Starts Gas Export to China', *OSW EastWeek* (Centre for Eastern Studies, 19 September 2012).

Ironically, intraregional competition on gas supply eastwards is obviously welcomed by China, which can easily diversify sources while enjoying a quasi-monopsonistic power on prices,[21] owing to it being in practice a single purchaser of a commodity. This is an irritant to Russia, which already suffers from successful resistance from the Western economies to sign long-term contracts at much higher than market prices once the crisis-hit demand for energy abated.

While gas and oil supply – where the main actors are powerful state companies – are the most important source of contention in the region, business exchanges that are key to effective and durable integration are also problematic because of poor judiciary and ineffective enforcement of contracts. When Kyrgyzstan and Tajikistan become members of the ECU they will be subject to the legal framework already in place for the enforcement of contracts and dispute resolution. The protection of individual property rights remains a problem in Kyrgyzstan, a member of the WTO since 1998, and Tajikistan, a member since March 2013, which indicates that implementation is likely to remain a problem for some time (see also Connolly, Chapter 4 of this volume).

The integration of other Central Asian states is unlikely in the foreseeable future. For both geographical and institutional reasons, Turkmenistan (bordering Iran, Afghanistan and the Caspian Sea) and Uzbekistan are unlikely to join the SES and EEU. Turkmenistan is effectively run by the President's family clan who control entire sectors of the economy and decide on import duties according to their own convenience, at the expense of the poorer sections of society which are hit by high import prices.[22] The judicial system in Turkmenistan is far below the level required for functioning markets, even in a region where such problems are rather endemic. Without an accepted supranational court for dispute resolution or, worst of all, the absence of compliance with its rulings, no meaningful economic integration may be expected.

---

[21] Pipelines International, 'The Pipelines Feeding China's Burgeoning Economy', *Pipelines International*, March 2011, http://pipelines international.com/news/the_pipelines_feeding_chinas_burgeoning_economy/055 358 (accessed 6 October 2012).

[22] Dudry Kuliev, 'Turkmenistan – Presidentskii Klan Delit Stranu', *Tsentr-Azia*, 23 November 2012, http://www.centrasia.ru/newsA.php?st=1353615480 (accessed 13 February 2013).

Similar problems can be observed in Uzbekistan, where confiscation of private assets has been endured by both Russian and Turkish companies.[23]

Nonetheless, for geopolitical reasons Russia will continue to compete for influence in the region. The United States – given persistent turbulence – will need to maintain a certain number of military bases and the EU is interested in diversifying gas and oil supplies from the region. With Kyrgyzstan and Tajikistan bordering China and keen to join the ECU and the EEU, one can speculate that Russia will move faster towards an eastward (rather than southward)-orientated Eurasian Economic Union, while trying to uphold relations with countries such as Uzbekistan and Turkmenistan, where security concerns tend to attract a number of other large and powerful external actors.

3. CONSTRUCTING THE 'EURASIAN BRIDGE'

The idea of the Eurasian Economic Union serving as a bridge between an integrated European economy and an increasingly integrated Asian economy, resulting in a mega common economic area, was voiced by Putin, Nazarbaev and other leaders at the 2012 Asia-Pacific Economic Cooperation (APEC) meeting in Vladivostok.

Ironically, Russia's vision came to the fore at a time when the EU's construct was beginning to expose serious failures and, in the Asia-Pacific region, antagonism is more visible than cooperation. It is not clear whether the idea of Russia serving as a bridge between the two continents was developed to bolster the support of Russians or mitigate the anxiety of an already economically weakened international community. Bridging Europe with Asia is an extremely ambitious goal. Nonetheless, rather than hampering ongoing integration projects, broader visions may help to boost the image of Russia as a peaceful and effective mediator at the global level. However, building such a bridge would entail, first of all, developing the backward Asian part of Russia: a tremendous task for Russia.

---

[23] The criminal indictment and nationalization of a subsidiary of the transnational Russian dairy and food product company, Wimm-Bill-Dann – ironically well known for good governance in Russia – is not encouraging: Eurasian Development Bank, above note 14, 303. See also Jim Nichol, 'Uzbekistan: Recent Developments and US Interests', Congressional Research Service, 3 August 2012, 7–8, http://www.fas.org/sgp/crs/row/RS21238.pdf (accessed 18 September 2012).

Putin presented this vision to businessmen as an advantage in relation to steadily growing Asian economies and an alternative to unstable global markets. Objective estimates of costs and benefits are difficult. Russian projections to 2020 show that improved infrastructure and transport in the Far East would allow a five-fold increase in transit from Europe to the Asia-Pacific region and spur competition.[24] By 2025 APEC countries may account for a third of Russian trade. This is linked to the steady decline (from 56 per cent in 2006 to 49 per cent in 2012) of the volume of EU bilateral trade with Russia, as well as the concomitant increase in trade with the Asia-Pacific region from 15 per cent to 23 per cent.[25] Framing Russia as an intrinsic part of the Asia-Pacific region, Putin linked his commitment to develop Siberia and the Far East to the robust growth in the Asia-Pacific region,[26] a policy allegedly welcome by Kazakhstan and other countries, such as New Zealand and Vietnam. Concerning security in the region, mutual interests between Russia and China are evoked. Putin promised that the production of foodstuffs, hydrocarbon and atomic energy will be enhanced to the benefit of all regional partners, citing cases of foreign partnership (such as the agreement between Exxon and Rosneft to tap energy reserves in Siberia, the Arctic and Black Sea).[27] China's plans to double its natural gas pipeline network by 2016 seemed to confirm Russia's expectations.

Russia plans to extend the 801 billion ruble East Siberian-Pacific Ocean pipeline (built to serve China) to its Far Eastern port of Kozmino in 2012 and further bolster Asia-Pacific energy ties since the launch of oil deliveries to China in 2011. Other projects include setting up a petrochemical complex on the Pacific coast to target the Chinese market. The Sino-Russian Eastern Petrochemical Company (49 per cent owned by Rosneft and 51 per cent by the China National Petroleum Corporation) will build a refinery in Tianjin with a total capacity of 13 million tons by

---

[24]   Vladimir Putin, 'Vladivostok – 2012: Rossiiskaia Povestka dlia Foruma ATES', *Kremlin.ru*, 5 September 2012, http://kremlin.ru/transcripts/16390 (accessed 13 February 2013).

[25]   Ilya Khrennikov and Scott Rose, 'Putin Looks East for Growth as Indebted Europe Loses Sheen', *Bloomberg*, 7 September 2012, http://www.bloomberg.com/news/2012-09-06/putin-looks-east-for-growth-as-debt-ridden-europe-loses-sheen.html (accessed 13 February 2013).

[26]   Putin, above note 24; 'Customs Union, Vietnam to Create Free Trade Zone: President', *Kazinform*, 10 September 2012, http://www.kazinform.kz/eng/article/2493319 (accessed 13 February 2013).

[27]   'Vladimir Putin Prinial Uchastie v Rabote Delovogo Sammita ATES', *Kremlin.ru*, 7 September 2012, http://news.kremlin.ru/news/16410; Pipelines International, above note 21.

2015 and 70 per cent Russian input. Russia is already advanced in planning and building nuclear stations in China – a business of interest to Japan. Other projects range from the production and storage of wheat to car plants financed by Japan.[28] While combining the network of energy pipelines across Central Asia is possible, it is time-consuming and exposed to mutual blackmail. In contrast, as discussed below, developing the Far East's structures appears, at least in principle, to be less problematic.

4. FROM THE ECU TO CHINA

Russia's efforts to benefit from trade with, and investment from, China and linking these efforts with pursuing the Eurasian integration project can be attributed to prioritizing the allocation of resources. While overtly ambitious, it would be wrong to dismiss this vision *per se*.

There are signs that the Asian economies as such may be interested in becoming more integrated. As explained in other parts of this volume, other countries manifest interest in the reshaping of economic and political relations in the Asia-Pacific region. Although Russia's trade with China is still low, it is rising fast: up to 33 per cent in 2012 compared with a significant decline in China's trade with Europe and Japan of 11 per cent. Expectations are that by 2015 it could reach $100 billion and by 2020 $200 billion.[29] Although this is still less than half the trade value with Europe, that projection bolsters Russia's contention that integration policies are not backward looking. Russia's integration policies keep an eye on security. The same is true for relations with China: a global competitor in all areas of power.

Politically, Russia is interested in the stability of the whole of Eurasia and seems to be ready to assume its costs. Yet this may not be sustainable. Nonetheless, as noted by some experts, during the economic crisis of 2008–09 Russia's investments in CIS countries were not suspended – as occurred with investment in non-CIS countries – but were

---

[28]   Khrennikov and Rose, above note 25. See also Putin speaking to the business community in Vladivostok, 'Putin Pozdravil Sechina', *Gazeta.Ru*, 7 September 2012, http://www.gazeta.ru/financial/2012/09/07/4758613.shtml (accessed 31 January 2013).

[29]   Zheng Yangpeng, 'China–Russia Trade Remains Robust', *China Daily*, 30 April 2012, http://www.asianewsnet.net/home/news.php?sec=2&id=30072 (accessed 30 September 2012); Vladimir Kozlovskii, 'RF i Kitai pereidut na svodobnuiu togovliu', *Rossiiskaya Gazeta*, 26 September 2012.

merely slowed down, possibly in an effort to uphold political ties.[30] A corporatist system such as that in Russia – and perhaps other post-Soviet countries' – is well positioned to enforce the immediate social costs of stability through economic integration; hence the overarching vision ought not to be dismissed outright.

5. SIBERIA AND THE FAR EAST: A RUSSIAN OR A EURASIAN BRIDGE BETWEEN EUROPE AND ASIA?

Russia beyond the Urals (from Siberia to the Far East) spans two-thirds of the country's territory and has been a 'neglected backyard'. Thus, massive investments will be necessary to bridge the Northern Chinese provinces, South Korea and Japan with Western Russia to effectively reach the European market. The economic agencies in Russia are well aware of the drain on resources this would entail during Putin's third presidential mandate (2012–18).

According to Putin's Presidential Decree on long-term economic policy, concrete projects for the development of the Far East should have been prepared by July 2012. A new Minister for the Development of Russia Far East was appointed in May 2012, in charge of coordinating projects and work in the region. The appointee was Viktor Ishaev, the former governor of Khabarovsk *krai* and plenipotentiary for the Far East. With the appointment of Shoigu as Minister of Defence in 2012, both the Far East – where most Russian military factories are located – and integration policies that would be favoured by a number of previously CIS-integrated factories acquired a new impulse (see also Cooper, Chapter 5 of this volume).

Institutional developments concerning the Far East remain obscure and probably a source of interministerial tension. The Ministry of Finance is opposed to a major redistribution of resources to a large underdeveloped and underpopulated area and development agencies are pushing for more vigorous financial policies. Progress so far is not significant, but the costs to the budget are already high. To rebuild and refurbish large areas of Vladivostok to host the September 2012 APEC meeting the government spent some $20 billion. The building of a new university in Vladivostok

---

[30]   Aleksandr Libman and Mikhail Golovninv, 'Trends in Investment Cooperation between CIS Countries and the Global Economic Crisis', in EDB, above note 14, 39.

is hoped to motivate bright young people not only from distant Russian areas but also from abroad.[31]

According to the Valdai Discussion Club Analytical Report, the advantages of developing Siberia and particularly the Far East lie mainly in the economic geography of the region and its wealth of water, agricultural land and forestry, all promising for further industrial development.[32] However, the main stumbling block is the poor transport infrastructure: for instance, there is no direct federal highway going as far as the Chinese border and Russia lacks modern high-precision equipment for roadworks and tunnelling. Attracting young Russians to the area would also pose problems as only 6.6 per cent of households are connected to gas supplies compared with the Russian average of 63.2 per cent. Perhaps migrant workers from less fortunate CIS countries would adapt.

The problem of how to attract investment is acute even if in the Far East competitive private businesses are blooming thanks to market forces unimpeded by state subventions or interference.[33] To boost investment, the government is considering economic preferences.[34] In addition, part of the revenues of large state companies (more than $3 billion) and money from the Reserve Fund would be transferred to the region.[35] Privatization revenues are also considered.[36] Although it is clear that there is a need for both state and private investment, neither is to be taken for granted under tight budget constraints on the one side, and the still low protection of property rights and contract enforcement on the other. It is not impossible that special economic zones or other bodies, previously dismissed, will be under consideration to facilitate the task.

---

[31] Oleg Barabanov and Timofei Bordachev, *Toward the Great Ocean, or the New Globalisation of Russia* (Valdai Discussion Club Analytical Report, July 2012).

[32] Ibid.

[33] Guido Friebel and Helena Schweiger, 'Management Quality, Firm Performance and Market Pressure in Russia', *Working Paper Nr 144* (EBRD, April 2012).

[34] Ansatoli Medetsky, 'Kremlin Backs Idea of Far East Tax Rebate', *The Moscow Times*, 19 September 2012, 5.

[35] 'Chast' Dividendov "Rosneftegaza" Budet Napravlena na Razvitie Dal'nego Vostoka cherez "Dochku" VEBa', *ITAR–TASS*, 26 September 2012, http://www.itar-tass.com/c9/529629.html (accessed 26 September 2012).

[36] 'MER: Dohody ot Sberbanka i "Rosneftegaza" Mogut Napravit' na Dal'nii Vostok', *RBK*, 20 September 2012, http://www.rbc.ru/rbcfreenews/2012092 0172822.shtml?print (accessed 13 February 2013).

The immediate costs of upgrading the infrastructure in the Russian territory located in Asia contrast with more distant and, to a large extent, unpredictable benefits from step-by-step ECU-SES-EEU integration policies. Whether this integration strategy is compatible with the accelerated development of the Far East becomes an important question for Russia itself, especially as the signs that the world economic crisis will abate before the end of the current decade are far from clear.

6. PERCEPTIONS OF THE EURASIAN PROJECT IN RUSSIA

Russian attitudes towards Putin's Eurasia project are mixed. There are concerns that Russia's economic drive towards the Asia-Pacific region may disturb China, which is eager to increase control of the region, and the US whose geopolitical interests in the Pacific area are also mounting. Some suggest that Russia should avoid intervening in the conflicts and historical disputes of other countries.[37] Many are concerned by how eastward-looking plans and financial commitments will impinge on society and businesses that are used to looking westwards. Others fear money will be wasted in government policies used to mobilize resources. Some (not necessarily pro-government supporters) offer their own proposals.[38]

In addition to nationalist feelings bolstered by integration projects the development of which is unpredictable,[39] the implications and feasibility of broader integration policies are examined dispassionately by some experts. The point that focusing on the development of the Far East is not necessarily compatible with a broader ECU taking in poor Central Asian

---

[37] Alexei Fenenko, 'Russia's Pacific Policy: A Myriad of Scenarios', *Valdai Discussion Club*, 15 December 2012, http://valdaiclub.com/russia_and_the_world/a161782283.html; Oleg Barabanov and Timofei Bordachev, 'Realism instead of Utopia', *Russia in Global Affairs*, 28 December 2012.

[38] For example, Fyodor Lukyanov, 'Nedorazumenie po-evraziiski', *Gazeta.ru*, 23 August 2012, http://www.gazeta.ru/column/lukyanov/4735037.shtml (accessed 17 November 2012); Anders Aslund, 'Putin's Eurasian Illusion Will Lead to Isolation', *The Moscow Times*, 21 June 2012; Aleksandra Samarina and Ivan Rodin, 'Ravnenie- na SSSR', *Nezavisimaya Gazeta*, 17 November 2012.

[39] Silvana Malle, 'Economic Modernisation and Diversification in Russia. Constraints and Challenges' (2013) 4 *Journal of Eurasian Studies* 1, pp. 78–99.

countries has been raised by Barabanov,[40] who also presses for immediate development activities in sub-regions – such as bridging the Far East with the North-Eastern regions of China primarily and making the Russian regions involved fully fledged participants in the EEU with their own representative in the Eurasian Union Commission. Ad hoc organizational structures, thus, become crucial both to prevent current ECU members from pulling decisions their own way against Russian interests, and to emancipate Russia's Eastern regions from Moscow's inertia or hostility.[41]

From such viewpoints, development plans for Siberia and the Far East appear as a quasi-alternative to a broadening of the ECU. This is because countries such as Kyrgyzstan and Tajikistan may put their own interests before those of integration based on WTO principles and requirements in the hope of winning concessions from Russia; thus, hampering the process of integration with the Asia-Pacific region.

7. CONCLUSIONS

It is not clear whether the idea of Russia serving as a bridge between the two continents was developed to bolster the support of Russians or mitigate the anxiety of an already economically weakened international community. Bridging Europe with Asia is an extremely ambitious goal. Ironically, Russia's vision came to the fore at a time when the EU's construct was beginning to expose serious failures and, in the Asia-Pacific region, antagonism is more visible than cooperation. Nonetheless, rather than hampering ongoing integration projects, broader visionary prospects may help to boost the image of Russia as a peaceful and hard-working mediator at the global level. However, building such a bridge would entail, first of all, developing the backward Asian part of Russia that represents two-thirds of her territory – a tremendous task for Russia.

---

[40]   Oleg Barabanov, 'Problems of Siberia and the Far East', *Valdai Discussion Club*, 4 August 2012, http://valdaiclub.com/economy/48480.html; Oleg Barabanov, 'Customs Union and Eurasian Union: Problems on the Road to Integration', *Valdai Discussion Club*, 11 April 2012, http://valdaiclub.com/near_abroad/41060.html (accessed 13 February 2013).

[41]   Sergei Karaganov, 'Russia Needs One More Capital in Siberia', *Valdai Discussion Club*, 2 July 2012, http://valdaiclub.com/economy/45483.html (accessed 4 September 2012).

From an Asian perspective, and under tight fiscal constraints, Russia may have to choose between prioritizing the enlargement of the ECU, in particular to Central Asia, or mobilizing resources for the development of Siberia and the Far East that in time could provide safer trade routes to China and the Asia-Pacific region. In Central Asia there are competing interests of various kinds from both China and the United States. They may interfere with Russia's efforts to control major oil/gas routes. Among Central Asian countries, only Kyrgyzstan and Tajikistan, once they become ECU members, would provide alternative routes and checkpoints for trade to and from China. Russia is keen to support financially their Eurasian partnership, but is afraid of the price to pay in implementing contracts.

There are also economic reasons to argue that Central Asian countries may be disturbed by Russia's cross-border integration with the Asia-Pacific region. To countries producing low value added goods, competing with China while not profiting from commodity exports because of the lack of capacity and capital could harm infant industries that would possibly become prey to Chinese companies. For Kazakhstan, trying to reap the benefits of its multi-vector strategy towards non-CIS countries and South East Asia, improved transit routes through the Far East and Siberia would not necessarily be welcome.[42]

Increasingly, if seen through the growing importance of China, Russia's own eastward-orientated development and growth may turn out to be more advantageous than broader economic integration across the post-Soviet space, if budget constraints turn out to be tighter than earlier envisaged.

But geopolitical interests in the stability of the area and the safety of transport routes and oil and gas pipelines are pre-eminent in Russia's approach to regional integration. Thus, one can expect that relations with Turkmenistan and Uzbekistan, the countries less prone to cooperation, will not be discontinued and even improved if the interests of third parties subside in time. However, immediate membership of the ECU is unlikely.

All in all, reliable transit routes westwards and eastwards through Siberia and the Far East would provide better support for a Eurasian union bridging Europe and Asia-Pacific than any other alternative. The project is tremendously costly but, contrary to extra-Russia integration plans, it should remain under the control of the Russian government. If interested private companies find a profitable business environment, the

---

[42] Barabanov (11 April 2012), above note 40.

region could take off within the foreseeable future. The mobilization of resources will need high political consensus: rising Russian nationalism cannot be excluded but it could be diluted into a purposeful and mutually beneficial goal: economic growth for all.

# 7.	Belarus: player and pawn in the integration game

Matthew Frear

## 1.	INTRODUCTION

Belarus is the smallest member of the tripartite Eurasian Customs Union (ECU) in terms of population, territory and economy. It has unfailingly participated in the Russia-led initiatives to foster economic integration in the post-Soviet space, alongside what is on paper the most ambitious integration project in Eurasia: the Union State of Russia and Belarus (USRB). Aleksander Lukashenko, ensconced as Belarusian president since 1994, has portrayed himself as a leading proponent of close integration while making it clear he views Belarus as an equal partner in regional bodies, not a subservient member.[1] The involvement of Belarus in the ECU and Single Economic Space (SES) is not unexpected, although Minsk has not been uncritical of the projects. As this chapter will argue, the reason behind the country's participation cannot simply be attributed to blind loyalty to its powerful neighbour to the east, Russia. Minsk has vigorously pursued its own agenda regarding Eurasian integration, albeit with varying degrees of success.

This chapter begins by examining the drivers for and the motivation behind the Belarusian leadership's engagement with regional integration projects. It is argued that the primary goal has not been integration *per se*, but rather securing beneficial deals from Russia, in particular on the energy front. Minsk has taken a highly instrumental approach, with integration traditionally exploited as a means to an end, rather than a goal in itself. The focus is on resolving specific problems of interest to Belarus, rather than seeking solutions to common problems across

---

[1]	Alexander Libman and Evgeny Vinokurov, *Holding-Together Regionalism: Twenty Years of Post-Soviet Integration* (Palgrave Macmillan, 2012) 91; Aleksandr Lukashenko, 'O Sud'bakh Nashei Intergratsii', *Izvestiya*, 17 October 2011, 1.

member states, with the authorities in Minsk taking a self-interested, instrumentalist approach to integration.

The chapter moves on to outline the initial implications of participation in the ECU for Belarus and the potential challenges that the country faces. The following sections then explore the rhetoric and reality of Belarusian implementation of Eurasian integration, as well as the way in which Belarus positions itself in the wider world. It highlights that while Minsk may support integration rhetoric, it is likely to be a fair-weather friend if economic benefits for Belarus are not forthcoming. Commitments may be made to cede sovereignty, but the Belarusian leadership will endeavour to pick and choose what they implement in practice, as they have demonstrated previously in the USRB. Belarus attempts to pursue integration on its own terms and with its own priorities, which will not always coincide with those of the other members of the ECU. Minsk has limited room for manoeuvre, politically and economically, to avoid engagement with Russia-led regional integration projects. Nevertheless it will seek to limit the surrender of control over the domestic levers of economic power for as long as possible in practice.

2. THE VIEW FROM BELARUS ON REGIONAL INTEGRATION

The most important political actor in Belarus is President Lukashenko. Since his election in 1994 there has been a personalization of power around the presidency and Belarus has transformed into an increasingly authoritarian regime.[2] The entire political system and all branches of government are highly centralized and hierarchical with ministries and parliament subordinate to the presidential administration. The composition of the ruling elites is frequently changed by Lukashenko and can include those who traditionally have close ties to Russia – for example, members of the old communist leadership or senior officials in the security and military services, as well as pragmatic, economic nationalists who are more open to cooperation with the West and are wary of Russian economic influence.[3] Lukashenko turns to these groupings as

---

[2]   Valerii Karbalevich, *Alyaksandr Lukashenko: Politicheskii Portret* (Partizan, 2010); Matthew Frear, 'An Anatomy of Adaptive Authoritarianism: Belarus under Aliaksandr Lukashenka' (PhD thesis, University of Birmingham, 2011).

[3]   Olga Belova-Gille, 'Difficulties of Elite Formation in Belarus After 1991', in Elena Korosteleva, Colin Lawson and Rosalind Marsh (eds), *Contemporary Belarus: Between Democracy and Dictatorship* (RoutledgeCurzon, 2003); Kamil

and when expedient for his own rule and they can be played off against one another.

This centralization extends also to the economy. According to official figures, 75 per cent of the economy remains under state control and directors of major state-owned enterprises are appointed and dismissed by the presidency. Additionally, patron-client networks with Lukashenko at the apex can be used to reward or punish senior officials and provide opportunities for opaque commercial dealings within the regime. There is no equivalent of the oligarchs found elsewhere in the region, with their own independent financial base. Some wealthy businessmen have emerged, but their success is attributable to close ties with the ruling circle around Lukashenko who can provide access to the national wealth.[4] As such there is no influential, independent business lobby to agitate for or against regional economic integration. Business and industry leaders may voice their opinions, but they can also be replaced if they fall out of favour. After almost two decades in power, decision-making in Belarus is focused on the short term and based on what will best serve the interests of Lukashenko and his allies remaining in control, rather than the longer-term interests of the country. This extends to the motivations behind participation in regional integration initiatives.

Belarus is almost exclusively dependent on Russia for its energy needs. Cheap gas and oil from Russia are essential for maintaining the relative success of the Belarusian economy and these subsidies can form up to 16 per cent of total gross domestic product (GDP).[5] It relies on Russia for 100 per cent of its gas imports and around 85 per cent of its oil imports following limited diversification since 2010. These economic subsidies from Russia have allowed Belarus to avoid any deep, painful economic

Klysinski and Agata Wierzbowska-Miazga, 'Changes in the Political Elite, Economy and Society of Belarus. Appearances and Reality', *OSW Studies No. 30* (Centre for Eastern Studies, June 2009).

4   Siarhei Bohdan, 'Are There Any Oligarchs in Belarus?', *Belarus Digest*, 1 May 2012, http://belarusdigest.com/story/are-there-any-oligarchs-belarus-9069 (accessed 6 November 2012).

5   Margarita M. Balmaceda, 'At the Crossroads: The Belarusian-Russian Energy-Political Model in Crisis', in Sabine Fischer (ed.), *Back From the Cold? The EU and Russia in 2009*, Chaillot Paper No. 119 (Institute for Security Studies, 2009); Belarus Digest, 'Belarus Reality Check 2012', *Belarus Digest*, 19 December 2012, http://belarusdigest.com/story/belarus-reality-check-2012-12486 (accessed 19 December 2012); Grigory Ioffe and Viachaslau Yarashevich, 'Debating Belarus: An Economy in Comparative Perspective' (2011) 52 *Eurasian Geography and Economics* 750; Leonid Zlotnikov, 'The Belarusian "Economic Miracle" – Illusions and Reality', in Fischer, ibid.

reforms and maintain energy-inefficient industries which provide employment. They enable the authorities to maintain a social contract with the electorate through public spending on social programmes, cheap electricity and petrol, and the preservation of a cycle in which salaries and pensions are increased on the eve of elections to win popular support. Subsidized energy has allowed Belarusian factories to refine crude oil and then export petroleum products to the West, generating up to 30 per cent of the revenues for the state budget. Up to three-quarters of Belarusian exports to the European Union (EU) are refined petroleum products (the remaining share made up of chemicals, machinery, agricultural products and textiles), which puts the national economy at risk if Russia restricts oil supplies.[6] It is with this background that Minsk has generally pursued integration initiatives as an opportunity to be rewarded with energy subsidies in return for remaining Russia's closest and most loyal ally in the region.

Belarus has been an active member of the Commonwealth of Independent States (CIS), headquartered in Minsk, as well as the Collective Security Treaty Organization, the Eurasian Economic Community (EvrAzES) and their precursors. Minsk has also developed a unique relationship with Russia beyond that of other republics in the post-Soviet space through the USRB. Belarus could be relied upon to provide rhetorical support for the numerous integration projects launched by Russia, in anticipation of economic support from Moscow in return, but there was little interest in the actual integration processes themselves.[7] There is no real ideological underpinning to, or unwavering geopolitical loyalty behind, Belarusian involvement in Eurasian integration. The rhetoric of Slavic unity and brotherhood can be invoked at times, but also ignored if it is not in the interests of Minsk.

The ECU and the SES follow in the footsteps of the more ambitious USRB; this project, however, highlights the challenges of implementing integration in practice. Presidents Eltsin and Lukashenko held a flurry of treaty signing ceremonies which proclaimed the formation of a Community (1996), then a Union (1997) and finally a new Union State (1999), which promised deeper economic integration alongside political

---

[6]   Sergey Mazol, 'Trade Policy of Belarus in the CIS Region: Specific Model or Country Specific Trade Policy for a Small Open Economy', *Berlin Working Papers on Money, Finance, Trade and Development No. 01/2012* (HTW/DAAD Partnership, January 2012) 12–13.
[7]   Libman and Vinokurov, above note 1, 43.

and military cooperation.[8] The two presidents pursued the project for their own domestic political advantages, often with mutually incompatible goals. The free movement of citizens was established and a customs union was partially created, although in practice some protectionist barriers remained in relation to each other's goods. The project has not fulfilled its ambitions of a genuine unified state.[9] Progress floundered on Minsk's demand to be treated as an equal partner. On issues such as potential monetary union or a new Constitutional Act for the USRB, Russia was unwilling to countenance an equal say for Belarus. The rhetoric supporting the USRB continues from both sides and joint USRB bodies exist, but the project is now mainly symbolic. Nevertheless the experience of, and lessons learnt from, this attempt at closer integration informs attitudes in both Minsk and Moscow for future Eurasian initiatives.

The USRB was initially a case when Lukashenko also actively pursued closer political integration for the prospect of taking on a leading role on the Russian political scene, in what has been described as an example of the tail trying to wag the dog.[10] Such ambitions were thwarted when Putin succeeded Eltsin to the Russian presidency in 2000 and since then the priority has been to trade the promise of military-political allegiance to Moscow for economic preferences which will help to keep Lukashenko in power in Belarus.[11] Lukashenko has had no compunction about using the rhetoric of defending Belarusian sovereignty against claims of a threat of Russian 'imperial mentality'[12] under Putin when it has suited him domestically. Belarus may sometimes be described at the

[8] Alex Danilovich, *Russian-Belarusian Integration: Playing Games Behind the Kremlin Walls* (Ashgate, 2006).

[9] Ruth Deyermond, 'The State of the Union: Military Success, Economic and Political Failure in the Russia–Belarus Union' (2004) 56 *Europe-Asia Studies* 1191; Wojciech Kononczuk, 'Difficult "Ally": Belarus in Russia's Foreign Policy', *CES Studies No. 28* (Centre for Eastern Studies, September 2008); David R. Marples, 'Is the Russia–Belarus Union Obsolete?' (2008) 55 *Problems of Post-Communism* 25.

[10] Karbalevich, above note 2, 516.

[11] Vyachaslau Pazdnyak, 'The Rise and Fall of Belarus' Geopolitical Strategy' (2011) 9 *Lithuanian Annual Strategic Review* 173; Pavel Usov, 'Mesto Belarusi v Geopoliticheskom Prostranstve: Vzglyad Iznutri' (2005) *Palitichnaya Sfera* 117.

[12] Dmitrii Sergeichik, 'Belarus' Voshla v Tamozhennyi Soyuz Po Printsipu "Pozhivem – Uvidim"', *Naviny Belorusskie Novosti*, 5 July 2010, http://naviny.by/rubrics/politic/2010/07/05/ic_articles_112_168474/ (accessed 7 November 2012).

most 'Soviet' of the new post-Soviet independent states, but Lukashenko is not interested in reducing his authority by becoming a mere vassal of Moscow. Belarusian participation in regional integration projects, including the ECU, is pragmatic, opportunistic, and focused on quick wins and short-term advantages, usually with an eye on the next national election.

The regime built around Lukashenko is the dominant force in Belarus. Alternative points of view from the opposition or the general public provide no real constraints. The opposition lacks consensus on how it views Eurasian economic integration.[13] Public opinion is generally positive towards the ECU and the SES, with approximately 60 per cent in favour, although somewhat less enthusiastic than in Russia or Kazakhstan.[14] However, Lukashenko has never offered the people of Belarus a referendum on issues such as the USRB or the latest regional integration initiatives. The support or otherwise of the general public is not essential for Minsk to pursue integration.

3. THE TERMS OF BELARUSIAN PARTICIPATION IN THE ECU

Having outlined the background to Belarusian engagement in Eurasian integration in general, this section looks at the ECU specifically. Forecasts from the Eurasian Development Bank have painted a rosy picture of 15 per cent additional GDP growth for Belarus by 2030 within the ECU and SES, but under the proviso that it complies fully with all the requirements demanded by these economic integration projects.[15] Minsk was not a particularly enthusiastic proponent of the ECU before its formation, anticipating little immediate economic benefit from it.[16] The state-controlled media has stressed two key advantages for Belarus. These are (i) the expansion of the markets for Belarusian products into Russia and Kazakhstan, and (ii) the potential for improved deals for the supply of energy commodities from Russia. In reality the consequences have not been so straightforward. This section first outlines how the ECU

---

[13]   Frear, above note 2, 199–201.
[14]   Igor Zadorin, Viktor Moisov and Ekaterina Glod, 'Monitoring Obshchestvennykh Nastroenii: Pervaya Volna' (2012) *Evraziiskaya Ekonomicheskaya Integratsiya* 7, 17–18.
[15]   Viktor Ivanter et al., 'The Economic Effects of the Creation of the Single Economic Space and Potential Accession of Ukraine', *Eurasian Integration Yearbook 2012* (Eurasian Development Bank, 2012) 23–6.
[16]   Libman and Vinokurov, above note 1, 49.

has created new challenges for the country, with Belarusian industry facing increased competition in the ECU's free market without resolving the long-standing trade disputes with Russia, including energy conflicts. It then looks at what the introduction of the Common External Tariff (CET) has meant for Belarus, and the likely impact of Russia's accession to the World Trade Organization (WTO) for the Belarusian economy within the context of the ECU.

Membership of the ECU offers Belarus access to a common market that includes Russia and Kazakhstan, but in reality accession has provided little extra benefit for Belarusian trade in the region. Minsk already enjoyed access to Russian markets through the existing agreements of the USRB and Russia still accounts for almost all of Belarusian trade with the ECU. While the rate of Belarusian exports to Kazakhstan has increased significantly since 2010, this was from a very low base and Kazakhstan still only accounted for less than one per cent of total Belarusian trade turnover in 2011.[17] China and Brazil remain larger trading partners for Belarus than Kazakhstan and the small Belarusian economy is actually relatively open to the rest of the world. Since 2011 Minsk has exported slightly more to the EU than its partners in the ECU, although less than its exports to the CIS as a whole.[18] Trade with the West is increasing in spite of economic sanctions and political opprobrium, which will be detailed in the next section of this chapter.

The readiness of Belarus to attempt to hold back the integration process in a bid to secure more favourable terms for its own participation is exemplified by the delay in final ratification of the ECU Customs Code.[19] The Agreement on the Customs Code was signed in November 2009 and was planned to enter into force on 1 July 2010. This coincided with a low point in relations between Belarus and Russia, who were engaged in a very public 'information war' over a variety of political and

---

[17]   Dzmitry Bruhavetski, 'Belarusian Commodities in Common Free Market Zone: Dumping, Devaluation and Oil in Exchange for Loyalty', *Studies & Analyses Nr 06/2012EN* (Belarusian Institute for Strategic Studies, 22 October 2012) 2–3.

[18]   Between January and November 2012, the EU accounted for approximately 39 per cent of exports, the ECU 36.5 per cent and the CIS almost 51 per cent. For official trade figures from the National Statistical Committee of the Republic of Belarus, see http://belstat.gov.by/homep/en/indicators/trade_balance.php (accessed 29 December 2012).

[19]   Sergeichik, above note 12.

economic disputes throughout 2010.[20] Minsk refused to ratify the agreement, hence making it impossible for it to enter into force. Lukashenko tied the question of the Code to the issue of Russia's retention of duties on exports of oil and petrochemicals to Belarus. ECU arrangements excluded export tariffs and taxation, leaving them to national laws, but Lukashenko went to the Court of EvrAzES in April 2010, arguing that a free trade area and customs union should not maintain such tariffs. Russia and Kazakhstan indicated that they were prepared to go ahead with the ECU without Belarus, and deprive the country of the existing economic benefits it already enjoyed. At the same time Belarus found itself embroiled in a new gas dispute with Russia threatening to cut supplies. Lukashenko ultimately signed the Code a few days later in July 2010 without securing the concessions he sought at that time. Nevertheless, Russia and Belarus did eventually agree a new oil deal in late 2010 with some of the improvements Minsk had sought, and Moscow promised that the wider issue of energy supplies would eventually be resolved within the context of the SES.

The ECU did not immediately resolve other long-running trade disputes between Russia and Belarus. While ECU membership may assuage some Belarusian fears that Russia could unilaterally close its borders to Belarusian exports, it also means that Belarus must open its own, traditionally protectionist, market to more competition from foreign products. Trade skirmishes with Russia have included the so-called milk and meat wars since 2009, as well as accusations of Belarus dumping sugar and other agricultural products on the markets of other ECU members, and even the suspension of flights between Minsk and Moscow in a dispute over airline routes in 2012.[21] At the same time the new integration structures do give Belarus some legal remedies to appeal to supranational bodies such as the Eurasian Economic Commission – as,

[20]   Matthew Frear, 'Friends or Foes? Developments in Relations between Russia and Belarus', *Russian Analytical Digest No. 87* (Center for Security Studies, November 2010); Kamil Klysinski and Wojciech Kononczuk, 'Lukashenka Has to Choose: Reforms or Concessions to Russia', *OSW Commentary Issue 42* (Centre for Eastern Studies, 27 October 2010) 1–3; Elena Korosteleva, 'Belarusian Foreign Policy in a Time of Crisis' (2011) 27 *Journal of Communist Studies and Transition Politics* 566, 572–5.
[21]   Siarhei Bohdan, 'Trade Wars with Russia: From Sugar to Airlines', *Belarus Digest*, 2 April 2012, http://belarusdigest.com/story/trade-wars-russia-sugar-airlines-8639 (accessed 28 October 2012); Bruhavetski, above note 17; Korosteleva, above note 20, 569–75.

for example, it has successfully done regarding Russian attempts to introduce legislation limiting foreign textiles on the Russian market.[22]

The CET agreed at the launch of the ECU in 2010 was almost exclusively based (92 per cent) on existing Russian duties, and Belarus had already harmonized almost all its tariffs (95 per cent) with Russia in the context of the USRB. Implementation of the CET resulted in the tariffs for Belarus increasing on 18.7 per cent of imported goods (notably motor vehicles, meat products, sugars, aluminium, certain articles of apparel and accessories) and decreasing on 6.7 per cent (in particular, mechanical appliances and electrical machinery, iron and steel, wool and fabrics).[23] Importantly for the business interests of those with links to the ruling elites in Belarus, the system of authorized 'special importers' was preserved. These economic bodies hold a monopoly on the import of certain lucrative commodities, such as alcohol, tobacco, fish and seafood.

Russian accession to the WTO in August 2012 further modified the terms under which Belarus will have to operate.[24] As noted in Connolly's chapter (Chapter 4), as an ECU member Belarus will be expected to open its market to cheaper and higher quality imports from WTO member states, but WTO member states will not have to lower their customs rates on goods originating from Belarus in return. This trade liberalization benefits Belarusian consumers who want to buy imported goods, such as domestic appliances, which are of better quality than locally produced televisions or refrigerators. It threatens Belarusian producers, not only on the domestic market but also in the face of increased competition for their exports on the lucrative Russian market. To support the Belarusian automotive industry at this time, Minsk successfully secured over 100

---

[22]   Tatiana Manenok, 'Konflikty v "Troike" Neizbezhny', *Nashe Mnenie*, 26 October 2012, http://nmnby.eu/news/express/4985.html (accessed 11 November 2012).

[23]   Irina Tochitskaya, 'The Customs Union between Belarus, Kazakhstan and Russia: An Overview of Economic Implications for Belarus', *CASE Network Series and Analyses No. 405* (Centre for Social and Economic Research, August 2010); Lucio Vinhas de Souza, 'An Initial Estimation of the Economic Effects of the Creation of the EurAzES Customs Union on Its Members', *Economic Premise No. 47* (World Bank, January 2011).

[24]   Kamil Klysinski, 'Consequences for the Belarusian Economy of Russia's Entry into the WTO', *OSW EastWeek* (Centre for Eastern Studies, 12 September 2012); Alexander Mukha, 'Vstuplenie Rossii v VTO: Riski Dlya Belarusi', *Nashe Mnenie*, 28 August 2012, http://nmnby.eu/news/analytics/4925.html (accessed 7 November 2012); Irina Tochitskaya, 'Russia's Accession to the WTO: Implications for Belarus' Trade and Industries', *Policy Paper Series* (IPM Research Center, June 2012).

exemptions for Belarus and Kazakhstan in the revised CET pertaining to goods such as trucks, tractors and buses following Russia's WTO accession. WTO membership has also seen Russia commit to reducing its agricultural subsidies, and in turn Moscow will increase pressure on Minsk to reform its heavily subsidized agricultural sector, which is still run on an inefficient collectivized model, to create a more even playing field. With the most optimistic prognosis, the earliest that Belarus could possibly join the WTO itself is 2014, and it will be the last of the current troika of ECU members to do so.

Belarusian participation in the ECU has not particularly expanded the market for Belarusian goods much beyond that which the country already enjoyed, and those goods now face more competition in the ECU from products which originate in WTO member states that are either cheaper and/or of higher quality. There will be increased pressure to open up the Belarusian market to goods from ECU partners and WTO members, challenging Lukashenko's economic system. However, there is also a potential incentive for modernization. It has become cheaper to import equipment and appliances from the West to upgrade Belarusian industry and improve efficiency. If Belarus complies with improved technical and sanitary regulation, as well the high international trade standards and practices of the WTO that by default Russian accession to the organization will require Minsk to introduce, Belarusian goods could become more competitive on international markets.

Belarusian participation in the ECU was a prerequisite from Russia if Belarus was to make any progress in maintaining and improving its lucrative energy deals with Moscow. These subsidies fuel the socially oriented Belarusian economy and provide a vital source of foreign income for the state budget through exports of refined oil products to the EU. Oil and gas commodities have been the primary focus of Belarus in the context of Eurasian integration, almost to the exclusion of all other factors. Nevertheless any cost–benefit analysis for Belarusian participation in the ECU cannot be limited to energy alone.

The continued supply of cheap gas from Russia may help to produce the electricity to maintain energy-inefficient industry, but changes to tariffs in the ECU and the accession of Russia and potentially Kazakhstan to the WTO mean that many of the products then produced by Belarusian factories will face increased competition in the common market of the ECU. Economic concessions from Moscow may allow Lukashenko to continue his practice of manipulating pensions and salaries around national elections, but in return there are expectations that Russian business will be allowed greater control over the Belarusian economy. Of particular interest have been state assets such as Belarusian oil refineries and gas pipelines, the MAZ automobile factory and the Belaruskali potash producer. Privatizing the so-called 'family silver' would reduce Lukashenko's central control over the economy. Minsk therefore has to maintain a difficult balancing act in its engagement with regional economic integration.

4. IMPLEMENTING EURASIAN INTEGRATION A LA BIELORUSSE

Despite its initial reticence, Belarus did join the ECU in 2010, but without the improved terms for energy supplies from Russia that it had sought up front. It has since become a more enthusiastic proponent of the SES, the next step in Eurasian integration.[25] This is primarily as a result of its prospective joint energy market, with the potential promise of allowing energy commodities to be delivered more easily from Kazakhstan and relieving some of Belarus's dependency on Russia, as well as the expectation that Moscow would supply oil and gas to Belarus at Russian domestic prices. This section explores how Belarus is likely to implement the latest wave of Eurasian integration projects in practice. It takes into account the administrative capacity of the state to fulfil the new requirements expected of it and also highlights the informal processes by which Minsk may circumvent obligations and preserve its room for manoeuvre in the face of Russian pressure to comply.

Eurasian integration is highly asymmetric, so while Russia may find surrendering power to supranational authorities in the integration process a challenge, as highlighted in Cooper's Chapter 5, Belarus will welcome having a voice at the top table in those same supranational authorities. The concept of 'one country – one vote' was key to Belarusian perceptions of the USRB as noted above, and Lukashenko has continued to emphasize the issue of equality in regional projects.[26] Any agreements that are reached at summits of the three heads of state will be ratified by

---

[25]   Alexander Chelin, 'Nuzhno Li Belarusi Edinoe Ekonomicheskoe Prostranstvo?', *Nashe Mnenie*, 7 February 2012, http://nmnby.eu/news/analytics/4436.html (accessed 7 November 2012); Gennadii Kosarev, 'Zachem Belarusi Speshit' v Evraziiskii Soyuz?', *Novaya Europa*, 24 January 2012, http://n-europe.eu/topics/2012/01/24/zachem_belarusi_speshit_v_evraziiskii_soyuz (accessed 7 November 2012); Tatiana Manenok, 'Pochemy Minsk Ne Boitsya EEP', *Nashe Mnenie*, 7 December 2010, http://nmnby.eu/news/analytics/2961.html (accessed 7 November 2012).

[26]   Lukashenko, above note 1.

the Belarusian legislature without question. The parliament in Belarus is a rubber stamp body devoid of any independent or opposition voices. There will be no genuine debate by deputies of any issues around regional economic integration.

In terms of implementing agreements, the Belarusian bureaucracy has had a reputation for having a large number of well-educated, competent staff. In a highly centralized political system such as Lukashenko's regime, however, the government has to take on a huge number of functions which can leave the civil service overstretched. Officials in government ministries also find themselves subordinate to, or in competition with, the ruling elites within the presidential administration, who make the real political decisions. The role of ministries is to implement decisions made by others and to take the blame for unpopular policies.

In 2012 Lukashenko announced that, as part of budget cuts, the number of government employees would be reduced by up to 30 per cent. As dissatisfaction rises, talented bureaucrats may decide to seek employment elsewhere, with many lured to higher salaries in Russia.[27] It remains to be seen how effective the administrative personnel left in Belarusian agencies will be and whether they can adapt to the demands made of them by new supranational institutions. Some of the most competent members of the state apparatus may be drawn to supranational bodies such as the Eurasian Economic Commission; however, Belarusians will make up only 6 per cent of the rank-and-file staff, proportionate to the country's relative size within the troika of member states.

With the judiciary subordinated to the presidency, the rule of law is weak in Belarus. The authorities can and do launch politicized anti-corruption drives against officials and businesses when it serves their interests. At other times those who have close ties with the rulers may find that they can avoid criminal proceedings for unfair practices. The authorities have shown that they are ready to summarily disregard ownership rights by, for example, passing a presidential *ukaz* which permitted them retroactively to deprive private owners of shares in two confectionary companies in 2012, allowing their effective expropriation by the regime. As will be outlined later in this section, the government appears even to have tacitly condoned illegal smuggling.

With the experience of the USRB, Lukashenko has demonstrated a track record of either interpreting certain concessions in the best possible

---

27   Yauheni Preiherman, 'Mortal Combat: Lukashenka v Bureaucracy', *Belarus Digest*, 5 November 2012, http://belarusdigest.com/story/mortal-combat-lukashenka-v-bureaucracy-11992 (accessed 7 November 2012).

manner for his domestic needs or walking away from agreements which do not suit him, claiming misunderstandings or misrepresentation.[28] Belarus can be expected to try and follow similar patterns of unreliable behaviour with the current Eurasian integration projects. Two examples can already be found in the cases of EvrAzES Anti-Crisis loans and the sudden sharp rise in the export of solvents and lubricants from Belarus.

Faced with a severe financial crisis in 2011, Belarus secured several tranches of loans from the Eurasian Development Bank EvrAzES Anti-Crisis Fund, which at Russia's behest came with strict conditions attached. The Belarusian government prevaricated on fulfilling the terms for each tranche and, although some payments were delayed, Minsk still received the fourth tranche in 2012 despite failing to fulfil its promises to privatize state companies. The stick of strict economic conditionality was partially applied,[29] but this could be trumped for political reasons by the perceived need for the carrot of further loans to ensure continued active support from Belarus for Eurasian integration.[30] The only asset which had been completely privatized was the Beltransgaz gas pipeline company, which was finally bought out by Russia's Gazprom in 2011 after almost a decade of broken promises from Minsk to sell it.

In spring 2012 accusations began to be made by local analysts, the independent media and Russian officials that Belarus was in effect smuggling refined oil products out of Belarus under the guise of solvents and lubricants, which did not require Minsk to pay export revenues to Moscow. Belarus is estimated to have made between US$1.5 and 2 billion from the grey economy through these means during 2012, earning the ire of Russia and demands for compensation.[31] The head of the State Customs Committee of Belarus has insisted that there was no wrongdoing. Belarus has been able to block attempts by Russia to request the Eurasian Economic Commission to extend the same customs duties

---

[28]   Libman and Vinokurov, above note 1, 99.

[29]   Yauheni Preiherman, 'How Not to Be Cheated by Belarus Authorities', *Belarus Digest*, 7 March 2012, http://belarusdigest.com/story/how-not-be-cheated-belarus-authorities-8228 (accessed 7 November 2012).

[30]   Alexander Mukha, 'Intergratsionnyi Kredit: Chetvertyi Transh', *Nashe Mnenie*, 26 November 2012, http://nmnby.eu/news/express/5009.html (accessed 3 December 2012).

[31]   Darya Firsava, 'Belarusian Solvents: A Tricky Path to Economic Growth', *Belarus Digest*, 7 August 2012, http://belarusdigest.com/story/belarusian-solvents-tricky-way-economic-growth-10438 (accessed 28 October 2012); Dmitrii Ivanovich, 'Rasplata Za Rastvoritel'nyi Biznes', *Nashe Mnenie*, 5 November 2012, http://nmnby.eu/news/express/4992.html (accessed 7 November 2012).

imposed on oil products to solvents and lubricants as well in a bid to close this loophole.

Despite the rhetoric of close fraternal relations between the two countries, Russia has become increasingly unwilling simply to write a blank cheque for the Belarusian economy as its relevance as a loyal ally on the Western border of Russia has diminished, and Moscow began to reduce its energy subsidies for Minsk in 2007.[32] If Minsk views regional integration as a means to secure energy subsidies, Moscow in turn is willing to use the threat of withholding deals on oil and gas as a means to secure influence for Russian business over the Belarusian economy and persuade Minsk to engage in economic integration. This is viewed from Minsk as an opportunity for predatory behaviour by Russian oligarchs in Belarus, and is often portrayed as such in the state media. As in the past with the USRB, both sides are often pursuing contradictory and even incompatible aims within Eurasian integration.

It should be noted that Belarus has traditionally had various allies within Russia willing to agitate for preferential economic treatment of the country, although some of their influence has waned under Putin.[33] These have included oil companies processing their product in Belarus refineries; Russian military elites who see Belarus as a bulwark against the West and (as noted in Cooper's chapter) support cooperation in the defence industry; the Russian Orthodox Church; and Russian regional elites nationwide who Lukashenko has assiduously courted over the years. Belarus will also be keen to work closely with Kazakhstan to coordinate their positions. High-level meetings have been held between senior figures from Minsk and Astana, such as the Presidents in May and the Prime Ministers in November 2012, in the run-up to important trilateral summits.

Lukashenko has demonstrated that he can be very adept at exploiting what limited leverage he holds over Russia.[34] This often comes into play during negotiations on the price and volume of oil and gas deliveries from Russia, which remain a matter negotiated bilaterally, usually on an annual basis at the end of the year, in a long drawn out process. They are informed by personal relations and increasingly a lack of trust. When Moscow demands concrete economic concessions in return for energy deals, Lukashenko instead emphasizes Belarus's geopolitical importance for Russia, close military ties, and emotional appeals to traditional

---

[32]   Balmaceda, above note 5; Klysinski and Kononczuk, above note 20.
[33]   Kononczuk, above note 9, 36–7.
[34]   Kathleen J. Hancock, 'The Semi-Sovereign State: Belarus and the Russian Neo-Empire' (2006) 2 *Foreign Policy Analysis* 117.

cultural and historical relations as adequate compensation. Lukashenko has shown that he can be a vocal defender of Belarusian sovereignty, haranguing Russia for betraying or trying to smother Belarus if he feels he is not getting a good deal. Lukashenko may not always be successful, but he has gained tens of billions of dollars' worth of benefits from Moscow and defied many predictions that he was destined to be outmanoeuvred or abandoned by Russia.

Based on past experience, Belarus will focus on trying to implement those elements of Eurasian economic integration which will be of particular benefit to securing Lukashenko's hold on power in Minsk. At the same time it will prevaricate or even act in an underhand manner to avoid fulfilling commitments it does not want to keep. On the other hand, Moscow has become accustomed to these tactics and will exert pressure, bilaterally and through the organs of the ECU and SES, to see commitments and promises turned into actions and policies.

5. BELARUS, EURASIAN INTEGRATION, AND THE WIDER WORLD

Having raised some of the complexities posed by the Russian factor, this section now summarizes the other external influences and alternative geopolitical vectors open to Belarus and how it positions itself in the wider global economy. Minsk would prefer not to have to commit to an exclusive Eastern or Western vector, seeking instead to enjoy the benefits of close ties with both the EU and Russia, while avoiding making any concessions to either. Minsk has also been actively looking to China and other emerging economies to diversify its options.

Looking westwards, Lukashenko's own statements often emphasize the interest of Belarus in maintaining cordial relations with the EU and Russia, with the country acting as a bridge, or sometimes a buffer, between Europe and Eurasia.[35] The EU has had limited leverage in the country during the Lukashenko presidency, which is frequently described by its detractors in the West as 'the last dictatorship in Europe'. Brussels has struggled to form an effective strategy on Belarus. Minsk has been open to the prospect of economic and technical cooperation with Brussels through the Eastern Partnership, but only without any preconditions in terms of democratization, which would threaten Lukashenko's hold on

[35]   Stefan Wagstyl, '"We Cannot Be a Closed Country" – Alexander Lukashenko Interview', *Financial Times: Belarus Special Report*, 18 November 2008, 2.

power. There is no interest amongst the incumbent authorities in Minsk in political conditionality from Brussels or EU membership, although there is much greater interest from the counter-elites in opposition.

Apart from democratic conditionality, the technical substance of interactions between Belarus and the EU is also becoming a challenging issue. As argued by Delcour and Wolczuk in this volume (Chapter 10), the export of the *acquis* is a key aim of EU policy. Yet Belarus is now a member of an alternative economic integration regime which is rapidly developing its own body of rules, something which remains unacknowledged in the EU approach towards Belarus. With isolation vis-à-vis the EU, if anything, Belarus has been mainly exposed to liberalizing and modernizing pressures from the ECU, especially in light of Russia's accession to the WTO. Rather than integration with the EU, it is the ECU membership that seems to confront the Belarusian government with the need to undertake essential economic reforms and speed up its negotiations on WTO membership.[36]

Having turned Belarus into a *cause célèbre* of its promotion of democracy, the EU has been reluctant to fundamentally review its policy towards Belarus, despite some periodical adjustments. The reduced level of interaction has deprived the EU of any effective leverage to promote change in Belarus, especially in light of Russia's political and economic support for Belarus. Russia, and increasingly the ECU as a whole, provide Lukashenko with explicit political support by condemning the EU's criticisms of, and sanctions against, Belarus. All of these factors appear to lock Belarus under Lukashenko into an ever tighter political and economic dependency on Russia, as exemplified by membership of the ECU, despite Belarus's ambivalence about the ECU itself.

The formation of the ECU and Belarus' membership is arguably the strongest test of the EU's capacity to devise a viable strategy on an 'unwilling country' in the Eastern neighbourhood. Yet, despite Belarus's membership of the ECU, the EU still regards itself as the only 'game in town':

> Belarus [is] becoming of outpost of Eurasian integration and will strengthen its role in the post-Soviet space. New EU policy is needed that will deal with Belarus not as a standalone state, but as an outpost of new Eurasian alliance. European and Eurasian integration [projects] should seek connections to gain more profit from cooperation, not cold war. The most interesting question is how soon the EU will understand that Belarus is ... [no] more a prodigal son that should ... [at some] time join [the] 'European family', but [an] outpost of

---

[36]   Klysinski, above note 24.

[a] powerful Eurasian alliance which has its own dynamics and logic of development.[37]

By relying on negative conditionality vis-à-vis Belarus in the shifting regional context, the EU remains locked into an ineffective strategy to the extent that its stance on Belarus may appear to have 'gone out of tune with reality'.[38]

Nonetheless, Belarus still needs the West. When relations have warmed between the two sides, such as between 2008 and 2010, one of Minsk's goals was undoubtedly to use the spectre of Belarus turning away from Russia to extract concessions from Moscow.[39] The EU and the United States have also imposed limited sanctions against the regime, most recently since the harsh crackdown against opposition forces following Lukashenko's contested re-election for a fourth term in 2010. It cannot be ruled out that Belarus will seek a thaw in relations again in the future, on its own limited terms, as a counterbalance to its large neighbour to the east. An early indicator of this would probably be the release of political prisoners. Having being burnt in the past, the EU is likely to demand more real concessions rather than vague promises in any future rapprochement.

While Belarus is heavily dependent on Russia economically and is currently politically ostracized by the West, it has sought to diversify its ties beyond this simple dichotomy. It looks towards developing economic links with China, the Middle East, Latin America and South East Asia. Disagreements with Moscow over oil have seen Belarus turn to other suppliers such as Venezuela and Azerbaijan, although these are insufficient to totally replace Russian deliveries.[40] The cornerstone of bilateral economic relations with Beijing will be the Chinese-Belarusian Industrial Park outside Minsk, the creation of which was approved in spring 2012. It remains to be seen what tangible results this cooperation will yield for

---

[37] Sergey Kizima, 'Lost Chances of the EU for Cooperation with Belarus' (2012) 3 *Baltic Rim Economies* 5.

[38] This mirrors the perception of the EU's lack of strategy on Central Asia, as referenced in Emilian Kavalski, 'Partnership or Rivalry between the EU, China and India in Central Asia: The Normative Power of Regional Actors with Global Aspirations' (2007) 13 *European Law Journal* 839, 852.

[39] Clara Portela, 'The European Union and Belarus: Sanctions and Partnership?' (2011) 9 *Comparative European Politics* 486, 495–8.

[40] Tatiana Manenok, 'Bezalternativnaya Neft', *Nashe Mnenie*, 15 November 2012, http://nmnby.eu/news/analytics/5001.html (accessed 15 November 2012).

Belarus, but Minsk is keen to portray Belarus as a convenient gateway to the ECU markets for Chinese business.[41]

The financial crisis which hit Belarus in 2011, at a time when relations with the West were worse than they had been in many years, left Russia-led bodies as the only reliable source of support Minsk could turn to in its time of need. This has left the country more beholden than ever to Moscow, with little room for manoeuvre, despite seeking to maintain ties with the EU, China and others. Belarus will continue to use its tried and tested tactics to secure the best possible deal for the incumbent leadership, and will also seek to make use of any new tools available to it through Eurasian integration initiatives, in a bid to avoid complete economic submission to Moscow.

6. CONCLUSION

Under Lukashenko, Belarus can be expected to continue to take an instrumental approach to Eurasian integration. It will support the rhetoric of Russia-led integration initiatives for as long as it is deemed to serve the narrow interests of securing the President's own domestic political position through tangible benefits for the Belarusian economy. Belarus could be viewed as taking a functionalist approach to regional integration only insofar as it addresses the perceived short-term needs of the rulers in Minsk, rather than the common needs of the region as a whole in the long term.

While Eurasian integration may offer some opportunities for economic modernization, the Belarusian authorities are willing to apply the brakes to integration, as they attempted to do in 2010, if it is perceived to damage Lukashenko's standing at home, weaken his authority or damage the commercial interests of the ruling elites around him and their ability to manipulate the economy. Even where they do meet their commitments on paper, the authorities in Minsk can resort to the grey economy, as demonstrated by the solvents and lubricants scandal in 2012, to bypass its obligations within the ECU or the SES.

Lukashenko has had two decades of practice in seeking to extract maximum concessions from Russia while maintaining room for manoeuvre in complying with agreements on its own part in return. Although Moscow has become less willing to tolerate such machinations, Minsk

---

[41]   Tadeusz Iwanski, 'Ukraine, Belarus and Moldova and the Chinese Economic Expansion in Eastern Europe', *OSW Commentary Issue 79* (Centre for Eastern Studies, 28 May 2012) 2–4.

still has allies in Russia who are willing to lobby on its behalf. Meanwhile, Russia is expecting Belarus to support integration through action, not just words. Were Belarus hypothetically to abandon Eurasian integration and reorient towards the EU, this would only come with democratization, which is not in Lukashenko's personal interests, and would end Russian energy subsidies, which would be disastrous for the economy. Minsk will hold out on making final, irreversible choices and passing the point of no return for as long as possible, and seek to keep its options open within and beyond Eurasian economic integration.

Belarus will pragmatically seek to monetize its geopolitical loyalty towards Moscow's regional projects, hoping that the potential embarrass-ment of such a close neighbour as Belarus not participating in Eurasian integration initiatives will outweigh any frustrations with Minsk's contin-ued attempts to avoid wholesale reform of its command economy and open it up to more external influence. The country will try to pick and choose the elements of integration it wishes to prioritize, such as the joint energy market of the SES, while avoiding opening up the Belarusian economy to outside influences which could undermine the ability of the leadership to keep a firm grip on the levers of power. Other actors involved in Eurasian economic integration, at the bilateral and supra-national level, will endeavour to counter those tendencies. The Belarusian authorities will look to develop tactics to best serve them through the next set of national elections rather than formulate coherent long-term strategies for integration. At times this may give the impression that Lukashenko is erratic and unpredictable, potentially praising Eurasian integration in one breath and condemning it in the next. Nevertheless, his wily political skills must not be underestimated as he has a lot of experience in playing these geopolitical and geo-economic games.

Finally, it is worth considering that Belarus could also bring its own risks and weaknesses to Eurasian economic integration. Its inflation rate is typically the highest in the CIS. The country saw two significant devaluations of the national currency in 2011 and further adjustments are widely expected. There may be concerns that Minsk will default on the international loans that become due from 2013 onwards. Lukashenko may hope that the need for Belarus to be seen to benefit from being involved in Moscow's regional projects, particularly as an example to Ukraine, means that it is too important for Russia to allow the Belarusian economy to collapse. There is the possibility, however, that in an expanded, wider Eurasian Economic Union that includes, for example, Ukraine and Kyrgyzstan, Belarus is seen to have become a liability and is cut loose. The ECU remains an opportunity and a threat to Belarus, with Lukashenko likely to remain a capricious supporter of integration.

Meanwhile Belarus itself could prove to be either an advantage or a disadvantage for further Eurasian economic integration. Minsk's high-wire balancing act of conceding just enough to regional economic integration to secure economic benefits without surrendering too much power to undermine the Lukashenko regime itself will remain a significant component of Eurasian integration for the foreseeable future.

8. Kazakhstan and Eurasian economic integration: quick start, mixed results and uncertain future*

Nargis Kassenova

1. INTRODUCTION

Eurasian economic integration has always been the official priority of Kazakhstan's government; therefore Kazakhstan's membership of the newly created Eurasian Customs Union (ECU) and Single Economic Space (SES), together with Russia and Belarus, seems to be a logical outcome of a consistent policy. However, as this chapter argues, the path that led to the current round of Eurasian integration was not that straight and clear, and the decision to pursue the ECU and SES option and its complexities can be better understood if placed in its political and geopolitical context.

The chapter starts with a brief overview of possible (and impossible) alternative options for economic integration explored by the Kazakhstani government or made available to it. To address the issue of why Kazakhstan has privileged the Eurasian vector of integration over the others, it assesses the relative importance of economics, politics, and geopolitics for decision-making on trade issues under President Nazarbaev. The official discourse is analysed along with other discourses provided by the academic and business community. Finally, the chapter looks at the first economic and political results of the ECU, discusses the prospects for Eurasian integration from the point of view of sustainability and utility taking into account the WTO accession of Russia and the forthcoming accession of Kazakhstan, and attempts an analysis of its implications for Kazakhstan's foreign policy.

---

* This chapter is an adapted version of the paper under the same name published in *Russie.Nei.Reports No. 14* (IFRI, November 2012), reprinted with the kind permission of IFRI.

2. POSSIBLE/IMPOSSIBLE ECONOMIC INTEGRATION ALTERNATIVES

Since early in its independence Kazakhstan's leadership has considered integration as an unavoidable necessity and a trend of the times, and focused on attracting investment and developing foreign trade options.[1] While this general goal was clear and uncontested, the ways and strategies for achieving it were less obvious.

2.1. Eurasian Integration

The first choice was (re-)integration with Russia, together with the rest of the post-Soviet space. The Kazakhstani leadership tried to stop 'the dangerous process of the chaotic disintegration' pregnant with inter-ethnic and inter-religious conflicts. The country's ethnic composition (Kazakhs 40 per cent, Russians 38 per cent, other minorities 22 per cent) at the beginning of independence made such a scenario of violent fragmentation deadly.

The economic factor has also played an important role. In 1991, 92.2 per cent of Kazakhstani export was going to countries of the Commonwealth of Independent States (CIS), predominantly to Russia, and the country's industries were still tightly linked to Soviet production cycles. In 1992–93 the Kazakhstani government made major efforts to stay inside the new Russian ruble zone, but failed.[2] In March 1994, President Nursultan Nazarbaev made a further attempt to stop disintegration and proposed the creation of a Eurasian Union during a meeting with the faculty and students of Moscow State University. At the time Moscow was not ready for this bold initiative, but it was reviewing its policy of 'going West' and 'shedding the burden' of Central Asia. In August 1994 the Russian Foreign Minister, Andrey Kozyrev, stated that Moscow was ready 'to go as far as and in the integration forms for which our partners (CIS states) are ready'.[3]

During the period 1995–96 Russia, Belarus, Kazakhstan and Kyrgyzstan formed a Customs Union (CU-95) which, for a number of

---

[1]   Nursultan Nazarbaev, 'Vmeste my mozhem soprotivlyatsya globalizatsii' *Nezavisimaya Gazeta*, 29 April 2001.

[2]   'Interview with Grigory Marchenko, Chair of the National Bank of Kazakhstan', *Kontinent*, 22 October–4 November 2013, 20 (107).

[3]   As quoted in Sergei Gretsky, *Russia's Policy Toward Central Asia* (Carnegie Moscow Center, 1997).

reasons, remained largely on paper.[4] In 2000 Vladimir Putin initiated the transformation of the CU-95 into a more realistic and functional organization – the Eurasian Economic Community (EvrAzES). In October 2007 Russia, Belarus and Kazakhstan signed the Treaty on the creation of the Customs Union and, in January 2010, the ECU was officially launched.

The bilateral trade statistics, however, show that despite the consistent efforts to integrate that had taken place since the mid-1990s, Russia's share in Kazakhstan's foreign trade had been decreasing by the time the ECU was created. In 1995 Russia accounted for 47 per cent of Kazakhstan's total trade turnover; in 2000 its share went down to 30.2 per cent, and in 2009 dropped to 17.4 per cent.[5]

2.2. Central Asian Integration

The second option was to focus on Central Asian integration. Post-Soviet Kazakhstan and four former 'Middle Asian' republics (Kyrgyzstan, Uzbekistan, Tajikistan and Turkmenistan) adopted a new 'Central Asian' identity. The common sense of vulnerability and high level of interdependence in terms of water management, gas distribution networks and electricity grids were significant drivers of regional cooperation and integration efforts.

In the early 1990s, having failed to interest Russia in the integration, the Kazakhstani leadership spearheaded the initiative to create the Central Asian Union. In 1994, Kazakhstan, Uzbekistan and Kyrgyzstan signed an agreement on the creation of the Single Economic Space. The commitments were made to push for free movement of goods, services, capital and labour, and coordination of budget, taxation, pricing, customs and currency policies. In order to make it operational member states set up the Interstate Council as the highest body, and the Executive Committee with functions of coordination, consultation and analysis. Tajikistan joined in 1998. In the same year, the organization changed its name from the Central Asian Union to the Central Asian Economic Union (CAEU). In 2006 the CAEU officially disappeared as a result of merger with EvrAzES.

In 2007 Nazarbaev again proposed the creation of the Central Asian Union. The idea was reiterated in his article 'Eurasian Union: From the Idea to the History of the Future', published on 27 October 2011 in

[4]   For a detailed overview, see Cooper's Chapter 2 in this volume.
[5]   Statistical Agency of the Republic of Kazakhstan, *Kazakhstan za gody nezavisimosti 1991–2010* (Statistical Agency, 2011).

Russian newspaper *Izvestiya*. Nazarbaev outlined his vision of the emerging Eurasian Union, but also argued that it did not prevent the creation of other structures, such as the Central Asian Union.[6]

With hindsight, the failure of Central Asian integration seems inevitable. Although it did make sense to stick together to withstand external pressures, this rationale/factor proved to be weaker than the structural constraints: different levels and paths of economic development and the overall weakness of economic and political systems. Importantly, the main economic interests of Central Asian states increasingly lay outside the region. In 1999, only 3.1 per cent of Kazakhstan's trade turnover was with members of the CAEU, and in 2009 it was just 2.7 per cent ($1.95 billion).[7]

2.3. Integration with Global Markets: WTO Membership and Free Trade Zone with China

The third option available in the 1990s was to focus on integration with markets outside the post-Soviet space. Joining the World Trade Organization (WTO) was deemed to be the main tool for pursuing this goal. In 1996 Kazakhstan submitted its official application to the Secretariat of the WTO. A working group with the participation of Kazakhstan's key trading partners was created, and negotiations started.

High rates of economic growth and increasing foreign trade in the early 2000s stimulated the will of the Kazakhstani government to join the WTO. In March 2006, President Nazarbaev devoted his annual address to the new strategy of making Kazakhstan one of the top fifty most competitive economies, in which he prioritized WTO accession as 'an additional tool of economic modernization and strengthening competitiveness of Kazakhstan in the world markets'.[8] There were plans to complete negotiations in 2009.[9]

---

[6]   Nursultan Nazarbaev, 'Evraziiskyi soyuz: ot idei k istorii budushego' *Izvestiya*, 27 October 2011.

[7]   Statistical Agency, above note 5.

[8]   Address of the President of the Republic of Kazakhstan, Nursultan Nazarbaev, to the People of the Republic of Kazakhstan', 1 March 2006, http://www.akorda.kz/en/page/page_address-of-the-president-of-the-republic-of-kazakhstan-nursultan-nazarbayev-to-the-people-of-kazakhstan-march-1-2006_13 43986805 (accessed 24 April 2010).

[9]   'Kazakhstan priostanovil peregovory po vstupleniyu v VTO', *Vesti.ru*, 12 June 2009, http://www.vesti.ru/doc.html?id=292462 (accessed 24 April 2010).

Outside the post-Soviet space, of particular importance and promise was the trade developing with two economic powerhouses of the Eurasian continent: the European Union (EU) and China. Both became major markets for Kazakhstani hydrocarbons and metals, and providers of manufactured goods. Starting in 2004 the EU surpassed Russia as Kazakhstan's main trading partner, and in 2009 its share in Kazakhstan's total trade turnover reached 40.2 per cent (against Russia's 17.4 per cent). China's trade with Kazakhstan has also been growing with geometric progression. In 1999 it accounted for 5.7 per cent of Kazakhstan's external trade and in 2009 13.2 per cent.[10]

The EU fully supported the prospect of Kazakhstan joining the WTO and provided considerable technical assistance to reach this goal. China joined the WTO in 2001, but did not actively push for Kazakhstan's accession. Beijing preferred to promote the creation of a free trade zone (FTZ). In 2003 Prime Minister Wen Jiabao, at a meeting with his Russian, Kazakh, Kyrgyz, Tajik and Uzbek counterparts, proposed to establish a FTZ in the framework of the Shanghai Cooperation Organization (SCO). Wen also proposed improving the flow of goods by reducing non-tariff barriers in customs, quarantine, standards and transport services.[11] The proposal for such regional integration did not receive an enthusiastic response.

Thus, the three options briefly introduced above (integration with Russia, the Central Asian Union, and WTO accession) were all indicated as priorities and therefore, officially, not presented as being incompatible. Although these three integration options did not exclude each other, they could not be prioritized and fully pursued at the same time. Such a multiple integration agenda inevitably implied tensions and inconsistencies in its implementation.

3. MOTIVATION BEHIND THE DECISION TO JOIN THE CUSTOMS UNION

In Kazakhstan there are no established political spaces for public discussion and contestations of major foreign and domestic policies. The key decision-maker is the President of the country, and the processes of adopting policies remain very opaque. Therefore, we can only speculate about the real motives of the decision to actively pursue the Eurasian

---

[10] Statistical Agency, above note 5.
[11] 'Chinese Premier Urges Economic Cooperation Among SCO Members', *China Daily*, 24 September 2003.

integration project on the basis of speeches and articles by, and interviews with the President and other high officials, as well as expert
opinions. The possible reasons can be divided into three categories:
(i) economic, (ii) political, and (iii) geopolitical.

3.1. Economic Reasons

The economic explanation was the official justification. In a December
2009 interview President Nazarbaev listed the benefits of the project for
the economic development of the country as follows. First, the ECU
creates a market of 170 million people instead of 16 million, which
should attract foreign investors. Second, the elimination of customs
tariffs in Russia and Belarus improves the opportunities for Kazakhstani
producers, making their goods more competitive in terms of prices (and it
is only there where they can realistically find a market), as well as being
beneficial for transporting Kazakhstani oil and gas. Third, tougher
competition with Russian and Belarusian goods would stimulate production.[12]

Officials also point out Kazakhstan's comparative advantage over
Russia and Belarus in terms of attractiveness for investors. It has a lighter
taxation regime and a relative ease of doing business.[13] It is hoped that
these conditions would also lure Russian companies to register in
Kazakhstan.

As for exposing Kazakhstani businesses to competition with Russian
and Belarusian producers, this is intended to prepare them for more fierce
competition in the framework of the WTO.[14] The ECU was presented as
some sort of a training camp for global trade.

These optimistic expectations, however, were not supported by publicly available studies of the potential gains and losses of joining the
ECU. Developing such studies would have been difficult, if not

---

[12] 'Nazarbaev's Interview to State Media', *Zakon.kz*, 23 December
2009, http://www.zakon.kz/157824-nursultan-nazarbaev-schitaet-sozdanie.html
(accessed 23 December 2009).
[13] Kazakhstan ranked 59 against Russia at 123 in 2011: World Bank and
International Finance Corporation, *Doing Business in 2011: Making a Difference
for Entrepreneurs* (2010) 4.
[14] 'Online Interview with Deputy Minister of Economic Development and
Trade, Timur Suleimenov', *Bnews.kz*, 30 March 2010, http://www.bnews.kz/ru/
conferences/view/27 (accessed 5 April 2010).

impossible, considering the speed of decision-making and implementation of the integration project, and also the fact that the option of WTO
accession was being pursued at the same time.

The most solid studies of these two options of trade integration were
carried out by the World Bank (WB) experts. It was argued that through
joining the WTO Kazakhstan would gain about 6.7 per cent of the value
of its consumption (or 3.7 per cent GDP) in the medium run and up to
17.5 per cent in the long run.[15] The largest gains would come from
liberalization of barriers to foreign direct investment (FDI) in the services
sectors, a reform of tariffs, improved market access, and reform of local
content regulation.

The WB experts were more sceptical about Kazakhstan's gains from its
participation in the ECU. In another report published in January 2012,
they developed three possible scenarios: (i) the current position with the
Customs Union, (ii) a pessimistic outlook, and (iii) an optimistic outlook.[16]

The first scenario assumes that the external tariffs, with some exceptions, are raised to the levels that prevailed in the spring of 2011. It is
estimated that in this case Kazakhstan would lose about 0.2 per cent in
real income per year as a result of participation in the ECU. It is also
estimated that tariff revenues collected in Kazakhstan will approximately
double, that the costs to businesses and consumers of imports will
increase, and that under the tariff umbrella resources are shifted to areas
of inefficient production. Consequently, the ECU would depress real
wages by 0.5 per cent and the real return on capital by 0.6 per cent.
Kazakhstan would trade less with the rest of the world and more with
Russia, Belarus and the rest of the CIS, resulting in less imported
technology from the more technologically advanced European Union and
other countries – leading to a loss of productivity gains in the long run.

The pessimistic outlook scenario assumes that the common external
tariffs are fully implemented and exceptions are eliminated. In this case,
Kazakhstan would lose about 0.3 per cent in real income per year.

The third scenario makes an optimistic assessment of how much the
ECU may lower the trade-facilitation costs involved in importing into or
exporting from Kazakhstan and how much Kazakhstan may benefit from

---

[15]   Jesper Jensen and David Tarr, 'The Impact of Kazakhstan Accession to the
World Trade Organization: A Quantitative Assessment', *Policy Research Working
Paper WPS 4142* (World Bank, March 2007).
[16]   World Bank Poverty Reduction and Economic Management Unit. Europe
and Central Asia Region, 'Assessment of Costs and Benefits of the Customs
Union for Kazakhstan', Report No. 65977-KZ, 3 January 2012.

a reduction in non-tariff barriers, such as in relation sanitary and phytosanitary conditions, in the ECU. It is assumed that the common external tariff is fully implemented. In this case the real income of Kazakhstan would increase by about 1.5 per cent of consumption per year.

Thus, the project of joining the WTO under the pre-ECU conditions would be more economically reasonable than the formation of the ECU, which implies that the motivation to privilege Eurasian integration over WTO accession is to be found elsewhere.

3.2. Political Reasons

The political explanation behind the decision to form the ECU focuses on regime security and group interests. This is the most difficult to reconstruct.

One line of thinking points to the growing concerns with regard to the security and stability of the country. The ongoing global economic crisis has affected Kazakhstan and endangered the prospects of its development. A worsening of the economy would fuel protest sentiments and could undermine the stability of the country. As President Nazarbaev argued in his article published in the Russian newspaper *Izvestiya* in March 2009, the crisis destroyed the illusions (of self-sufficiency) fuelled by high prices of natural resources, and in order to survive and prosper now countries would need to pull their efforts together.[17]

Another factor that creates the potential for instability is the lack of clarity over political succession. In 2009 President Nazarbaev turned 69, and there is no apparent groomed 'heir' to the position who would create a smooth transition.

External factors, such as the potential for growing instability in Central Asia and Afghanistan, together with fears of 'colour revolutions', have also contributed to the sense of insecurity in Kazakhstan. All of these factors could have resulted in the Kazakhstani leadership leaning more towards Russia, the traditional patron who can provide the regime with certain guarantees in terms of security.

Another line of thinking tries to answer the question '*cui prodest?*' to find out if any powerful business group would benefit particularly from the ECU arrangements. Here the prime suspects are the oil and gas producers who potentially can obtain better and cheaper access to

---

[17] Nursultan Nazarbaev, 'Evraziyskiy ekonomicheskiy soyuz: teoriya ili realinost', *Izvestiya*, 19 March 2009.

pipelines crossing Russia and Belarus. In December 2010 the ECU members agreed to introduce unified norms and standards on oil and oil products and equal tariffs on the transportation of oil and oil products in the framework of the SES.[18]

3.3.   Geopolitical Reasons

The geopolitical explanation behind the decision underlines the necessity of making a choice among great powers and defining the 'civilization' to which Kazakhstan belongs. This implies that the period of uncertainty and balancing reflected in Kazakhstan's multi-vector foreign policy is no longer sustainable. This position was expressed at the roundtable devoted to the ECU:

> The Customs Union is, first of all, an instrument of regional integration, and in this sense, a national protection instrument. We need this integration to protect our national sovereignty. This will be our new civilizational identity.[19]

Although officials try not to stress the geopolitical meaning of the ECU, at the same roundtable Kuandyk Bishimbayev, Deputy Minister of Economic Development and Trade, stated:

> The Customs Union should be considered in the context of geopolitical processes. [...] What economic gravity pole we will be drawn to? And choosing the Customs Union, we clearly choose the economic gravity pole.'[20]

The 'moment of truth' had been brought closer by the global economic crisis. In the article published in March 2009 (referred to above), Nazarbaev argued that the crisis made clear the necessity of pulling efforts together, and 'in the long term there is no alternative to Eurasian integration'.[21]

The alternatives to Eurasian integration were briefly introduced earlier in the chapter. Since Central Asian integration in economic terms is not of major interest for Kazakhstan, only two other options should be considered from the geopolitical point of view: joining the WTO as

---

[18]   Tulkin Tashimov, 'Diversifikatsiya neftedvizheniy', *Expert Kazakhstan*, 13 December 2010.

[19]   Bahytzhamal Bekturganova, Roundtable, 'Kazakhstan v tamozhennom soyuze: chto delat dalshe?', organized by the Institute of Political Solutions, 19 April 2011, http://www.ipr.kz/print/kipr/3/1/27/ajax (accessed 28 April 2011).

[20]   Ibid.

[21]   Nazarbaev, above note 17.

promoted by the West (both the EU and the USA), and economic integration with China.

The Western vector has been always a strong competitor with the Russian vector because of the appeal of the West as the source of investment, technologies, legitimacy and security assistance. The only two factors that have constrained the Kazakhstani leadership's desire to deepen relations with Washington and the European capitals have been the concern not to anger Moscow and the fear of Western democratization agendas.

This tension between the pro-Russian and pro-Western directions of Kazakhstan's foreign policy surfaced when the Kazakhstani government had to make the decision to join the WTO or the ECU first. According to Wikileaks, in February 2009, Prime Minister Karim Massimov met with US Ambassador Hoagland and said that he needed a clear signal from Washington that Kazakhstan is welcome in the WTO. Upon receiving such a signal, he promised to stall the ECU formation process.[22] This means that Kazakhstan needed stronger support from the West to find the determination to pursue WTO membership without Russia.

As for integration with China, this option was never pursued by the Kazakhstani government. The fears that the country will be overwhelmed by the Chinese economic, demographic and eventually political power are clearly present in Kazakhstani society. Some experts have expressed the opinion that the ECU and further integration with Russia are to constrain the growing Chinese influence in Central Asia.[23] Interestingly, President Nazarbaev sought to refute this in his 2011 article in *Izvestiya*: 'some Western experts rushed to state that the Eurasian Union is to become a defence against the so-called Chinese economic expansion. There is nothing more remote from the truth than this statement'.[24]

The Kazakhstani policy toward China seems to be complex. On the one hand, despite growing fears of the Chinese might, Astana continues to deepen relations with Beijing. Over the last several years they have grown stronger with the acquisition of prime energy assets by Chinese companies (which account for 26 per cent of investments in the oil and gas sector and 20 per cent of oil produced in the country) and massive

---

[22] Tikhon Alexeyev, 'Kak prodali Kazakhstan tamozhennomu soyuzu', *Respublika*, 9 September 2011, 31.
[23] 'Tri vektora dvizheniya', *Liter*, 18 March 2011.
[24] Nazarbaev, above note 6.

loans (estimates range between \$15 and \$19 billion) taken from China by the Kazakhstani government and businesses.[25]

On the other hand, Astana continues to reject Beijing's proposals for free trade zones. As mentioned earlier, in 2003 Prime Minister Wen Jiabao suggested the establishment of a FTZ in the framework of the SCO. In June 2011, President Hu Jingtao visited Kazakhstan and made a six-point proposal to boost bilateral cooperation.[26]

While not ready for a fully fledged FTZ with China, the Kazakhstani government has agreed to build a free economic zone (FEZ) on the border. In 2006 the two countries began constructing the Khorgos FEZ that is to become fully operational in 2018.[27] It is expected that the venture will give a boost both to bilateral trade and to trade between China and Europe.[28]

Thus, Kazakhstan wishes to benefit from the opportunities that cooperation with China presents, but is hesitant to find itself in the full embrace of its Eastern neighbour. From this perspective, Eurasian integration could serve as a counterbalance.

4. EURASIAN ECONOMIC INTEGRATION: RESULTS AND IMPLICATIONS

The ECU having existed for almost three years allows one to draw some preliminary results and compare them with the initial expectations. The range of opinions regarding the gains, losses and implications of Kazakhstan's participation in the project remains broad and polarized.

---

[25] Nursultan Nazarbaev's speech at the presentation of the Astana–Almaty high-speed railway project in Beijing, 22 March 2011, http://temirzholy.kz/kz/press_center/news/page_795 (accessed 24 April 2011); 'Groznoie obayanie nefti', *Exclusive*, 8 October 2012.

[26] 'Hu Proposes Measures to Boost Cooperation with Kazakhstan', *China Radio International*, 14 June 2011, http://english.cri.cn/6909/2011/06/14/2741s642736.htm (accessed 17 June 2012).

[27] 'In April 2012, the Khorgos FEZ Opened for Human Traffic, Tourists and Investors', Khorgos International Centre of Boundary Cooperation, September 2012, http://www.mcps-khorgos.kz/smi-review/prezentatsiya-dlya-investorov-i-smi-transportno-logisticheskogo-khaba-«khorgos»-stantsiya (accessed 13 October 2012).

[28] Joanna Lillis, 'Kazakhstan: Astana Sees Free-Trade Zone as Antidote to Dutch Disease', *Eurasia.Net.org*, 31 May 2010, http://www.eurasianet.org/print/63587 (accessed 17 June 2012).

The analysis is made more difficult by a series of significant developments that have taken place since the start of the ECU in 2010. In January Russia, Kazakhstan and Belarus launched the SES to promote the freedom of movement of capital, people and services and promised to create the Eurasian (Economic) Union by 2015. In the meantime, in December 2011 Russia joined the WTO; Kazakhstan is finalizing its negotiations and expects to join the organization in 2013. This very complex dynamic creates confusion, but at the same time it sheds light on the nature of the planning and decision-making of participating governments.

4.1. Economic Results and Prospects

Government officials continue to enthuse about the ECU and its benefits. To prove that it has lived up to the high expectations, they provide figures that show an increase in trade turnover and Kazakhstan's exports. In 2010, the turnover between Russia and Kazakhstan increased from $12.4 billion to $17.9 billion, and between Kazakhstan and Belarus from $421 million to $865 million. The reported numbers for 2011 are even more impressive. Kazakhstan's trade with Russia reached $22.7 billion (although with Belarus it decreased to $698 million).[29]

What accounts for such hikes in the figures? First, the increase is less considerable when compared with the pre-crisis 2007 and 2008 figures – Russia–Kazakhstan trade turnover stood at $16.2 billion and $20 billion accordingly.[30] Second, the increase in foreign trade turnover was as a result of higher prices on main export items: oil (a 38.8 per cent increase), ferro-alloys (24 per cent) and steel (31.8 per cent).[31] In 2010 mineral products accounted for 75 per cent of Kazakhstan's total export, and metals and metal goods for 13.5 per cent.[32]

It is also worth noting that Kazakhstan has a considerable deficit in its trade with its ECU partners. In 2011 Kazakhstan exported $7.5 billion to

---

[29]   Statistical Agency, above note 5.

[30]   Ibid.

[31]   Report of the Minister of Kazakhstan for Economic Integration, Zhanar Aitzhanova, at the Roundtable 'Influence of Changes in the Foreign Trade Policy in Connection with the Launch of the Customs Union on the Economy of Kazakhstan at the Majilis of the Parliament of Kazakhstan, 16 May 2011, Ministry of Economic Development and Trade, http://www.minplan.kz/pressservice/482/37253 (accessed 10 August 2011).

[32]   Statistical Agency of the Republic of Kazakhstan, *Kazakhstan 2010* (Statistical Agency, 2011).

Russia and Belarus and imported $15.9 billion.[33] The structure of the trade is not in Kazakhstan's favour either: it was exporting mostly minerals and importing manufactured goods.[34]

The share of exports to Russia and Belarus grew insignificantly in 2010 – from 8.3 per cent of total exports in 2009 to 10.1 per cent, and decreased to 8.5 per cent in 2011. At the same time, Russia could increase its share of exports to Kazakhstan from 31.3 per cent in 2009 to 39.4 per cent in 2010, and 41.4 per cent in 2011, while the share of the European exports fell from 29 per cent in 2009 to 24.3 per cent in 2010, and 20.4 per cent in 2011.[35] Thus, we can conclude that Russia's position has strengthened, in part thanks to trade diversion.

This trend is as a result of the considerable increases in tariffs. To a large extent, common external tariffs were approximated to the Russian tariffs. According to Deputy Minister of Economic Development and Trade Timur Suleimenov, 47.7 per cent of tariffs were brought in line with Russia, 45 per cent left at the Kazakhstani level of 2009, and 5 per cent were reduced (for the remaining 2.3 per cent the classification of tariffs was changed).[36]

According to the study conducted by the Almaty-based research centre, Rakurs, following accession to the ECU, for the entire economy the simple mean ad valorem equivalent (AVE) tariff rate has increased from 6.45 per cent to 12.1 per cent, and the weighted mean AVE tariff rate from 4.3 per cent to12.67 per cent. If, before the ECU, Kazakhstan had a liberal trade regime, its level of tariff protection now became higher than that in the low- and middle-income countries, and above the average in the world.[37]

As a result, Kazakhstani producers using imported Western equipment and materials were severely affected. Tariffs on equipment increased by 10–20 per cent, and on materials (previously imported with zero tariffs)

---

[33]   Statistical Agency of the Republic of Kazakhstan, *Kazakhstan in 2011* (Statistical Agency, 2012).

[34]   'Vzryvnaya poroda. Dolya syrya v torgovle mezhdu RK i RF vyrosla v neskolko raz', *Forbes Kazakhstan*, February 2012, 2.

[35]   Statistical Agency 2012, above note 33; Adil Urmanov, 'Torgovlya na vynos', *Karavan*, 7 May 2012, 5.

[36]   Online interview with Timur Suleimenov, above note 14.

[37]   Oraz Jandosov and Leila Sabyrova, 'Tariff Protection in Kazakhstan: Before and After the Customs Union', *Discussion Papers 5.4* (Rakurs Center for Economic Analysis, May 2011).

by 20 per cent.[38] Thus, high technology products assembled in Kazakhstan went up in price and became non-competitive. Ironically, Kazakhstani producers, who were previously worried about the negative effects of the WTO, are now waiting for it as a salvation as it would bring back liberalization of trade.[39]

Some representatives of small and medium enterprises describe the situation as a disaster.[40] Instead of the promised simplification, the documentation became more voluminous and confusing. The new unified electronic customs base was prepared in a hurry and is full of deficiencies. Overall, the new customs regulations are seen as cancelling out the achievements of the past decade and throwing Kazakhstan back to the early 2000s on some positions and even back to the 1990s on others.[41]

According to the business community, higher tariffs protect Russian producers at the expense of local producers. While Russian goods have full access to Kazakhstan, Russian authorities at the local level have been using double standards to block Kazakhstani goods with the help of various non-tariff barriers. Generally, there is a fear that Russian companies will dominate the Kazakhstani market and reshape it to their liking.[42] There is a widely shared opinion that Russian companies use aggressive marketing tactics, actively resort to political and administrative resources, possess much larger capital, and use anti-competitive methods.[43]

The only sector that has benefited from the new protective barriers is the budding automobile production industry. Tariffs on cars increased 30 to 40 times, making imports from third countries prohibitive. In the first half of 2011, car sales went up by 160 per cent: Russian cars accounted for 40.3 per cent, locally assembled 31.7 per cent, and imported from

[38] 'Rify tamozhennogo soyuza', *Kazakhstan: The International Business Magazine*, (2011) 4.
[39] Gennady Shestakov, 'Vstupleniye v VTO mozhet stat spaseniyem dlya Kazakhstana', *Kursiv*, 13 May 2010, 18 (342).
[40] Interview with the Executive Director of the Forum of Entrepreneurs of Kazakhstan, 11 October 2011.
[41] 'Rify tamozhennogo soyuza', above note 38.
[42] Remarks made by business representatives at the AmCham Economic Policy Forum 'The Customs Union and the WTO Accession: Regional and Global Aspirations. Focus on Russia and Kazakhstan', 15 October 2012, Almaty.
[43] 'Tamozhennyi soyuz Kazakhstana: slovo praktikam', *Exclusive*, 1 March 2010.

third countries 23 per cent. The improved market reportedly stimulated the interest of investors.[44]

As for the oil and gas sector, the expected benefits have been slow in materializing. The 2010 agreement on unified norms and standards on oil and oil products and equal tariffs on transportation of oil and oil products in the framework of SES does not regulate tariffs on oil exported outside the SES. Thus, Russian transit tariffs for Kazakhstani exporters remain twice as much as those paid by domestic oil companies. Kazakhstani gas exporters do not have equal access to Russian gas infrastructure and have to sell gas at the border.[45]

Another great hope and promise of the ECU was the inflow of foreign companies attracted by a bigger market, Kazakhstan's more liberal taxation regime and better business environment. The country was envisaged to become the 'springboard for MNCs to enter Russia'. Some experts remain sceptical about the potential, arguing that it is unlikely that companies would wish to set up production so far from main markets in the European part of the ECU.[46]

So far, what is happening is the relocation of Russian and Belarusian companies to Kazakhstan. As of January 2012, there are 8,600 Russian and Belarusian companies registered in Kazakhstan, accounting for 55.4 per cent of all foreign companies. This is a 16.8 per cent increase compared with the previous year (against a 6.5 per cent increase for all foreign companies).[47]

The government is also very proud of the fact that the ECU has brought in considerable budget revenues. According to Deputy Minister of Finance Ruslan Dalenov, in 2010 Kazakhstan could receive more than $1.2 billion, while previously it was receiving $600 million a year in customs duties.[48] Astana was able to negotiate receiving 7.33 per cent of the total ECU import tax (its share in 2007–08 was less than 3.5 per cent of the aggregate collected by the three states).[49]

---

[44] A. Vorotilov, S. Rudenko and I. Dorokhov, 'Prazdnik obshei bedy', *Forbes Kazakhstan*, September 2011, 1.

[45] Gulnur Rakhmatulina, 'Vliyaniye tamozhennogo soyuza na ekonomich-eskoe razvitiye Kazakhstana. Perspektivy integratsii v neftegazovom sektore' (2012) 1(14) *Evraziyskaya Ekonomicheskaya Integratsiya* 77.

[46] 'Soyuzniki ili souzniki? Tamozhennyi soyuz: poltora goda spustia', *Exclusive*, 14 September 2011.

[47] 'Alikhan Smailov: za pyat let prodovolstviye podorazhalo na 73 per cent', *Kursiv*, 15 March 2012.

[48] Roundtable, above note 19.

[49] Online interview with Timur Suleimenov, above note 14.

The numbers look impressive. However, experts point out that this increase has taken place at the expense of consumers. Prices on food and electronic appliances from non-ECU member countries went up. Russian goods did not become cheaper, partially as a result of a stronger ruble. As a result, prices on meat, dairy products and vegetable oil almost doubled.

Finally, the argument that the ECU will serve as a training camp for joining the WTO becomes less relevant in view of the Russian membership of the organization, and Kazakhstan's accession expected by 2013.[50] It is still not clear what conditions have been negotiated by the Kazakhstani side, but considering the agreement among ECU member states that they will adopt the tariffs agreed by the member that joined the WTO first, it seems likely that the AVE tariff will be the same or close to that currently agreed by Russia – 7.15 per cent (in 2009 Kazakhstan's AVE tariff was 5.9 per cent).[51]

The business community is also concerned that the WTO accession once again would introduce confusion in the regulations, similar to that created by the ECU. It does not help that the results of negotiations on accession conditions are not made public and Kazakhstani entrepreneurs do not know what to expect and prepare for.[52]

4.2. Political Impact

If the security of the regime was a motivation behind the decision to advance integration with Russia, the effect so far has been mostly negative. First, the creation of the ECU has pushed up the prices on basic goods, creating the potential for social tensions. Second, it has impacted upon millions of 'self-employed' people engaged in small trade with third countries, particularly China, and consequently their families. Third, it has given the nationalists another issue around which they can mobilize popular support and criticize the government.

---

[50] 'Kazakhstan Aims to Conclude WTO Talks by 2013', *RIA Novosti*, 27 January 2012, http://en.rian.ru/business/20120127/170980037.html (accessed 28 January 2012).

[51] 'Strany TS primut tamozhennye tarify strany, pervoi vstupivshei v VTO', *Vlast.kz*, 28 March 2012, http://www.vlast.kz/?art=149Vlast (accessed 24 April 2012).

[52] Remarks made by business representatives at the AmCham Economic Policy Forum, above note 42.

Over the three-year period 2009–11, food prices in Kazakhstan increased on average by 23.7 per cent. Over the last five years food prices have increased by 73.5 per cent.[53]

The ECU is not the only culprit responsible for these price hikes; however, it has clearly made a contribution. One of the factors behind this inflation was the increase in fuel prices (28–29 per cent growth for gas and 34 per cent for diesel fuel) as a result of the opening of the customs borders between Russia, Kazakhstan and Belarus. Kazakhstani prices on fuel, which used to be the lowest among the ECU member states, started to become level with those in Russia.[54]

The government understood the destabilizing potential of this trend and created the Price Commission under the First Deputy Prime Minister, Umirzak Shukeyev.[55] In July 2011 the President also signed a law on state regulation of production and circulation of certain types of oil product that capped retail prices on fuel.[56]

Another problem created by the ECU is the loss of income accruing to small traders and their dependants by the raised tariffs on imports from third countries. It was estimated that an army of 2.5 million of so-called self-employed people were engaged in small trade, which consequently involves their families.[57] The loss of income led to personal tragedies and fuelled discontent. Ironically, the problem is partially alleviated by corruption of the Kazakhstani customs. According to Russian importers, the quantity and quality of Chinese counterfeit products reaching the Russian market via Kazakhstan has increased dramatically as a result of the ECU.[58]

Finally, while a considerable proportion of the Kazakhstani population welcomes the union with Russia, certain vocal groups believe that the ECU and the forthcoming SES undermine Kazakhstan's sovereignty. On 8 June 2010, on the eve of the launch of the ECU, the movement In Defence of Sovereignty – unifying 50 organizations, democratic opposition parties, youth organizations, media and intelligentsia representatives – published a letter addressed to the people of Kazakhstan. The main

---

[53] 'Alikhan Smailov: za pyat let prodovolstviye podorazhalo na 73 per cent', above note 47.
[54] Rakhmatulina, above note 45.
[55] Viktoriya Panfilova, 'Nazarbayeva prosyat vyiti iz Tamozhennogo Soyuza', *Nezavisimaya Gazeta*, 14 September 2011.
[56] Rakhmatulina, above note 45.
[57] 'Soyuzniki ili souzniki?', above note 46.
[58] Presentation of Dmitry Fedorkov, Brand Production Director, Baiersdorf (Russia) at the AmCham Economic Policy Forum, above note 42.

message was that Kazakhstan's accession to the ECU and SES has led to the loss of political sovereignty. The authors argue that in the ECU Kazakhstan has delegated its foreign economic policies to a supranational body and, with the introduction of the SES, it will have to delegate its domestic economic powers as well. Astana would need to coordinate with Moscow its macroeconomic policies, budget deficit parameters, inflation, currency exchange rates, oil and gas pricing scenarios, agricultural subsidies and technical regulation. With time it is planned to establish a single currency and tariffs on gas and electricity. All this, in the opinion of the authors, means the revival/resurrection of the union state.[59]

Surprisingly, these anti-integration sentiments eventually found some support among important policy experts firmly implanted in the Nazarbaev regime. Thus, the Secretary of the ruling Nur Otan Party, Yerlan Karin, gave a strong response to the proposal for the creation of the Eurasian Parliament made by the Russian Duma Speaker, Sergei Naryshkin, denouncing it as 'unrealistic in the short and long term' and 'in breach of the sovereignty and the Constitution of Kazakhstan'.[60]

Such a lack of consensus in society on the desirability and extent of Eurasian integration raises the question of how sustainable the project is, especially considering the similar lack of consensus in Russia and Belarus. So far, the project has been driven by the political will of President Nazarbaev and President/Prime Minister Putin, and it is not clear what will happen when they leave the political scene.

4.3. Geopolitical Implications

It is too early to assess the geopolitical impact of the ECU; however, it is possible to make a preliminary analysis of the effect it has had on Kazakhstan's multi-vector foreign policy and the balancing acts that Astana had been so good at. How strong is the tilt of Kazakhstan toward Russia? How will it affect Kazakhstan's relations with two of its major economic partners – the EU and China – who also happen to be two

---

[59] 'Vstupleniye Kazakhstana v tamozhennyi soyuz i edinoe ekonomicheskoe prostranstvo vedet k potere politicheskogo suvereniteta strany!', *Zona.kz*, 8 June 2011, http://www.zonakz.net/articles/?artid=29733 (accessed 8 June 2011).

[60] 'Ideya sozdaniya evraziyskogo soyuza dazhe ne obsuzhdaetsya', *Vremya*, 19 September 2012. A similar stance has been taken publicly by Presidential Adviser Yermukhamet Yertyspayev, *Tengrinews.kz*, 20 September 2012, http://tengrinews.kz/kazakhstan_news/ertyisbaev-razgovoryi-o-sozdanii-evraziyskogo-parlamenta-poka-prejdevremennyi-220606 (accessed 22 September 2012).

other poles of geopolitical power in the Eurasian continent? And what will be the impact on Kazakhstan's relations with the rest of Central Asia?

The creation of the ECU and SES showed that the leadership of Kazakhstan decided to subordinate its trade and economic policies to Russia. However, over the three-year period there have been important changes in the decision-making mechanisms, indicating that the Kazakhstani leadership has had second thoughts with regard to the degree of this subordination. In the first supranational body, the Commission of the Customs Union, 57 per cent of votes belonged to Russia and 21.5 per cent each to Kazakhstan and Belarus. The decisions were made with two-thirds of the votes, providing for Russia's clear dominance in deciding international trade issues. In the Eurasian Economic Commission (EEC) that was substituted for the Commission of the Customs Union with the launch of the SES in January 2012, there is equal distribution of votes following the model of the European Commission.[61]

At the same time, the unequal weight of the economies of the member states is reflected in the distribution of quotas for staff of the EEC: 84 per cent for Russian citizens, 10 per cent for Kazakhstani citizens, and 6 per cent for Belarusian citizens. Consequently, the financing of the EEC was decided as follows: Russia 87.97 per cent, Kazakhstan 7.33 per cent, and Belarus 4.7 per cent.[62] This gives certain leverage for Russia to shape the SES.

With the launch of the SES in January 2012, Astana might have reached the limit of its integration ambitions. At the March summit of EvrAzES it blocked Moscow's initiative to reorganize the community into the Eurasian Economic Union with the request not to hurry.[63]

The absence of any noticeable changes in Kazakhstan's multi-vector foreign policy also seem to indicate that the tilt toward Russia has been smaller than it appeared in 2009–10. On a trip to Turkey in October 2012 Nazarbaev even allowed himself statements critical of the Russian historical role, saying that in 150 years of being the colony of the Russian empire and then the Soviet Union, Kazakhs have almost lost

---

[61] See Cooper (Chapter 2) and Dragneva (Chapter 3) in this volume.

[62] 'Pismo ministra po delam ekonomicheskoi integratsii Zhanar Aitxhanovoi', *Vremya*, 27 September 2012.

[63] 'Lukashenko: transformatsiyu EvrAzES pritormozil Kazakhstan', *Newsru. com*, 21 March 2012, http://www.newsru.com/finance/21mar2012/lukashenko. html (accessed 22 March 2012).

their traditions, customs, language and religion. He called on Turkic peoples to unite and become an effective force in the world.[64]

Kazakhstan continues to pursue closer relations with the EU and China. While in political terms there are some constraints – Astana is increasingly intolerant of European democratization and efforts to promote human rights, and remains concerned with the implications of the rise of China – the economic pull factor of their giant economies remains strong. In fact, the SES in no way can substitute European and Chinese markets for Kazakhstan – in 2010 Kazakhstan's exports to Europe stood at $32 billion (53.2 per cent of all exports) and to China $10.1 billion (16.8 per cent).[65] Significantly, unlike Europe and China, Russia and Belarus are not major sources of technologies, investment and best practices. In this regard, the ECU and SES do not present a challenge to Europe and China. However, their formation, to some extent, re-establishes the traditional role of Russia as 'the window to Europe', and Kazakhstan again attaches itself to the Russian modernization train.

As for Kazakhstan's relations with the rest of Central Asia, the impact of the ECU and SES has already been considerable. To fulfil its membership obligations, Kazakhstan has adopted stricter regimes to regulate the export of goods and strengthened its southern borders. These measures have hindered intraregional trade and, in particular, have undermined the economy of Kyrgyzstan, which is dependent on the re-export of Chinese goods. It was reported that in 2010–11 the number of wholesale traders in the country dropped by 70–80 per cent, and the number of retail traders by 30–40 per cent.[66]

Although both Kyrgyzstan and Tajikistan have announced their interest in joining the ECU and both are encouraged by Russia and Kazakhstan, such an expansion in the near future is probably unlikely as a result of the massive problems that it would entail. Moscow can continue to entertain broader geopolitical ambitions, but the realities on the ground dictate the more feasible goal of making the relatively prosperous 'core' of the post-Soviet space integrate and work.

In this sense, the formation of the ECU and the SES could result in the institutionalization of the fragmentation of Central Asia. Overall, the region of Central Asia is increasingly becoming a zone of potential instability given the absence of proper political succession mechanisms,

---

[64]   'Idem prezhnim kursom', *Karavan*, 19 October 2012.
[65]   Statistical Agency, above note 33.
[66]   'Kyrgyzstan: tamozhennyi soyuz udaril po torgovtsam s rynka Dordoi', *Ferghana.ru*, 1 November 2011, http://www.fergananews.com/news.php?id= 17566 (accessed 3 November 2011).

growing economic disparities, nationalism and Islamism. Russia and Kazakhstan do not seem to have a plan of how to address these challenges.

5. CONCLUSION

The creation of the ECU in 2010 and the SES in 2012 constitutes a major breakthrough for the Eurasian economic integration project, promoted by Kazakhstani President Nursultan Nazarbaev since early 1990s. While a union with Russia has been always an official priority, other trade integration alternatives have been pursued by the Kazakhstani government as well. In strong competition with the ECU option was the prospect of joining the WTO, thus advancing Kazakhstan's integration with global markets and making the country's economy more competitive. The tension between these two options remained until 2009, when the decision was made to join the ECU first.

The analysis of the possible motives (economic, political and geopolitical) to explain why the Kazakhstani leadership privileged integration with Russia over joining the WTO shows that economic reasons emphasized in the official discourse did not play the main role. Political reasons seem to have been more prominent.

The overview of the results of the two years of the existence of the ECU shows that they have been mixed at best, despite the continued enthusiasm of government officials. The introduction of higher external tariffs hurt Kazakhstani producers (except for exporters of minerals and metals) and consumers, while the opening of the customs borders did not result in major increases in Kazakhstani exports to ECU member states. It remains to be seen on what conditions Kazakhstan will be joining the WTO, and whether this can partially alleviate the negative impact of the ECU.

As for the political impact, the Eurasian integration project allowed the mobilization of nationalist forces around the issue and gave them a strong argument in opposing the government. The inflation stimulated by the ECU has increased the potential for instability in the country. The fact that Eurasian integration is promoted largely by the political will of the Presidents, and there is a lack of public consensus regarding the usefulness of the ECU, SES and future Eurasian Economic Union, the sustainability of the project is not ensured.

In geopolitical terms, the formation of the ECU and the SES has not affected noticeably the traditional multi-vector foreign policy of Kazakhstan. The lack of internal dynamism and resources of the Eurasian economic integration project means that it does not constitute a major challenge to Europe and China, two major trade partners of Kazakhstan. However, it does, to some extent, re-establish the traditional role of Russia as a 'window to Europe'.

The ECU has created a bigger challenge for Kazakhstan's Central Asian neighbours – in particular, Kyrgyzstan. To fulfil its obligations towards its ECU partners, Kazakhstan has strengthened its southern borders and introduced stricter trade regimes. Unless Kyrgyzstan and Tajikistan are engaged in the integration project, as promised by President Putin and President Nazarbaev, the development of the SES will mean further fragmentation of the region of Central Asia. Such integration, however, seems unlikely in the near future because of the serious challenges that it would entail.

PART III

The ECU and its ramifications for the European Union

9. The impact of the Eurasian Customs Union on EU–Russia relations

Hiski Haukkala

1. INTRODUCTION

The Grand Narrative of EU–Russia relations since their inception in the early 1990s has been the EU's repeated attempts at 'constructive engagement' with a view to 'binding' or 'tying' Russia closer into Europe and its key institutions. These attempts at inclusion have nevertheless always had a rather uneasy coexistence with exclusion: at no point has Russia been deemed a serious candidate for full accession to any of the leading European bodies, be it the European Union or NATO.[1] This exclusionary dynamic, which more recently has increasingly been gaining features of wanton self-exclusion by Russia itself, has been a factor that has hampered the achievement of some of the EU's strategic objectives vis-à-vis Russia.

The main underlying objective for the EU in its dealings with Russia has revolved around attempts at tying the country into an EU-centric – or, alternatively, concentric – order. In this reading 'Brussels' and its institutions are the unipole with Russia envisaged as a more or less passive recipient of norms, values and a whole gamut of policy best practices originating in and promoted by the EU. It should be pointed out that although Russia has been granted several privileges by the EU – such as a role of special 'strategic partner' as well as a much more lenient application of political conditionality in the process – in essence, Moscow has been subjected to the same objectives, principles and policies as the rest of the EU's Eastern neighbourhood. For all intents and

---

[1] Mark Webber, *Inclusion, Exclusion and the Governance of European Security* (Manchester University Press, 2007).

purposes they have been based on the EU's claim of normative hegemony in Europe, built on asymmetrically sovereignty-challenging approaches.[2]

It should be pointed out that, at least initially, Russia also subscribed to this agenda: in the early 1990s Moscow was repeatedly voicing its ambition to join the 'community of civilized states', a process that was seen as entailing the largely one-sided adoption by Russia of Western liberal standards of democracy and market economy.[3] Although during Vladimir Putin's leadership this rhetoric has largely subsided, some of the calls for closer integration and cooperation with the EU put forward by Putin, especially in the early 2000s, were based on at least a tacit acceptance of the rules of the game propagated by the EU.

When viewed against this backdrop, the formation of the Eurasian Customs Union (ECU) between Russia, Belarus and Kazakhstan, and the ambition to rapidly develop it into a fully fledged Eurasian Economic Union (EEU) in the future, is potentially a very significant development. Although largely stemming from the Commonwealth of Independent States (CIS) and the Eurasian Economic Community (EvrAzES) – both institutions which, more often than not, have been seen as rather moribund organizations with serious defects in terms of turning their ambitions into practice – the ECU can potentially be seen in a different light. The reason for this is, firstly, Vladimir Putin's apparently firm decision to invest a good deal of political and economic capital into the project and make it the lynchpin of his second presidency.[4] This determination has, secondly, resulted in a situation in which the formation of the ECU and its myriad of institutional structures has progressed rapidly, giving some grounds for an assessment that it has more dynamism and staying power than its predecessors (see Dragneva, Chapter 3 of this volume).

The ECU can be seen as a significant break in the main post-cold war narrative outlined above in at least three overlapping respects. First, philosophically it rejects the notion of an EU-centric unilateral order in which the transference of norms and values is entirely one-sided. Second, politically it seeks to build an alternative pole that has the potential to augur a more bipolar setting in Europe, at least for the time being. To a

[2] Hiski Haukkala, *The EU–Russia Strategic Partnership: The Limits of Post-Sovereignty in International Relations* (Routledge, 2010).
[3] Robert English, *Russia and the Idea of the West: Gorbachev, Intellectuals, and the End of the Cold War* (Columbia University Press, 2000).
[4] Hannes Adomeit, 'Putin's "Eurasian Union": Russia's Integration Project and Policies on Post-Soviet Space', *Neighbourhood Policy Paper 04* (Centre for International and European Studies, July 2012).

degree this can be seen as an attempt by Russia to delineate its privileged sphere of influence – or interests – in a more clear and institutionalized manner. Third, and largely as a consequence of the previous two points, it has repercussions both for EU–Russia relations as well as the policies the EU has been promoting in its Eastern neighbourhood, the analysis of which is the task of this chapter.

The argument will be developed in three parts. First, an analysis highlights the changes which the adoption and development of the ECU can be seen to have had on EU–Russia relations and, indeed, on the EU's policy towards Russia. It is argued that the ECU is in fact a logical outcome of the frictions the EU and Russia have faced in developing integration and cooperation and, at the same time, it can be expected to contribute to further problems between the two squabbling 'strategic partners'. An examination of the potential impact of the ECU on the so-called 'common neighbourhood' between the EU and Russia – a term the use of which Moscow has quite tellingly never officially endorsed – will then follow. The main point made is that, most likely, it is in the realm of the EU's neighbourhood policies that the biggest impact of the ECU can be expected, especially if Russia is successful in attracting into its ranks other countries from Eastern Europe in addition to Belarus. Indeed, one way of reading the ECU is to see it as an instrument used to blunt the EU's European Neighbourhood Policy (ENP), especially in view of the Deep and Comprehensive Free Trade Agreement currently developed and promoted by the EU, which can be seen as having the potential to break, or at least lessen, Russia's grip on certain key countries, such as Ukraine. The chapter ends with some conclusions which seek to tease out the essential impact of the ECU on EU–Russia relations in the foreseeable future.

Before proceeding it should be pointed out that this analysis is offered with the caveat that it is based on a reading of current achievements and declarations by Russia and the other participants in the ECU and a fairly straightforward extrapolation of these trends. As is argued in other chapters in this book, it is not at all given that all the pronouncements will be easily fleshed out, however, and this should be borne in mind throughout the present chapter.

2. THE IMPACT OF THE ECU ON EU–RUSSIA RELATIONS

One way of viewing the development of the EU–Russia relationship since its inception in the early 1990s is to envisage it as an ongoing debate, perhaps even a contestation, concerning the nature, depth and breadth of the post-cold war order in Europe. In the most concrete terms the issue has boiled down to Russia's place in that order and to what extent free trade, deep economic integration and political relations between the EU and Russia are feasible to begin with, and on what rules they should be based. It should be emphasized that at the level of official documents and declarations the parties have been able to agree and mutually ratify an ambitious and wide-ranging road map for closer economic integration and political cooperation. That said, EU–Russia relations have been largely predicated on the EU's insistence on a one-sided transference of its own norms, values and practices into Russia. This has been particularly so in the realm of economic relations, where, since the adoption of the Partnership and Cooperation Agreement (PCA) in 1994,[5] the aim has been nothing less than an eventual free trade area between the EU and Russia.

To be sure, economic integration always entails a certain degree of normative convergence and, as a highly developed legal system and single market, the EU is no exception. As is the norm in EU external trade relations, the onus in the case of Russia has been put on the need to converge towards the EU norms and standards. Therefore Article 55 of the PCA states unequivocally that 'the Parties recognize that an important condition for strengthening the economic links between Russia and the Community is the approximation of legislation', and how it is the task of Russia to 'endeavour to ensure that its legislation will be gradually made compatible with that of the Community'.[6] In addition, the EU has insisted on political conditionality based on liberal values. Taken together, this double expectation of convergence constitutes the essence of the EU's claim for normative hegemony.

The PCA still forms the contractual foundation between the EU and Russia. That said, it is by no means the only instrument between the parties as over the years the two have been busily engaged in the

---

[5] The PCA was fully ratified and entered into force in December 1997. It was originally adopted for a period of ten years and it expired in December 2007. Article 106 of the PCA does, however, state 'that the Agreement shall be automatically renewed year by year provided that neither Party gives the other Party written notice of denunciation of the Agreement at least six months before it expires'. To date this has not transpired so the PCA is still the main contractual foundation between the EU and Russia.

[6] Agreement on partnership and cooperation establishing a partnership between the European Communities and their Member States, of one part, and the Russian Federation, of the other part [1997] OJ L 327, 3–69.

adoption of a whole series of different policy templates to augment and complement the PCA. Therefore, the aim of eventual free trade and the need for normative convergence were also reaffirmed in the Four Common Spaces documents in 2005.[7] To a degree the Common Spaces can be seen as an attempt to reinvigorate the process of economic integration between the parties as well as locate the areas where deepened cooperation between the EU and Russia would be particularly feasible. More recently, the EU and Russia have also adopted a Partnership for Modernization that springs from an original bilateral partnership between Germany and Russia, a process that has rapidly resulted in a web of bilateral partnerships between Russia and the majority of EU member states, as well as at the EU level. The parties have also been engaged in negotiations since 2008 to replace the PCA with a new basic agreement, although it seems that the format and content of the agreement has also turned into a matter of contention.

All in all, it is hard to avoid the impression that the energies that the EU and Russia have devoted to the adoption of ever more policy platforms and instruments have partly been attempts at creating a semblance of progress in the relationship. That said, the new initiatives have had a hard time covering up the lack of actual deliverables between the parties and to a degree they have, to quote Michal Emerson, amounted to little more than a mere 'proliferation of the fuzzy'.[8] Although officially all the key building blocks of EU–Russia relations are still in place and even their continuation and potential deepening is being discussed, the actual institutionalized practices seem to verify this sceptical observation.[9] Regardless of its long sought after accession to the World Trade Organization (WTO) in August 2012, Russia has largely failed to meet its obligations listed in the PCA to adapt its legislation to meet EU standards, or the process has at least been very slow and

---

[7] Agreed at the EU–Russia Summit in Moscow in May 2005, the Four Common Spaces document can be seen as an attempt to operationalize the commitments taken by both parties in the PCA. These Common Spaces cover economic issues and the environment; issues of freedom, security and justice; external security, including crisis management and non-proliferation; and research and education, including cultural aspects. The 2005 document was at the time touted as a comprehensive roadmap for the development of EU–Russia relations. The actual implementation of the documents has, however, left a lot to be desired. For more about the document, see http://www.eu-un.europa.eu/ articles/en/article_4490_en.htm (last accessed 6 June 2013).

[8] Michael Emerson, 'EU–Russia Four Common Spaces and the Proliferation of the Fuzzy', *CEPS Policy Briefs No. 71* (CEPS, 1 May 2005).

[9] For a fuller discussion, see Haukkala, above note 2, 176–7.

uneven. The underlying reason for the basic reluctance of Russia is clear: it is an economy based on exports of natural resources and this has only increased during the 2000s; therefore there has been fairly little incentive to rapidly develop a deep free trade arrangement with the EU. Russia's internal development has also shown that perhaps even since the early 1990s the country has in fact been moving away from and not towards Western democratic ideals and human rights standards.[10] As a consequence, and as exemplified by the chronic difficulties the EU and Russia have faced in negotiating a new post-PCA basic agreement, the parties no longer seem to be able to arrive at a jointly shared vision concerning the future of their relations.

All in all, it seems evident that under Putin Russia has increasingly come to reject the notion of a unipolar Europe based on the EU's hegemonic norms, values and principles. This rejection seems to have been developing gradually in three stages. In the first instance, already visible during the 1990s, Russia made little or no headway at all in terms of converging towards the EU standards, while nevertheless still paying official lip service to them and the ideals that underpin them. In the second period, since the early 2000s, Russia, and especially through its leader Vladimir Putin, started to disassociate itself from most of the objectives and principles propagated by the EU. The new narrative emerging from Moscow has revolved around the notion of how 'the West' – usually understood to be represented by the United States, but at times by the EU as well – took advantage of Russia's temporary weakness in the early 1990s and imposed an alien set of policies and principles on Russia while side-lining the country politically in Europe. A good deal of criticism has been levied against the role of the Organization for Security and Cooperation in Europe (OSCE) in becoming the tool of the US and the Western part of the continent, but also NATO and the EU have increasingly earned their share of criticism for adopting similar 'unilateral' practices. Although the rhetoric coming from Moscow has at times been quite belligerent, the essential gist of the Russian argument seems to have been defensive: for Russia, and especially Putin, the issue is a need to uphold Russia's own traditions and principles, not the full implementation of Western norms and standards. Therefore the main task at hand is to cordon off alien influences to

---

[10]   M. Steven Fish, *Democracy Derailed in Russia. The Failure of Open Politics* (Cambridge University Press, 2005); David R. Cameron and Mitchell A. Orenstein, 'Post-Soviet Authoritarianism: The Influence of Russia in Its "Near Abroad"' (2012) 28 Post-Soviet Affairs 1.

enable the indigenous and somehow more organic and 'natural' development of Russia.

That said, the very make up and contours of the ECU betray more than
a whiff of copycat integration and institutionalization, as not only the
overall aims (the four freedoms, eventual common currency, and so on)
but also the whole institutional make-up of the proposed Eurasian
Economic Union is built on the EU model. Emulation of Western
practices has, of course, a long pedigree in Russia and more often than
not it has not amounted to much more than suboptimal and inconsequential simulacra.[11] Yet it is hard to escape the impression that, on this
occasion at least, imitation is indeed the highest form of flattery: despite
its current problems and long-term challenges, and the increasingly flat
rejection by Russia of meeting the EU's standards and expectations,
'Brussels' is still nevertheless seen as a worthy model to be followed by
Moscow when it seeks to promote Eurasian integration. This has been
openly admitted by Putin, who has noted how the aim of the ECU is to
make good use of the positive experiences of EU integration while
avoiding some of the mistakes made in the process.[12] Interestingly,
Russia's Mid-Term EU Strategy from 1999 already hinted that Russia
would be keen to use the EU as a model in developing integration in the
CIS area, a promise seemingly made good with the adoption of the
ECU.[13]

Nevertheless, in the third and most recent stage, Russia has abandoned
its basically defensive stance as Moscow has taken a more active role in
promoting its preferred vision of order beyond its own borders. Therefore, with the formation of the ECU, Russia has started to invest in a
more institutionalized bipolar setting in Europe, with Moscow as the
leading power in the other half of the continent. The methods for
achieving this are clear and familiar: it is the rebuilding and reassertion
of control over key infrastructures and industries in the CIS with a view
of maintaining and even enhancing Russia's dominant position in the
Eurasian economic area.[14] Obviously it is too early to declare the mission
completed; the current composition of the ECU with only three countries
hardly makes it a representative body even in the CIS area, but Russia's

---

[11] Hiski Haukkala, 'A Norm-Maker or a Norm-Taker? The Changing Normative Parameters of Russia's Place in Europe', in Ted Hopf (ed.), *Russia's
European Choice* (Palgrave Macmillan, 2008).

[12] Adomeit, above note 4, 8.

[13] Haukkala, above note 2, Chapter 6.

[14] Katri Pynnöniemi, 'Russia and Eurasian Economic Space: The Case of
"Strategic Partnership 1520"', *EU-Russia Paper 6* (CEURUS, July 2012).

vision seems to be clear: the Customs Union and the eventual Eurasian Economic Union is expected to attract the majority, if not perhaps even all, of the post-Soviet states under the wings of Russia's leadership.

Although the ECU's role as an augur of a more bipolar setting in Europe seems clear – and can in itself account for Russia's willingness to promote the project – other motivations can also be detected behind the initiative. It seems to be the case that for Russia the ECU entails a certain element of delicious diplomatic tit-for-tat. For years Russia has been grappling and becoming increasingly frustrated with the basic incompatibility between the division of competences at the member state and EU level in several key issues, ranging from visa freedom to trade politics, and Russia's own preference for conducting key economic and political relations in Europe on a bilateral basis. In a sense, therefore, it is hard to escape the impression that the Kremlin must be delighted when it now finds itself in a position to point out to the European Commission that it is no longer in a position to discuss, for example, certain trade-related issues bilaterally with Brussels as they now belong to the exclusive competence of the ECU and its newly founded Eurasian Economic Commission.

When one keeps all of this in mind, it is hardly a surprise that the EU has greeted the emergence of the ECU with mixed feelings, to say the least. In fact it seems clear that the EU has taken a relatively negative stance towards the formation of the new body. There is an element of irony here as officially the EU has been keen to present itself as a promoter of regional integration and cooperation elsewhere in the world, but the difficulties the EU has had in coming to grips with the formation and development of the ECU have been plain to see.

In the first instance the adoption of the ECU was interpreted as a tactical ploy to sidetrack, or at least to slow down, Russia's WTO entry.[15] To a degree this could have been the case as it seems clear that the Russian leadership and several key industries – and indeed the population at large – had some serious misgivings about joining the trade body, as they still do. Yet, more recently it has become obvious that the ECU has not only persisted despite Russia's entry but it has also acquired increasingly ambitious features. In the process it has proved that the ECU is a more purposeful endeavour, and hence more consequential for the EU, than was originally envisaged. In other words, the initiative cannot

---

[15]   George Bovt, 'Russia: Customs Union Instead of WTO?', *EurActiv*, 9 April 2010, http://www.euractiv.com/global-europe/russia-customs-union-wto-analysis-429487 (accessed 14 December 2012).

be discounted as yet another inconsequential acronym emerging, and soon falling into oblivion, in the post-Soviet space.

The key issue that has highlighted the EU's reluctance to come fully to terms with the ECU has been the fact that it has refused to recognize the ECU as an equal negotiating partner, something Russia has repeatedly requested.[16] This is not just a snub aimed at the fledgling new Eurasian Economic Union, as the recognition *problematique* has both practical and symbolic aspects to it. The practical side deals with the fact that not all of the ECU members – both current and, especially, foreseeable – are WTO members. The fact that not all of them enjoy equal access and roles in world markets or positions in the world trade body makes it practically impossible to treat the ECU as a negotiating partner on a par with the EU.[17] The situation is further complicated by the fact that the European Commission currently has a mandate only for bilateral negotiations with Russia as well as other countries in the ECU; gaining a new mandate that would authorize the Commission to deal with the ECU directly would require the adoption of a new mandate by the Council, which seems politically unlikely and difficult to secure. Finally, as argued by Dragneva in this volume (Chapter 3), whether the ECU is actually endowed with a separate legal personality is not a straightforward question.

The key reason for the EU's apparent lack of enthusiasm to greet the ECU with open arms is the clear scepticism towards the basic political and economic viability of the project in the Union. For example, Peter Balas, the Deputy Director General for External Trade in the European Commission, has noted how the ECU reflects more political than economic considerations and how the Commission has some serious doubts whether the depth and speed of integration to which the ECU is aspiring is in fact feasible.[18] According to the EU, Russia's implementation of its WTO commitments represents a litmus test for the ECU's promise to promote economic integration and modernization in line with international standards. Indeed, most of the economic analyses concerning the ECU seem to indicate that the overall economic impact is either close to zero or perhaps even negative.[19] For example, neither Belarus nor Kazakhstan has to date experienced, nor can they readily expect, any

---

[16]   Olga Shumylo-Tapiola, 'The Eurasian Customs Union: Friend or Foe of the EU?', *The Carnegie Papers* (Carnegie Endowment for International Peace, October 2012) 3.

[17]   'The Eurasian Customs Union: What's In It for the EU?', Event Transcript (Carnegie Endowment, 24 October 2012) 3.

[18]   Ibid.

[19]   Shumylo-Tapiola, above note 16, 15.

substantial economic gains from participation in the ECU (see Frear and Kassenova in this volume, Chapters 7 and 8). On the contrary, it seems that they have suffered from the higher external tariffs they have been forced to implement to conform with the Russian trade tariffs as part of the Customs Union, as argued by Connolly in this volume (Chapter 4). What is more, there seems to be some evidence that the ECU lacks economic dynamism and creates merely trade diversion – that is, it redirects trade from other external partners to intra-ECU trade – but does not seem to be creating new trade opportunities and fresh markets for the participants.[20] For the moment, therefore, it seems the EU has adopted a policy of 'wait and see'. In the meantime the EU is insisting on business as usual – on a bilateral basis – with the member states of the ECU, a stance that has clearly managed to irritate the Russians.

None of this should be taken to mean that the EU and/or its Commission have refused to have any dealings with the ECU. On the contrary, working-level exchanges have taken place both in Brussels and in Moscow. Yet the symbolic aspect of the issue should not be under-estimated either. Should the Commission accept the ECU fully as its equal, it would also simultaneously tacitly accept and consequently legitimize the existence of an increasingly bipolar setting in Europe. This is, of course, not something that the EU officials themselves would openly admit; in fact, when questioned about the topic during back-ground interviews conducted for this chapter in November 2012, they flatly rejected this interpretation – yet it seems a plausible hypothesis to keep an eye on. It seems unlikely that the potentially revolutionary ramifications of the ECU on the EU's own preferred *modus operandi* would have gone entirely unnoticed in the European Commission, or indeed in the wider EU.

It could be that the issue of recognition is a wider theme in Russia's role in Europe that is worth noting. It seems that Russia has a hard time winning equal recognition for any of its regional cooperation schemes, as exemplified by the reluctance that NATO and the OSCE have shown towards embracing the Russia-led Collective Security Treaty Organ-ization in the field of security. This is, of course, taken as an insult in Moscow – a fact that seems to irritate the Russians further, spoiling the political mood between Moscow and its Western partners as well as

---

[20]   Rilka Dragneva and Kataryna Wolczuk, 'Russia, the Eurasian Customs Union and the EU: Cooperation, Stagnation or Rivalry', *Briefing Paper REP BP 2012/01* (Chatham House, August 2012) 2.

stimulating the Kremlin into basically intensifying its efforts to build and win recognition for these bodies.

3. THE CHALLENGES POSED BY THE ECU IN THE 'COMMON NEIGHBOURHOOD'

Since the 'Big Bang' Eastern enlargement of 2004 the EU has had a much larger stake in its Eastern neighbourhood. At least since the Orange Revolution in Ukraine the same year the EU has also had to deal with Russia's growing suspicion over the EU's ambitions and activities in the region.[21] In fact, it can be argued that the EU has become locked into an integration competition with Russia. Although the EU has done its best to convince the Russians that it is not interested in exclusive spheres of influence but is seeking consensual win-win outcomes instead, Moscow has decided to treat the EU's presence in the region largely in a classical zero-sum manner. This is mainly because the Russian elites frame international relations in general in terms of fierce competition and consequent spheres of interests and influence.[22] This has been reflected in the fact that Russia decided to opt out of the value-laden ENP and consequent Eastern Partnership and has insisted on, and been granted, a more interest-driven strategic partnership instead. In addition, Russia has taken a series of steps to counter the EU's impact in Eastern Europe and has increasingly put forth its own policies that in effect have undermined the Union's influence in the region. As Leonard and Popescu have noted, in certain respects Russia has, in fact, had a much more robust strategy and policy in place than has been appreciated either in the EU or the US.[23]

To better understand the Russian reactions, a closer look at Moscow's evolving responses to the EU's neighbourhood policies is in order. Initially it seemed evident that Russia did not take the EU's neighbourhood policy seriously, relegating the question of its own participation in the scheme, or the role of the whole topic in EU–Russia relations, to the

---

[21]   Hiski Haukkala, 'The Three Paradigms of European Security in Eastern Europe: Co-operation, Competition and Conflict', in Sven Biscop and Richard G. Whitman (eds), *The Routledge Handbook of European Security* (Routledge, 2013) 159–69.

[22]   Dmitri Trenin, 'Russia's Spheres of Interest, not Influence' (2009) 32(4) *The Washington Quarterly* 3.

[23]   Mark Leonard and Nicu Popescu, 'A Power Audit of EU–Russia Relations', *European Council on Foreign Relations*, 7 November 2007, 17.

status of a non-issue. The first wake-up call for Russia was Ukraine's Orange Revolution in 2004, which showed that Russia could not take its own standing in the CIS area for granted. But it was the evolution of the ENP, and especially the emergence of a more ambitious and institutionally more robust Eastern Partnership in 2009, that finally changed Russia's tack.

The EU's strategy of developing hard law contractual frameworks with a view to eventual EU association for the Eastern partners has raised the stakes and changed the nature of the game for Russia. On the one hand, the process has raised the spectre of loosening Russia's grip in several key post-Soviet states – Ukraine, in particular. On the other hand, the potential success of systemic transformation along the EU model in Eastern Europe could result in a situation where Russia's own system could be exposed to unfavourable comparisons with its Western neighbours, with potentially devastating political consequences for the standing and legitimacy of Russia's current elites. In light of this it seems hardly surprising that Russia has repeatedly deplored the EU's attempts at 'carving its own sphere of influence in the East' and has not made its growing displeasure a secret. On the contrary, Russia has actively started to take steps to blunt the edge of the EU's policies in the region.

Energy-rich Russia can use a whole array of mechanisms, both positive and negative, that are not necessarily at the Union's disposal to foster bilateral relationships in Eastern Europe. Russia's biggest asset may be its ability to engage in business deals with countries with which the EU finds it hard to engage. In short, Russia can offer economic benefits that the EU at times cannot match because Russia does not have any problems in supporting authoritarian regimes. A particular case in point has been Central Asia, where Russia has for years been operating at full economic and political speed, while the EU still contemplates the merits and possible limits of engaging with countries with severe problems in their democratic and human rights credentials.[24] In Eastern Europe too – the main arena for the EU's neighbourhood policies – the same lesson seems to apply: it has been largely thanks to political and economic support from Moscow that President Lukashenko has been able to hold on to power for so long in Belarus.[25] Moscow has also been trying to lure back President Viktor Yanukovych's Ukraine with a set of preferential gas deals that have kept the country's crisis-ridden economy afloat while

---

[24] Neil J. Melvin, 'The European Union's Strategic Role in Central Asia', *CEPS Policy Briefs No. 128* (CEPS, March 2007).

[25] Arkady Moshes, 'Avenue of Independence: Will Russian-Belarusian Relations Take the Ukrainian Path?' *Russia in Global Affairs*, 7 July 2010.

actually lessening the prospects of successful economic modernization and eventual integration with Europe.[26]

As a consequence, Russia seems increasingly to position itself as a counter-force to the EU's approaches to their 'common neighbourhood'. Indeed, Russia seems to be investing increasing political and economic energies into developing alternative models of economic modernization and societal development to those promoted by the EU. To date, however, it seems that Russia's effectiveness has been hindered by two factors: first, Moscow has failed to come up with an idea or theme to provide its policies with sound intellectual underpinnings that would have wider international resonance; second, Russia's own lack of credibility, given its weak integration into the world economy. As a consequence, and compared with the magnetic pull of the EU, Russia's 'soft power' has been lacking.[27]

This is where the ECU enters the scene. To a degree the Customs Union can be seen as an exception to Russia's previous tendencies just to coerce countries in the post-Soviet space to take heed of Moscow's interests. It seems to have a more forward-oriented and aspirational side in the form of joint institutions based at least ostensibly on supranationality and emphasis on economic growth and prosperity.[28] Yet the underlying realities seem to suggest a much more mixed picture. Despite the accent put on the expected positive outcomes of closer Eurasian integration, Russia's invitations for other CIS countries to join the initiative always seem to be laced with subtle, and at times less than subtle, threats of economic hardships imposed by Russia if the invitation is not duly heeded (see also Delcour and Wolczuk, Chapter 10 of this volume). In addition the EU has voiced less than veiled concerns over the voluntary nature of accession to the ECU. One instance that highlights this tendency is the return of energy into an openly used foreign policy instrument by Russia. It seemed that the 2009 gas crisis with Ukraine made Russia publicly downplay the role of energy as an instrument of its foreign policy. More recently, however, there seems to be more than anecdotal evidence that this is no longer the case. For example, in September 2012 in the space of a few days both Moldova and Ukraine were faced with a situation where Russia linked the future prices of natural gas to the countries' willingness to seriously consider joining the ECU and giving up their pretentions of pursuing closer integration with

---

[26] Adomeit, above note 4.

[27] Andrei P. Tsygankov, 'If Not by Tanks, then by Banks? The Role of Soft Power in Putin's Foreign Policy' (2006) 58(7) *Europe-Asia Studies* 1079.

[28] Dragneva and Wolczuk, above note 20.

the EU.[29] In a similar vein Putin has characterized Belarus's relatively affordable prices of natural gas as 'integration discounts', making it no secret that the price of commodities and the political choices of CIS countries are indeed inextricably linked in the eyes of Russia.[30]

4. CONCLUSIONS

For bilateral EU–Russia relations the ECU can be seen as a codification or slow institutionalization of the present inertia and lack of dynamism between the parties. In this respect the changes are not major in economic or political terms. More likely, the biggest change is diplomatic if/when the EU, and especially its Commission, are forced to deal with the ECU instead of insisting on discussing and settling issues bilaterally with Russia and the other countries in the ECU.

As mentioned above, potentially the most radical repercussions from the ECU can be expected in the region covered by the EU's own ENP. All in all, the ECU can be seen as a serious attack against the EU's normative hegemony in Europe. Instead of accepting an EU-centric/concentric order in Europe, Russia has clearly made a bid for a more bipolar setting and seeks to cement its own position as the other important pole in Europe. Although it is obviously too early to argue that the EU has lost its position as the main magnet in Europe, it seems safe to conclude that the ECU and Russia's role in its rapid development presents the starkest challenge to date to both the EU's objectives as well as its preferred solutions and policies in Eastern Europe.

That said, one could argue that the European choice of Ukraine, or any other neighbour, is not the EU's business: the EU is not in the business of aggressive association and integration but it moves more consensually and essentially through invitation. At the same time it is worth taking note that should Ukraine opt for the Eurasian integration path, it seems safe to conclude that Russia would have managed to undo the majority of the EU's objectives in the East and Moscow could in turn be congratulated for achieving a truly bipolar setting in Europe. Yet most of these developments still lie in the future and are, therefore, largely speculative. The important point for the EU to keep in mind, however, is that the stakes in Eastern Europe are getting higher at the same time as the EU's

[29]   See 'Kremlin Pressures Ukraine to Join Alliance', *The Moscow Times*, 17 September 2012; Agata Wierzbowska-Miazga, 'Russia's Energy Ultimatum to Moldova', *OSW EastWeek* (Centre for Eastern Studies, 9 September 2012).
[30]   Adomeit, above note 4, 4.

own capacity is on the decline as a result of its own internal economic and political problems. It could be that the EU's own relative weakness in fact spurs the prospects of Eurasian integration in the future regardless of the indigenous potential the ECU otherwise might have.

Indeed, it is too early to conclude that Russia will be able to realize its goals, at least in full, for three reasons. To begin with both Russia's ability to lead and the Eurasian region's basic propensity to engage itself fully in an integration process are to be doubted: the post-Soviet area is not easily subordinated to a single organizing principle. On the contrary, it is a mosaic of different, at times even conflicting, layers of authority and interests that compete for institutional and economic resources.[31] A detailed analysis of these issues must remain outside the scope of this chapter, but suffice it to say there are at least three serious reservations concerning the long-term feasibility of the ECU. The ECU itself is far from having fully secured foundations. As has already been noted, the economic rationale seems weak and this alone could result in its eventual undoing. It is also too early to tell whether the institutions adopted will work and whether they, as well as the ECU member states, can and eventually will implement their commitments in a timely and consistent manner (see Connolly and Dragneva in this volume). Furthermore it seems evident that with potential expansion, especially to Central Asia, many of the bilateral and/or regional problems and issues will be exported to the ECU; it could be that over time it will suffer the fate of the CIS and will become increasingly dysfunctional as an organization (see Malle, Chapter 6 of this volume).

Second, it is to be doubted whether Russia can sustain, let alone increase, its ability to act as a credible pole even in the post-Soviet space. This is not the place to discuss the future of Russia, but it seems evident that it faces severe domestic, economic and societal challenges that could make it difficult for Moscow to act as the fully credible leader of the post-Soviet region. The rise of China has the potential to challenge Russia's pre-eminence, especially in Central Asia but potentially elsewhere in the region as some of the loans granted by China, for example, to Belarus seem to suggest.

Third, the history of CIS integration has shown that the 'newly independent states' are just that – a rather motley collection of increasingly independently minded states that are busily building their own identities and statehood while seeking to preserve and even buttress their own sovereignty and freedom to manoeuvre (see also Cooper, Chapter 2

---

[31]   Pynnöniemi, above note 14, 13–14.

of this volume). Therefore it seems unlikely that the rest of the CIS will simply fall in line with the visions put forward by Russia concerning the future of Eurasian integration. For example, in January 2013 the President of Kazakhstan, Nursultan Nazarbaev, announced unilaterally that the project should remain purely economic and should steer clear of any pretentions for a political union. For Nazarbaev there simply will be 'no return to the USSR'.[32]

This does not mean that the idea of Eurasian integration is doomed, however. What it does seem to imply is that to succeed Russia must be much more willing to pool and share its own sovereignty and compromise with others to accommodate their interests as well. The supranational elements of the ECU must not remain on paper only. The irony here is that to succeed with its own Customs Union, Russia must in fact come to terms with some of the same post-sovereign principles it has found so hard to accept in its relationship with the EU.

But it is doubtful whether Russia will find it easy or comfortable to compromise, let alone agree to be potentially outvoted by its Eurasian partners. Indeed, it remains to be seen if other members act as equal partners rather than mere objects of Russia's policies. At least the policy towards the development of the ECU to date seems to suggest that it has been largely based on an uneasy mix of economic benefits and coercive tactics and thus could mean that the process will meet its limits sooner rather than later (see Delcour and Wolczuk, Chapter 10 of this volume). It could very well be, therefore, that the impact on EU–Russia relations and the challenge presented to the EU by the ECU would be less existential than some of the preceding analysis might imply. That said, it seems evident that the ECU, even in its current incarnation, manages to bog down the EU's neighbourhood policy while essentially negating the prospects for any new basic agreement between the EU and Russia for the foreseeable future. The sobering conclusion of these developments and this chapter must therefore be that the narrowing of horizons between the EU and Russia that has been in process since at least the turn of the millennium seems set to continue also in the future, and the ECU – if it successfully persists – could turn out to be the final nail in the coffin of current attempts at successfully integrating Russia into Europe.

---

[32] Aleksandra Jarosiewicz, 'Kazakhstan Distances Itself from Moscow's Integration Projects', *OSW EastWeek* (Centre for Eastern Studies, 23 January 2013).

10. Eurasian economic integration: implications for the EU Eastern policy*

Laure Delcour and Kataryna Wolczuk

1. INTRODUCTION

The European Union (EU) has sought to exert its influence in the post-Soviet space by promoting economic integration with partner countries. Alas, in many respects, this strategy is not fully compatible with the needs, capabilities and expectations of partner countries. This is because the EU offer rests on a tight connection between economic integration and the extensive adoption of the *acquis communautaire* – a particularly challenging and costly proposition for the neighbouring states. Initially the EU promoted economic convergence through soft law – that is, with a low degree of legally binding obligation. Such an integration formula had initially imposed limited constraints on the partner countries' relations with other economic actors, such as Russia and the Commonwealth of Independent States (CIS). However, in the late 2000s the EU introduced a more legally binding framework – an Association Agreement – as a key instrument to achieve its key objective of the promotion of domestic reforms in its Eastern neighbours.

The Eurasian Customs Union (ECU) has started to impinge on, and hinder the achievement of the EU's objective in the region. This is because Russia has started to use the new regime to contest the EU's

* Preparation of this chapter was greatly facilitated by a collaborative research project conducted by the authors entitled 'Exploring the Role of the EU in Domestic Change in the Post-Soviet States', jointly funded by the ESRC and ANR as part of the scheme 'Open Research Area in Europe' (ESRC research grant (RES-360-25-0096), ANR-10-ORAR-014-01). See http://euimpacteast.org.

normative power in their common neighbourhood[1] (against the backdrop of stagnation in bilateral relations between the EU and Russia). It could be argued that through the ECU Russia is making its own quest to become a normative power, in the sense outlined by Diez, as an actor 'whose conception of its foreign policy role and behaviour is bound to particular aims, values, principles, as well as forms of influence and instruments of power in the name of a civilization of international relations'.[2] In essence, the emergence of the ECU means that the EU is no longer the only actor promoting deep economic integration premised on regulatory convergence in the post-Soviet space.

Russia's aspirations to be a normative power are treated with scepticism in the countries in the common neighbourhood: in contrast to the EU, the ECU is not regarded as a credible source of modernization through rule-based economic integration. Nevertheless, the dependency of these countries on Russia is conditioned by security, political and economic factors.[3] By exploiting these dependencies – especially with regard to trade, energy and security – Russia is able to alter the costs and benefits associated with the economic integration of these countries with the EU.

While Russia's credibility is low with regard to delivering rule-based economic integration, owing to its preponderance of economic power the country exercises a constraining role on the neighbouring countries that seek closer economic integration with the EU. This is especially so because the EU and Russia adopt different temporal perspectives vis-à-vis the countries in the common neighbourhood: the EU emphasizes the long-term benefits of integration, whereas for Russia the ECU's existence and quest for expansion is a much more pressing issue, thereby exerting a strongly constraining force on the influence of the EU in the region in the immediate future. While Russia may not be able to preclude the countries in the common neighbourhood from pursuing closer relations

---

[1]   The common neighbourhood consists of the post-Soviet states which participate in the Eastern Partnership, i.e. Armenia, Azerbaijan, Belarus, Georgia, Moldova and Ukraine. On normative contestation, see Rilka Dragneva and Kataryna Wolczuk, 'Russia, the Customs Union and the EU: Cooperation, Stagnation or Rivalry?', *Briefing Paper REP BP 2012/01* (Chatham House, August 2012).

[2]   Thomas Diez, 'Constructing the Self and Changing Others: Reconsidering Normative Power Europe' (2005) 33(3) *Millennium Journal of International Studies* 613, 617.

[3]   These dependencies were frequently referred to by officials and experts during the authors' interviews in Georgia and Armenia in November 2011 and Ukraine and Moldova in April and May 2012, respectively.

with the EU, it can introduce a series of factors which make the eventual choice in favour of the EU more costly and risky for these countries.

In order to illustrate the constraining role that the ECU can play, this chapter will focus on the EU's relations with the Soviet successor states – Ukraine, Belarus, Moldova, Azerbaijan, Georgia and Armenia – in the context of the European Neighbourhood Policy (ENP) and the Eastern Partnership. This analysis of EU policy is important because the implications of the ECU can only be properly gauged by considering the nature of the EU's own strategy in terms of objectives and instruments against the backdrop of the preferences of the partner countries. We will then proceed to outline the constraining role of the ECU by focusing on Russia's strategy in relation to Ukraine, in particular Russia's campaign to force Ukraine to abandon the landmark Association Agreement with the EU and join the ECU instead. Ukraine is a particularly suitable case study to illuminate the implications as, first, it was the first country to conclude the negotiations on the Association Agreement; and, second, it is largest and economically most important country in the Eastern neighbourhood which could benefit most from access to the EU market. It will be argued that although Russia has not been able to persuade Ukraine to join the ECU (yet), the emergence of the ECU weakens the 'market power' of the EU as it lowers both the short-term prospects for entering into binding commitments vis-à-vis the EU as well as the long-term prospects for implementation of these commitments.

2. THE EU POLICY IN THE EASTERN NEIGHBOURHOOD: RELIANCE ON MARKET POWER

With the ENP, and even more so with the Eastern Partnership, the EU has engaged in an intensive process of policy diffusion to post-Soviet countries. Both the ENP and the Eastern Partnership are premised on the view that convergence with the EU norms and rules will ultimately bring stability and prosperity to the Eastern neighbourhood, as was the case in post-war Western Europe and in post-cold war East-Central Europe. The EU has made it clear, however, that the reinforcement of its ties with Eastern partners is distinct 'from the possibilities available to European countries under Article 49 of the Treaty on European Union'; in other words, accession is not an option.[4]

---

[4]   European Commission, 'European Neighbourhood Policy: Strategy Paper', COM(2004) 373 final, Brussels, 12 May 2004, 3.

In this section we argue that EU policies in the Eastern neighbourhood are not closely matched with, and suited to, the needs, capabilities and expectations of partner countries. This is because the EU's offer rests on a tight connection between the adoption of the *acquis communautaire* and closer integration with the EU. While being the lynchpin of EU integration, the *acquis* is, however, a questionable blueprint for a feasible and cost-effective reform process in the Eastern neighbourhood. The essential gap between EU policies and the needs of Eastern partners is evidenced in the incongruity between the nature of the EU's offer and transformation processes in the Eastern neighbourhood.

The ENP and the Eastern Partnership were initiated and driven by the EU, both in terms of content and the methodology of economic integration. Even though their implementation is at least formally guided by the joint ownership principle, these policies are largely shaped by the EU's *modus operandi*, the specificities of its policy-making process and the contingencies of the context in which they are designed. A fragmented policy process and increasing heterogeneous preferences within the EU are prominent factors accounting for the substance, aims and instruments of both the ENP and the Eastern Partnership. With member states still playing a significant role in the decision-making process, EU foreign policy is primarily shaped by complex internal considerations. This institutional context ultimately shapes the EU integration strategy in the post-Soviet area, which is strongly constrained by the remits of internal consensus.

Upon conceding that the ENP suffered from the incongruence between the incentives offered to, and commitments required from, partner countries, with the Eastern Partnership the EU clarified and reinforced its offer around three major pillars: (i) the 'upgrading' of contractual relations with Association Agreements with deep and comprehensive free trade areas (DCFTA) with each country; (ii) progressive visa liberalization in exchange for creating a secure environment; and (iii) deeper cooperation to enhance the energy security of the partners and the EU.[5]

The offer of an Association Agreement with the DCFTA represents a watershed in the EU's relations with the partner countries because of an upgrade of the contractual basis towards a more legalized framework for economic integration. The DCFTA goes beyond a 'standard' FTA agreement by eliminating non-tariff trade barriers. The creation of the DCFTA

---

[5] European Commission, 'Eastern Partnership', Communication to the Council and to the European Parliament, COM(2008) 823 final, 3 December 2008, 4.

entails a profound impact on the regulatory framework of the country associated with the EU in a wide range of areas. Furthermore, the regulations have to be implemented in their entirety – no selectivity is permitted. This is to ensure the credibility of commitment and prevent selective implementation based on self-serving interpretations of the country entering into an association with the EU, as was the case under the Partnership and Cooperation Agreements (PCAs) dating back to the 1990s. It is a deliberate shift from vague and low-binding reform guidance to a regime with very detailed obligations with regard to the adoption of the extensive sections of the *acquis*.[6] Yet the Association Agreements stop short of acknowledgment of membership prospects. Flexing its 'market power', the EU requires the adoption of the economic *acquis* in third countries which are granted access to the single market to protect the coherence of the internal market, reflecting the centrality of sector-specific, technical international rules to the EU as an international organization and foreign policy actor.[7]

The shift in the EU's policy paradigm towards functional cooperation aimed at regulatory convergence through the Association Agreements, DCFTA and visa liberalization in the Eastern Partnership in a way camouflages the lack of consensus on the ultimate strategy vis-à-vis the Eastern partners. In this context, the EU exports primarily what it already agrees upon – its corpus of norms and rules, the *acquis communautaire*. While the import of the *acquis* was singled out as a major accession criterion under the enlargement process designed in the 1990s, since the last wave of enlargement the *acquis* has also emerged as a key link connecting EU members with each other in a context of growing heterogeneity:

> Portugal and Poland might not agree on various aspects of the EU's political relations with Ukraine; both Portugal and Poland agree, however, that the

---

[6]   The text of the Association Agreement with Ukraine, as released on the *Kyiv Post* website in December 2012, consists of extensive appendices containing Ukraine's detailed commitments with time frameworks for their implementation, http://www.kyivpost.com/content/ukraine/text-of-association-agreement-between-eu-ukraine-317197.html (accessed 6 December 2012).

[7]   Sandra Lavenex and Frank Schimmelfennig, 'EU Rules Beyond EU Borders: Theorizing External Governance in European Politics' (2009) 16(6) *Journal of European Public Policy* 791; Chad Damro, 'Market Power Europe' (2012) 19(5) *Journal of European Public Policy* 682.

export of the EU *acquis* to Ukraine is a good thing from the point of their national interests.[8]

Therefore, the export of the *acquis* serves as a backbone of consensus within the EU's relations with the Eastern partners.

Nevertheless, the EU's strategy is fundamentally contradictory since neighbours are unlikely to join the EU in the foreseeable future: after all, why should the partner countries accept the *acquis* with no prospect of becoming members? The EU addresses this ambiguity by presenting the *acquis* as a driver for modernization which is beneficial for partner countries, regardless of membership prospects. Increased convergence with EU legislation is defined as a key precondition for integrating with the EU in economic and political (but not institutional) terms. The export of the *acquis* is thus invested with multiple functionalities in the Eastern Partnership – something which, as will be argued below, does not always resonate in the partner countries.

The diffusion of technical rules embedded in the *acquis* takes place without much consideration given to the constraints, capacities and dependencies of partner countries. The DCFTA scheme reflects a very broad understanding of trade encompassing not only tariffs but also non-tariff barriers and new areas of growth. Partner countries are expected to pursue convergence with trade-related and internal market *acquis* – that is, to incorporate approximately 95 per cent of the EU's corpus of rules.[9] This implies wholesale institutional and regulatory reform in key sectors of the EU internal market and trade policy (for example, food safety, competition, intellectual property rights). Clearly some EU requirements are irrelevant.[10] Georgia, for example, is required to implement EU norms on cable cars and lifts although it does not produce these products,[11] whereas Moldova needs to comply with rules for the production of silk worms even though the country does not produce any silk. In many areas, such as the regulation of state aid and

---

[8]   Alexander Duleba, Vladimír Ben and Vladimír Bilčík, *Policy Impact of the Eastern Partnership on Ukraine: Trade, Energy, and Visa Dialogue* (Research Center of the Slovak Foreign Policy Association, 2012) 78.

[9]   Ibid.

[10]   See Patrick Messerlin, Michael Emerson, Gia Jandieri and Alexandre Le Vernoy, *An Appraisal of the EU's Trade Policy Towards its Eastern Neighbours: The Case of Georgia* (CEPS, March 2011).

[11]   Ibid.

competition, the countries are expected to converge with the EU regardless of their developmental priorities, actual capacities and economic profiles.

While exporting the *acquis*, the EU pays little attention to the political economy of the reform process and often glosses over economic linkages (or the absence of them) between the post-Soviet countries themselves. The EU demands the implementation of the DCFTA in a hegemonic fashion – that is, as if the partner countries were not dependent on other markets and were solely interested in economic integration with the EU. While the partner countries import machinery from the EU, their own exports to the EU are relatively modest and consist mainly of low value added items. Moldova exports its main agricultural commodity – fruits and vegetables – mainly to Russia and the CIS market; the CIS market accounts for 40 per cent of Georgia's exports (compared with 20 per cent to the EU). Ukraine's trade with the EU constitutes just less than one-third of its overall trade and is the lowest amongst all the partner countries (see below). In addition, Armenia, Belarus, Ukraine and Moldova are heavily reliant on Russian energy supplies, which further underscores their dependency on Russia, something the EU is not able to alleviate.[12]

While technical conditions imposed by the EU are difficult or even impossible to fulfil in some cases, the EU has made it clear that it considers its enhanced offer under the Eastern Partnership as a package and would not accept integration *à la carte*. In other words, it is not possible for partner countries either to opt out of parts of the package or to receive an offer other than the comprehensive Association Agreement with DCFTA, regardless of the unsuitability of the offer and related institutional and economic implications for the country. For instance, the EU rejected the proposal of the Georgian authorities to sign a simple free trade agreement instead of a DCFTA.[13] This 'take it or leave it' approach means that approximation with a large part of the *acquis* cannot be escaped if Eastern partners intend to develop close ties with the EU regardless of the actual costs and benefits of such comprehensive integration with the EU. Clearly, linking progress in the overall bilateral relationship to regulatory sectoral reforms provides the EU with stronger leverage. However, it is clear that the EU has been acting as 'a regional normative hegemon that is using its economic and normative clout to

[12] Authors' interviews in Armenia, Ukraine and Moldova in November 2011, April 2012 and May 2012, respectively.
[13] Authors' interviews with Georgian officials and experts in November 2011.

build a set of highly asymmetrical bilateral relationships that help to facilitate an active transference of its norms and values'.[14]

The EU strategy induces an incongruity between the tools the EU uses and the reforms undertaken by partner countries – something which, as will be argued below, Russia exploits by stressing the *immediate* benefits of ECU membership. The problem is two-fold. First, while requiring significant up-front costs to be borne by partner countries in the short term, the EU predominantly offers long-term benefits rather than rapid respite for their economic difficulties. Second, EU assistance is the main policy tool at the EU's disposal to bridge the discrepancy between short-term costs and long-term benefits, but its application is often outpaced by political and economic changes in the post-Soviet partner countries. We will now explore these points in more detail.

Most EU requirements entail substantial costs for partner countries to be expended before they can reap any benefits. DCFTAs offer the best illustration of this. The EU requires extensive and costly reforms that have to be implemented over a relatively short period of time. It introduced key sectoral recommendations that had to be fulfilled before negotiations for DCFTAs could be launched with Moldova, Georgia and Armenia. In the food safety area, for instance, these recommendations involved onerous steps (for example, the creation of laboratories and the establishment of bodies responsible for inspection) to be taken rather rapidly, whereas partner countries will only eventually be able to export to the EU at some unspecified time in the future, if at all. Indeed, even in the longer term, not all Eastern neighbours will reap benefits; some of them, such as Armenia and Georgia have few products which are likely to be competitive on the EU market. Where countries are likely to be competitive, the EU often resorts to protective measures by introducing product quotas, as is the case with dairy products in Ukraine. Following a long-established tradition, the EU negotiating position is about highlighting the benefits of the capacity of the EU single market rather than making market access sufficiently attractive for the partner country. This negotiating position is perceived as protectionist, something which weakens the EU 'power of attraction'.

The Russian and CIS markets are likely to remain more important for agricultural production for all partner countries. Yet the preconditions for regulatory convergence put forward by the EU are not only costly in themselves but may entail losing the Russian/ECU market (as a result of

[14]   Hiski Haukkala, *The EU–Russia Strategic Partnership: The Limits of Post-Sovereignty in International Relations* (Routledge, 2010) 47.

increased costs of production, a new regulatory framework and regulatory divergence with the ECU) while not gaining access to the EU market and/or not being sufficiently competitive to benefit substantially to offset the costs. Therefore, gaining access to the EU relies on partner countries adopting a long-term vision with the determination to integrate their countries with the EU, regardless of short-term economic and political costs.

The EU's strategy requires adoption of reforms in a short period of time – five to eight years – while the positive impact of these changes (if at all) may not be immediately visible. Thus, as was the case during enlargement, the ENP/Eastern Partnership relies on 'deferred gratification' along the lines of 'reforms now, benefits later'.[15] But it also becomes all too apparent that the scale and type of domestic adjustment envisaged under the ENP/Eastern Partnership present a particular challenge for the post-Soviet states; they all suffer from poor governance and insufficient institutional and administrative capacity, as outlined by Connolly (in Chapter 4). In many instances, diffusion of the *acquis* is designed to address the very problems which hamper the convergence with the *acquis*, such as political instability, absence of the rule of law, weak administrative capacity, corruption and frozen conflicts.[16]

Governments that have reformed in line with EU requirements, having incurred the associated costs, have come under pressure to demonstrate the beneficial results of integration with the EU for their domestic electorates. Yet, so far domestic expectations are growing while meeting EU conditions has yielded few tangible benefits for the general public in partner countries, which have suffered economic hardship, especially owing to the global crisis. This makes the EU's strategy dependent on contingency: a favourable domestic political context and a lack of alternative opportunities in the region, neither of which necessarily occur at any one time. As a result, there is a disjuncture between the EU's focus on economic and governance dimensions, on the one hand, and the political and economic realities, as well as geopolitical predicaments of these countries, on the other.[17]

---

[15] European Commission, 'On Strengthening the European Neighbourhood Policy', COM(2006) 726 final, 4 December 2006, 3.

[16] Kataryna Wolczuk, 'Convergence without Finalité: EU Strategy towards Post-Soviet States', in Karen Henderson and Carol Weaver (eds), *The Black Sea Region and EU Policy: The Challenge of Divergent Agendas* (Ashgate, 2010).

[17] Helen Wallace, 'The European Union and its Neighbourhood: Time for a Rethink', ELIAMEP Thesis, Hellenic Foundation for European and Foreign Policy, April 2009.

At the same time, the credibility of the EU to deliver the benefits it supposedly offers is not always sufficiently high, especially in respect of those which require the repeated consensus of the member states rather than the Commission. Given the internal divergences amongst EU member states, for example, it is not clear whether the EU will be able to deliver on its promises relating to a visa-free regime – the most substantial benefit for Eastern neighbours in the short term. In Ukraine, the way in which the member states have implemented the visa facilitation agreement has dented the EU's credibility to enact its own commitments. As regards Georgia, problems and inconsistencies among EU member states in the issuing of Schengen visas were criticized by President Saakashvili.[18] Full visa liberalization is even more politically sensitive for the EU. It took five months to assess Moldova's completion of Phase 1 under the Visa Liberalization Action Plan, which indicates considerable difficulties within the EU regarding some countries in more sensitive areas.[19] This is despite the fact that the government of Vlad Filat in Moldova invested considerable political capital in making European integration a priority for Moldova after being elected in 2009, and has been reliant on EU's 'reward' for its commitment and compliance.

Second, under the Eastern Partnership, the EU offers increased assistance with a view to bridging the mismatch between EU requirements and benefits stemming from EU-induced reforms. EU assistance supports partner countries in the approximation process and therefore offers the most immediate incentive to reform. Some even argue that the proliferation of instruments and increased funding compensate for the lack of overarching vision.[20] Arguably, while the wide range of assistance instruments under the European Neighbourhood and Partnership Instrument (ENPI) (particularly budget support) is designed to allow for better adjustment to the needs of partner countries, in practice EU assistance is fraught with cumbersome procedures, especially at the programming stage which requires a number of steps and consultations.[21] These procedures hamper any adjustments which are nonetheless frequently

---

[18] Mari Nikuradze, 'Georgians Struggling to Get through European Visa Maze', *Democracy & Freedom Watch*, 20 March 2012, http://dfwatch.net/georgians-struggling-to-get-through-european-visa-maze-56012 (accessed 30 March 2012).

[19] Authors' interview with a Council official, Brussels, October 2012.

[20] Elena Gnedina and Nicu Popescu, 'The European Neighbourhood's Policy First Decade', Kadir Has University, Istanbul, July 2012.

[21] Laure Delcour, 'Lessons Learnt from the ENPI. Recommendations for the ENI', Briefing for the European Parliament, AFET Committee, 2012.

needed in a fast-changing environment to build up an effective domestic alliance for reforms. In addition, under the ENPI, the EU has focused on cooperation with the governments of partner countries that are central to the core of EU policy, while other key stakeholders in the reform process are neglected when it comes to EU assistance. In particular, support to the private sector has been limited, which in turn raises questions as to the capacities of businesses to make the adjustments required by approximated legislation (as is the case for small-scale farmers with food safety requirements or food processing plants).

Overall, the EU's policy towards its Eastern neighbours is primarily informed by internal developments, negotiations and compromises. It aims to transfer those norms through methods that are not contested internally and that have proved to be successful in cementing EU integration – that is, the *acquis communautaire* and functional cooperation. But, as a result, the EU strategy is not attuned to the regional context, nor is it sufficiently sensitive and responsive to the needs and capacities of partner countries.

While promoting economic integration, the EU has pursued a technocratic and law-oriented approach with the key interlocutors being political elites and state officials.[22] Little attention has been paid to engaging non-state domestic actors and securing a broader societal support, which means it has not been able to build a wide support base within the countries. There are three reasons for this. First, the voluntary nature of seeking closer integration seemingly absolves the EU of promoting the benefits of integration inside the partner countries.[23] Second, many aspects of the reforms promoted by the EU are highly technocratic and relate to a wide range of policies and institutions, such as intellectual copyright, regulation of state aid, migration legislation and phytosanitary standards, making it difficult to target and engage non-governmental organizations and a broader domestic audience. Third, the ENP and Eastern Partnership have seen a proliferation of instruments, tools, funds

---

[22]   Rilka Dragneva and Kataryna Wolczuk, 'EU Law Export to the Eastern Neighbourhood and an Elusive Demand for Law', in Paul Cardwell (ed.), *EU External Relations Law and Policy in the Post-Lisbon Era* (TMC Asser Press, 2011).

[23]   The viewpoint that the benefits of integration with the EU for the partner countries are not only overwhelming but also self-evident emanated strongly from the officials of the EU institutions and member states, especially the European External Action Service. With the benefits being so obvious, it is up to the governments in the partner countries to enact the EU's reform guidance. Authors' interviews in Brussels in October 2012.

and initiatives, often framed in highly technical terms, which are difficult to grasp by those domestic actors lacking an intricate knowledge of EU policies. Despite the promotion of wide-ranging and far-reaching reforms, the requirements of and benefits from integration with the EU have not been conveyed in accessible terms in the partner countries.

3. THE ECU AS RUSSIA'S FOREIGN POLICY TOOL IN THE NEIGHBOURHOOD

Until the launch of the Eastern Partnership in 2009, the EU had mainly relied on soft law instruments, such as the Action Plans, to promote domestic change in the Eastern neighbourhood. The Action Plans were compatible with the existing multilateral and bilateral agreements in the CIS.[24] From the Russian perspective, the harmonization required by the PCA and early ENP (that is, until 2009) was not deemed to be achievable by the post-Soviet countries, and therefore was not likely to affect Russia's interests in the post-Soviet space. However, the Eastern Partnership entailed a move from the soft law approach based on persuasion and assistance to a comprehensive, binding and detailed legal framework structuring relations between the EU and its Eastern neighbours. As argued above, while lacking a membership perspective the Eastern Partnership nevertheless aims to anchor participating countries in the EU's 'sphere of influence' in the legal framework of the Association Agreement with DCFTA. The EU's shift to hard law contractual frameworks altered the nature of relations between the EU and countries in the Eastern neighbourhood and the significance of this shift was not lost on Russia. The launch of the Eastern Partnership in May 2009 provoked the strongest reaction of the Russian leadership to any kind of EU initiatives in the post-Soviet space. In Russia's view, the Eastern Partnership violated an implicit consensus on the nature of EU engagement in the region – that the EU would eschew assuming a dominant position in the common neighbourhood and thereby constrain Russia's own strategy in the region.[25] As a result, the pursuit of comprehensive, legally binding agreements meant that it was not only the EU's relations with the

[24] Antoaneta Dimitrova and Rilka Dragneva, 'Constraining External Governance: Interdependence with Russia and the CIS as Limits to the EU's Rule Transfer in the Ukraine' (2009) 16(6) *Journal of European Public Policy* 853.
[25] Andrei Zagorsky, 'Eastern Partnership from the Russian Perspective', Friedrich Ebert Stiftung, Spring/Summer 2010.

countries of the Eastern Partnership that were significantly altered, but also its relations with Russia.

The Eastern Partnership provided a further impetus for Russia to create its own highly legalized integration regime. The rapid formation of the ECU with its ambitious plans for (deepening) integration was accompanied by the quest to include other post-Soviet states, not only to ensure the viability of the ECU through enlargement (see Chapter 11) but also to counter the influence of the EU in the region. Symptomatically, however, while the deepening of the ECU stems from a complex interplay of preferences of the member states, the quest for widening has been driven solely by Russia.

Russia has been promoting the ECU in states participating in the Eastern Partnership that have the prospect of concluding an Association Agreement with the EU, such as Moldova and Armenia. Ukraine – the largest and most important country in the common neighbourhood – was the first to open negotiations on the DCFTA in 2008 and to close them (in late 2011), although by then the EU had refused to sign the Agreement. As far back as 2010–11, Russia launched a campaign to draw Ukraine into the ECU while simultaneously eroding support for the Association Agreement.

The arguments and instruments used in the pro-ECU campaign in Ukraine are worth examining, as they reveal the determination to bring Ukraine in. Russia has promoted the ECU as a worthy counterpoint to the EU in terms of economic integration, while explicitly capitalizing on the above-mentioned weaknesses in the EU's strategy. The campaign has promoted the considerable and immediate benefits of participation in Eurasian integration (as opposed to the disadvantages and costs associated with integration with the EU) as well as the prospect of using negative economic conditionality (punishing Ukraine in the case of non-accession). The rationale for joining has been put forward by the Russian leaders, Vladimir Putin and Dmitrii Medvedev, in numerous bilateral meetings with the Ukrainian leaders, in the Russian and Ukrainian media as well as analytical reports, which have been widely disseminated and discussed in the Ukrainian media.[26]

---

[26]   See, for example, Eurasian Development Bank (EDB), *A Comprehensive Assessment of the Macroeconomic Effects of Various Forms of the Deep Economic Integration of Ukraine with Member States of the Customs Union and the Common Economic Space within the EurAsEC* (EDB, 2012); Sergei Glaz'ev, 'Tamozhnyi Soyuz v ramkakh EvroAzES I Ukraina' (2010) 10 *Mezhdunarodnaya Zhyzn* 168.

3.1.   Russian Efforts to Expand the ECU to Ukraine

Whereas previous integration initiatives in the post-Soviet space were justified in terms of historical, cultural and linguistic commonalities, the rationale for the ECU is presented differently. The dominant justification for membership of the ECU is that prospective members can join a modernizing regime for economic integration based on international law. The argument that the ECU, as a progressive economic project, would bolster growth of the existing and prospective member states echoes that of the EU on the role of the DCFTA in the neighbourhood. Russia's argument, however, is more specific and more closely tailored to the circumstances of the individual countries.

It has been argued by Russia that, through increased trade and enhanced growth rates, membership of the ECU would also enable Ukraine to modernize rapidly, thereby avoiding the issues which characterize Ukraine's integration with the EU, as pointed out above. The campaign highlights the prospects for equalization of technological levels, industrial cooperation and a common strategy of development. Therefore, joining the ECU would enable Ukraine to develop a competitive advantage, something the country has not been able to achieve on its own. By accruing the benefits of the re-creation of a technological research and development complex within the ECU, Ukraine would improve its competitiveness. Ukraine's lack of competitiveness is, in particular, highlighted as an obstacle to benefiting from increased trade with the EU. According to estimates, under the DCFTA, EU imports to Ukraine would increase by 10 per cent, leading to a further 5 per cent deterioration in the trade balance, which means that 'Ukraine stands to lose up to 1.5 per cent of its GDP base volume' by pursuing economic integration with the EU.[27]

Much emphasis was put on Ukraine's disadvantaged position vis-à-vis the EU and the latter's protectionism, implying that Ukraine would integrate on unfavourable terms. In its campaigning Russia emphasized the EU's economic protectionism by drawing public attention to the fact that some Ukrainian agricultural products would remain subject to quotas. In contrast, the ECU would allow Ukraine unrestricted access to the Russian market, particularly for agricultural products, a sector of considerable importance and potential to Ukraine. The credibility of such pledges, however, will be addressed below.

---

[27]   EDB, ibid., 29.

In addition to citing broad, long-term developmental benefits, Russia has also stressed immediate economic gains, relying particularly on the offer of a reduced gas price to Ukraine. For example, Putin offered a reduction of the gas price to $160 per 1,000 sq m upon Ukraine's accession to the ECU during his meeting with Yanukovych in October 2012. As argued by Frear in Chapter 7, energy is excluded from the ECU's trilateral regime and remains agreed on a bilateral basis between its members, enabling Russia to use the 'energy discounts' vis-à-vis third countries at its discretion. However, this bilateral strategy to enlarge the ECU would bear major costs for Russia itself, something which does not appear to feature in Russia's discussion on the ECU in general and Ukraine's potential accession in particular (see Cooper in Chapter 5 and Dragneva and Wolczuk in Chapter 11).

The overall economic benefit of joining the ECU would apparently amount to $219 billion between 2011 and 2030 (that is, at an annual average of $12.2 billion).[28] While the actual basis for these estimates is rather unclear, the aim of this kind of argument has been to emphasize the substantive, immediate and sustainable economic benefits to Ukraine. Without a doubt, the campaign in terms of incentives and punitive measures has been tailored to powerful domestic actors, especially with regard to the energy sector. The profitability of Ukraine's major export industries, metallurgy and chemicals, depends on low energy prices, because of the high energy consumption used in their production. This profitability has been affected by the global economic crisis and further dented by the high energy prices negotiated by Ukraine with Russia during the energy crisis in January 2009.

While the EU relies on the promotion of deep economic integration in terms of long-term modernization benefits and assistance, Russia uses a broader portfolio of instruments in a more targeted and timely way. Besides short-term economic gains and long-term modernization, Russia also invokes the threat of resorting to punitive measures, such as economic and other sanctions, against Ukraine. These are primarily justified in economic terms, such as the negative implications of the EU–Ukraine DCFTA for Russia.[29] Russia expressed concerns about

---

[28] Ibid., 30.
[29] The expected impact of the EU–Ukraine DCFTA is unlikely to be significant for Russia in terms of impeding trade flows between Ukraine and Russia, or affecting the Russian economy. If anything, the DCFTA will open new business possibilities for numerous Russian-owned companies in Ukraine, especially in light of Russia's adoption of international and EU norms. Very few analysts outside Russia consider the implications for Ukraine–Russia economic

being flooded by Ukrainian products which have been displaced from the domestic market by EU imports. In such an event, President Putin has threatened that 'we will have to introduce protective measures'.[30] The Deputy Prime Minister of Russia has also referred to the complications in Ukraine's relations with Russia 'on all fronts'.[31] Although there is no sound basis for such predictions, Putin warned: 'I'm confident that ... both Kazakhstan and Belarus will immediately demand that Russia closes its customs border'.[32] The measures which Russia could introduce range from applying anti-dumping tariffs, limiting imports of Ukrainian food products through the application of phytosanitary standards, to lowering the quotas for pipes – a key export for Ukraine.[33] Russia has a history of deploying selective, targeted sanctions towards states that pursue a policy that Russia regards as unfriendly. Therefore, Russia's threats to resort to such sanctioning measures are credible to Ukraine.

A major and particularly damaging measure for Ukraine would be the cancellation of the bilateral Russia–Ukraine Free Trade Area Agreement of 1993. However, this has not been explicitly mentioned so far, mainly because a blanket withdrawal would be too harmful to Russian business interests in Ukraine. It is worth pointing out that the 1993 agreement does not represent strong legal protection against Russia's trade sanctions because it is rather general and vague and a list of exempted categories are annually agreed in bilateral negotiations. At the same time, the enforcement of the new multilateral CIS Free Trade Area Agreement, which came into force in 2012, would limit the impact of Russia's withdrawal from the bilateral agreement with Ukraine.

It is the prospect of Russia resorting to punitive economic measures vis-à-vis Ukraine, rather than the interest in economic modernization, that has caused greatest concern amongst domestic state actors and key oligarchic business groups in Ukraine, against the backdrop of the

---

relations, so no reliable, independent studies exist to verify the various claims made by the Russian officials.

[30] See http://podrobnosti.ua/power/2011/04/12/763729.html (accessed 11 January 2012).

[31] See http://arkadeysladkov.livejournal.com/877365.html (accessed 11 January 2012).

[32] Vladimir Putin, 'New Integration Project for Eurasia: A Future which is Being Born Today', *Izvestiya*, 3 October 2011.

[33] Oxford Economics, 'The Impact of an FTA between Ukraine and the EU', unpublished report prepared for the Foundation for Effective Governance (2012).

importance of trade with Russia and the CIS for the Ukrainian economy.[34]

While indicating Russia's determination to bring Ukraine into the ECU, the campaign regarding Ukraine also underscores the continuous reliance on the mix of positive and, especially, negative conditionality with regard to energy and trade, closely tailored to the domestic circumstances and needs of the 'target' countries. Russia does not suffer from the 'knowledge problem' which characterizes so many policies of Western international actors.[35] Such country-specific differentiation is much weaker in the EU strategy, as is argued above.

In addition to economy-related arguments, a political rationale in favour of ECU membership is put forward. Membership of the ECU is presented as a less asymmetrical arrangement than the association offered by the EU. Through the Association Agreement, Ukraine would be required to align itself with EU rules without membership and without having any say in setting them. In contrast, the ECU, being a multilateral organization, would provide Ukraine with full membership rights. More-over, the ECU would facilitate relations between its member states and the EU. It is argued that the countries in the 'common neighbourhood' could integrate with the EU faster and on more favourable terms if they do so 'together with Russia'. This reflects the desire and expectation prevailing in Russia that the ECU would enter into an *interregional* dialogue with the EU, as expressed by Putin during his visit to Brussels in December 2012. A year earlier, Putin had predicted:

> Soon the Customs Union, and later the Eurasian Union, will join the dialogue with the EU. As a result, apart from bringing direct economic benefits, accession to the Eurasian Union will also help countries integrate into Europe sooner and from a stronger position.[36]

This confidence in being able to secure the best deal for the Russia-led bloc is underpinned by the prevailing view in Russia that the country cannot be offered less than other post-Soviet states because of Russia's strategic role and a strong bargaining position vis-à-vis the EU.[37]

---

[34]   Razumkov Centre, 'EU–Ukraine–Russia Relations: Problems and Prospects' (2012) 4–5 *National Security and Defence* 133.

[35]   Thomas Carothers, 'The Rule of Law Revival', in Thomas Carothers (ed.), *Promoting the Rule of Law Abroad: In Search of Knowledge* (Carnegie Endowment for International Peace, 2006).

[36]   Putin, above note 32.

[37]   Arkady Moshes, 'Russia's European Policy under Medvedev: How Sustainable is a New Compromise?' (2012) 88(1) *International Affairs* 17; Laure

In sum, Russia's stance in relation to both the EU and ECU member states is apparent. First, Russia has contested EU policy in the countries in the neighbourhood without confronting the EU directly. Thus, Russian objections to the EU–Ukraine DCFTA were raised with Ukraine rather than at the bilateral level with the EU. Second, it is notable that the campaign to draw Ukraine in has been conducted exclusively by Russia, with other ECU member states hardly commenting on Ukraine's proposed membership. This indicates Russia's confidence in using its dominant position within the ECU to pursue its foreign policy aims with the tacit consent of other member states, underscoring the asymmetries with the ECU itself.

Nevertheless, the key drawback is that the single-handed promotion of the ECU by Russia signals continuity despite all the change. The drive to expand the ECU before it has demonstrated its viability and ability to add value to the member states through sustained implementation makes it appear as a top-down, geopolitical project of Russia. In Ukraine this merely reinforces this perception of the ECU as an 'upgraded' vehicle for asserting Russia's domination. Using trade sanctions and energy dependency, while 'inviting' the new members, fuels the suspicion that the ECU is a vehicle for Russia's domination of the 'near abroad'.[38] In other words, Russia has little credibility as a multilateral actor and promoter of modernized, rule-based governance in the post-Soviet space. With Russia at its helm, the ECU's modernization potential is assessed as low by Ukrainian experts:

> The main problem is that the main obstacles to Ukraine's economic development are now associated with the non-economic factors distorting the overall institutional basis for the country's functioning. No economic preferences obtained from Eurasian integration will remove those obstacles. However, successful integration with European socio-economic standards offers solutions to those vital developmental tasks faced by Ukraine.[39]

Therefore, Russia's quest to become a normative power, as outlined by Diez, is received with much scepticism.[40] The ECU may be a more

Delcour, *Shaping the Post-Soviet Space? EU Policies and Approaches to Region-Building* (Ashgate, 2012); Zagorsky, above note 25, Chapter 4.

[38]   Razumkov Centre, above note 34.

[39]   Ibid.; see also Igor Burakovsky et al., *Costs and Benefits of FTA between Ukraine and the European Union* (Institute For Economic Research and Policy Consulting, 2010).

[40]   Diez, above note 2. Even in Armenia, which is regarded as one of the most pro-Russian states in the post-Soviet space, the EU is regarded as a viable source

robustly institutionalized regime with a high degree of delegation, but the hegemonic position of Russia in such a supranational organization with its questionable ability to 'do rules' reduces the willingness of neighbouring states to enter the organization.

4. UKRAINE BETWEEN THE ECU AND EU: INTEGRATION PUZZLES AND CONSTRAINTS

For the countries in the common neighbourhood the conclusion of the Association Agreement and the emergence of the ECU mean a hardening, in legal terms, of the integration regimes with regard to both Europe and Eurasia. For Ukraine, this change of legal basis for structuring relations with the EU and Russia – two key external actors – represents a watershed in its foreign policy since independence.

Until now, the post-Soviet countries (with the notable exception of the Baltic states) have not significantly re-oriented their trade away from Russia/CIS. East-Central European countries started to do so in the early 1990s, willing to bear the political and economic costs of re-orientation towards the EU.[41] The remaining post-Soviet states have maintained multi-vector economic and foreign policies. The legal context of the CIS has provided little constraint on such policies. The PCAs with the EU, as well as the multilateral and bilateral agreements with the CIS, lacked detail and did not contain mutually binding commitments.[42] This allowed the countries between Russia and the EU to be selective and flexible in terms of modes of economic integration. For example, within the framework of the CIS FTA, Ukraine has engaged in very intensive cooperation in trade development (including FTA issues), standardization, agriculture and transportation, while not being a fully fledged member of the organization.[43] This soft law mode of integration has

---

of modernization, whereas Russia tends to be mentioned in the context of security. Authors' interviews with Armenian experts and officials in Yerevan, November 2011.

[41]   Stephan Haggard et al., 'Integrating the Two Halves of Europe: Theories of Interests, Bargaining, and Institutions', in Robert Keohane, Joseph Nye and Stanley Hoffman (eds), *After the Cold War: International Institutions and State Strategies in Europe, 1989–1991* (Harvard University Press, 1993) 173.

[42]   See Rilka Dragneva, 'Is "Soft" Beautiful? Another Perspective on Law, Institutions, and Integration in the CIS' (2004) 29 *Review of Central and East European Law* 279.

[43]   Katharina Hoffman, 'Regional Integration in the Post-Soviet Space', PhD thesis, University of Birmingham (in preparation). See also Roman Wolczuk,

allowed Ukraine to 'pick and choose' degrees of economic integration with Russia/CIS across different sectors. Because of its soft law basis, the CIS FTA (which came into force in 2012) is also essentially compatible with the concluded Association Agreement.

With the creation of the ECU, Russia has made regional economic integration a matter of hard and precise obligations premised on *ex ante* regulatory convergence, along the lines envisaged by the Association Agreement. The legal formula for economic relations with the EU and Russia has changed dramatically as a result. The context of the DCFTA, the emergence of the ECU and, especially, Russia's vigorous promotion of Ukraine's membership compound the challenges in EU–Ukraine relations.

First, Ukraine faces high economic costs of regulatory convergence with the EU and in providing improved access for EU goods to the Ukrainian market. While beneficial for Ukrainian consumers and in the long term leading to modernization, competitiveness and growth, in the short term it imposes significant costs on many Ukrainian producers.[44] Thus, the economic incentives offered by the Union – prospects of market access and assistance – may not do enough to stimulate *per se* a far reaching and comprehensive process of convergence with the EU owing to the aforementioned disincentives.[45]

Second, integration with the EU has for the first time become contingent on meeting the EU's explicit democratic conditionality requirements. After some hesitation in 2010–11, the EU adopted a principled position and resorted to using the Association Agreement – a key tool at its disposal – to pressurize the Ukrainian authorities to address EU concerns over the deterioration of democratic standards. The signing and ratification of the agreement has been on hold since late 2011 owing to political prosecutions of certain opposition figures – the two most conspicuous cases being the former Prime Minister, Yulia Tymoshenko, and a former Minister of the Interior, Yuriy Lutsenko. These prosecutions have been condemned by EU institutions and member states as a conspicuous breach of democratic standards and European

---

'Ukraine – A Partial but Reluctant CIS Member', in David Dusseault (ed.), *The CIS: Form or Substance?* (Aleksanteri Institute, 2007).

   [44]   Burakovsky et al., above note 39.

   [45]   Gabriella Meloni, 'Is the Same Toolkit Used During Enlargement Still Applicable to the Countries of the New Neighbourhood?', in Marise Cremona and Gabriella Meloni (eds), *The European Neighbhourhood Policy: A Framework for Modernisation?*, Working Paper No. LAW 2007/21 (European University Institute, Florence, 2007) 100; Duleba, Ben and Bilčík, above note 8.

values. But, by making economic integration contingent on upholding democratic standards, the EU has introduced significant political costs for the Ukrainian authorities: meeting EU conditions will affect the prospects of remaining in power for the ruling elites, who have sought to consolidate their power to render ineffective any challenge to their rule. Such a trade-off between relations with Europe and consolidating power means that the pursuit of association with the EU carries direct political risks for President Viktor Yanukovych and the ruling Party of Regions.

Therefore, economic integration with the EU is costly in both economic and political terms for the Ukrainian authorities in the short term. But when offering economic integration to Ukraine and exercising democratic conditionality, the EU has not considered the costs associated with abandoning and revising Ukraine's relations with other economic partners. The integration costs to Ukraine in terms of its knock-on effects on relations with other economic partners, especially Russia, have not been factored in.[46] This predicament is exacerbated by Russian efforts to persuade Ukraine to participate in the ECU.

As argued above, in contrast to the EU, Russia's credibility to deliver rule-based economic integration beneficially to all partner countries is low. It has been noted in Ukraine that the Russian promises of benefits of ECU membership to Ukraine, especially with regard to energy prices, are all based on non-binding statements.[47] But for Russia the stakes in the region are high. This is expected to lead to Russia's willingness to resort to punitive measures if Ukraine concludes the Association Agreement with the EU, thereby compounding Ukraine's political and economic difficulties.[48]

The EU is unwilling to help the Ukrainian authorities owing to its disillusionment and fatigue with Ukraine under President Yanukovych. It is indicative that the EU has not stepped up its promotion of the Association Agreements even when Russia started to exert the countervailing pressure on Ukraine to join the ECU instead. This creates the impression that the EU is indifferent towards the region, perhaps confirming the perception of the Eastern Partnership as a 'third tier' policy of the EU.[49] So while the EU's highly technocratic approach, with its focus

---

[46] Olga Shumylo-Tapiola, 'Ukraine at the Crossroads: Between the EU DCFTA and Customs Union', *Russie.Nei.Reports* No. 11 (IFRI, April 2012); authors' interviews with Ukrainian experts and officials in Kyiv in April and May 2012.

[47] Razumkov Centre, above note 34.

[48] Oxford Economics, above note 33.

[49] Gnedina and Popescu, above note 20.

on rule-based functional cooperation, is a source of credibility, it simultaneously creates a distinct perception of itself as a disinterested and
detached actor. The EU promotes what is beneficial for Ukraine in the
long term but relies largely on the Ukrainian authorities to realize these
benefits, even at the cost to their own political prospects and economic
sanctions from Russia.

Therefore, EU strategy is largely premised on lengthening the time
horizons of the political class in the neighbouring countries. Enlargement
has created a favourable framework for lengthening the time horizons of
the political elites in the accession countries: the prospect of EU
membership has stretched the time framework for decision-making on
ambitious, comprehensive and costly reforms in East-Central Europe.[50]
But the EU lacks similar leverage or mechanisms for extending the
horizons in the neighbourhood policy. This absence becomes especially
significant in the context of Russia's 'integration behaviour' in the region.
While experts agree that Eurasian integration does not offer the prospect
of long-term modernization, the economic crisis and high energy prices
are conducive to a shortening of time horizons and prioritizing immediate
economic benefits. Moreover, Ukraine's economic integration with the
ECU would entail no immediate 'power costs' for the incumbent
authorities in Ukraine – that is, there is no democratic conditionality
associated with joining the ECU, an important consideration in light of
the presidential elections of 2015.

It is worth pointing out that this normative rivalry over Ukraine is not
just a matter of a short-term 'either-or choice' but a longer-term contestation. Even if and when the Association Agreement is signed and
ratified, its implementation will be prolonged, costly and highly sensitive
in political and economic terms for numerous domestic actors in Ukraine.
This is not only because of high costs but also the myriad of divergent
preferences amongst the domestic state and business actors. Ukraine has
a strong record of signing up to international agreements which are then
not complied with.[51]

Many business groups have a strong interest in the ECU in terms of
maintaining access to the Russian market and/or securing cheaper energy

---

[50]   Wade Jacoby, 'Inspiration, Coalition, and Substitution: External Influences
on Postcommunist Transformations' (2006) 58(4) *World Politics* 623.
[51]   Julia Langbein and Kataryna Wolczuk, 'Convergence without Membership? The Impact of the European Union in the Neighbourhood: Evidence from
Ukraine' (2012) 19(6) *Journal of European Public Policy* 863.

resources.[52] Russia accounts for 28.9 per cent of Ukraine's exports whereas the EU accounted for 27.6 per cent in 2011.[53] Therefore Ukraine is highly sensitive to the requirements of convergence with the EU, where it may entail losing the Russian/ECU market. This is especially likely for the products with which Ukraine is unlikely to gain access to the EU market because of the high costs of meeting regulatory requirements, protective measures adopted by the EU and/or Ukrainian products not being sufficiently competitive to benefit sufficiently to offset costs (such as dairy products).

By offering strategically important incentives, Russia is well positioned to put forward conditions that may make it more difficult for Ukraine to implement its commitments vis-à-vis the EU. This is because Russia has a good grasp of economic and political stakes in the post-Soviet countries and is able to react quickly where and when it matters to Russian interests. Despite extensive engagement in, and assistance to, Ukraine, the EU lacks the same degree of agility. With the EU and Russia deploying different temporalities and using various incentives and disincentives, Ukraine faces a significant dilemma.

Ukraine's concerns about continuous access to the ECU market are evidenced in its agreement to become an 'associated member' of the ECU, after the initial '3+1 formula' was rejected by Russia. According to President Yanukovych, Ukraine will be adapting its regulatory framework to the rules of the ECU as long as 'they do not contradict Ukraine's international obligations'.[54] However, it is not clear if these commitments relate to membership of the WTO or the DCFTA with the EU. Nevertheless, it is clear that with both the ECU and the EU promoting *ex-ante* regulatory convergence, Ukrainian state and non-state actors face the prospect of convergence with two advanced economic integration regimes. Such simultaneous adaptation represents a difficult balancing act for Ukraine with its inefficient state institutions and influential business actors who are able to shape state policies and legislation to suit their preferences. By altering the costs and benefits of convergence with

---

[52]   A. Zanuda, 'Ukraina Posyliuye Spivpratsiyu z Mytnym Soyuzom', BBC Ukrainian website, 28 August 2012, http://www.bbc.co.uk/ukrainian (accessed 30 August 2012).

[53]   Ukraine's imports from Russia account for 35.3 per cent and this share is determined by energy resources, whereas Ukraine's imports from the EU represent 36.6 per cent. Eurostat data available at http://trade.ec.europa.eu/doclib/docs/2006/september/tradoc_113459.pdf (accessed 1 March 2013).

[54]   Viktor Yanukovych, 'Ya by khotiel provodid' proshlyi god pozitivnymi vaspomnieniami', *Komsomolska Pravda v Ukraine*, 4 January 2013.

the EU at the national and sectoral level, the ECU will affect the prospects for the conclusion and implementation of the DCFTA. For the countries in the common neighbourhood the regulatory compatibility of the two integration regimes will be a key issue for the foreseeable future.

5. CONCLUSIONS

The EU regards itself as the primary source for socio-economic modernization in the post-Soviet space, with the requirement for regulatory convergence with EU norms as its key mechanism. The Association Agreements consist of hard law, legally binding commitments, but a higher degree of legalization cannot make up for the EU's lack of a blueprint for political and economic relations with the post-Soviet states, or these countries' limited interest in and capacity for convergence with the EU for the sake of long-term developmental benefits.

Nevertheless, for Russia, the EU's exercise of 'normative power' in the post-Soviet space has resulted in important lesson learning. Russia has upgraded its approach to regional integration by prioritizing economic integration with a high degree of institutionalization and legalization to assert its position in the post-Soviet space. Russia now lays claims to normative competence and has begun to compete in a field where the EU had hitherto exercised a monopoly in the post-Soviet space.[55] With a complex pattern of dependencies on the EU and Russia displayed by the countries in the common neighbourhood, the emergence of the ECU has multiple and far reaching implications for the EU.

For many countries in the common neighbourhood, Russia's promotion of the ECU appears to be selling 'old wine in new bottles'. This is especially evident with the use of tried-and-tested mechanisms of influence – such as selective economic sanctions or 'loyalty discounts' on energy prices – to promote integration with the new regime. This creates the perception of the ECU as an 'instrument of Moscow's foreign policy' in the region rather than a new multilateral platform for structuring economic relations. Nevertheless, the countries in between have to find a formula for economic interactions with the new organization. The case of Ukraine is highly instructive. It is unlikely that Russia's campaign will be successful in persuading Ukraine to become a fully fledged member of the ECU and Eurasian Economic Union. Nevertheless, Russia's leverage over Ukraine in terms of energy and market access is likely to make its

---

[55]   Dragneva and Wolczuk, above note 1.

economic integration with the EU even more costly and risky in the short term and thereby weaken Ukraine's regulatory convergence with the EU.

For the partner countries, the coexistence of European and Eurasian integration regimes entails working out their priorities and strategies within the overlapping spheres of integration. The difficulty is compounded by the different temporalities promoted by the EU and Russia, with each of them relying on asymmetries vis-à-vis the countries in the neighbourhood. This growing complexity would seem to necessitate from the EU a more self-reflective, purposeful and contextualized policy towards the post-Soviet states to effectively promote economic integration. This is unlikely to be forthcoming in the context of political and economic crises in the EU, and the common neighbourhood will remain caught in the overlapping spheres of integration, resulting in a highly precarious regional context.

11. Commitment, asymmetry and flexibility: making sense of Eurasian economic integration

Rilka Dragneva and Kataryna Wolczuk

1. INTRODUCTION

Eurasian regionalism seems 'an idea whose time has come', to para-phrase Katzenstein's expression on Asia.[1] After several failed or un-fulfilled initiatives in the post-Soviet world, the Eurasian Customs Union (ECU) has emerged as a functioning project with important domestic and international implications. This volume set out to examine the ECU integration process, its institutional architecture and key driving forces behind it. The analysis has revealed a complex regional phenomenon where deep economic integration and legalized design have been pursued in response to a precarious balance of motives. While these motives vary across the ECU's three member states – Russia, Belarus and Kazakhstan – it is the political and geopolitical demands that prevail. This outcome is unambiguously connected to the nature of their political systems, which can broadly be described as non-democratic.[2]

While independently neither of these features is unique, it is their combined role which sets the Eurasian case apart from other integration projects. This chapter 'unpacks' the ECU's characteristics by pointing out the key driving forces behind the countries' commitment to Eurasian integration, the limits of that commitment and the institutional responses

---

[1] Peter Katzenstein, 'Regionalism and Asia' (2000) 5(3) *New Political Economy* 353, 361.

[2] None of the ECU member states – Belarus, Kazakhstan and Russia – can be considered a democracy but the countries differ in terms of their authoritarian features and tendencies. Therefore, to avoid getting preoccupied with the specific classification of their respective political systems (such as a hybrid regime, electoral authoritarianism, and so on), we adopt the broad category of 'non-democracy' when referring to the political systems of the member states.

– both part of the formal design of integration and the systemic political and socio-legal context – in structuring cooperation.

2. THE ECU: KEY FEATURES AND CONTRADICTIONS

The ECU has emerged and matured within a short period of time in what can be described as a 'big bang' development. This approach has been effective in getting the project off the ground and generating momentum; its continued rapid advance and the pronounced ambition driving it are much in evidence. There are several features of this process which stand out in particular.

Firstly, this pursuit of deep economic integration reveals a deep-seated ambition. Following on from the launch of the ECU in 2010, the economic agenda was expanded to the coordination of a range of economic policies, free movement of factors of production, and the harmonization of standards within the Single Economic Space (SES) declared in 2012. At the same time, working towards a Eurasian Economic Union (EEU) was seen by the ECU partners as the next logical step in regional relations. Where the consensus behind this drive seems to be coming under pressure is in relation to the formation of a fully fledged monetary union and the spillover to other areas of integration. Yet, as shown in this volume, this Union is conceived by some of its member states not just as a vehicle for economic integration but also for cooperation in areas such as foreign policy and defence.

Secondly, the drive towards advanced economic integration has been bolstered by the creation of a highly institutionalized and binding legal regime.[3] While the regime exhibits many problems, as analysed in this volume, it represents a departure from the more typical and less successful integration *à la carte* which was a feature of the Common-wealth of Independent States (CIS). A common customs regime, significantly influenced by the trade-related and transparency requirements of

---

[3]   As explained in Chapter 3, we have used the conceptual framework of the legalization literature to describe the strength and scope of legal coordination in international relations, in particular, Kenneth W. Abbott et al., 'The Concept of Legalization' (2000) 54(3) *International Organization* 401. See also James McCall Smith, 'The Politics of Dispute Settlement Design: Explaining Legalism in Regional Trade Pacts' (2000) 1 *International Organization* 137; Kal Raustiala, 'Form and Substance in International Agreements' (2005) 99 *American Journal of International Law* 581.

the World Trade Organization (WTO), has become part of domestic regulation. Extensive delegation of key domestic policy-making powers to a common institution, the Eurasian Economic Commission (EEC), has occurred. The commitment for cooperation has been strengthened through the directly binding effect granted to the EEC's decisions as well as improved dispute resolution through the Court of the Eurasian Economic Community (EvrAzES).

These features suggest a similarity with the European integration model which is heavy on legalization and institutionalization, with rigid decision-making processes and functional spillover into new areas of integration. In contrast, most non-Western regional projects, including the ECU's predecessors in Eurasia, can be described as relatively 'light' on institutionalization, acting on initiatives of the member states rather than supranational institutions, and putting a premium on informality, flexibility and consensus. While borrowing design elements from the European Union (EU) is not unheard of,[4] the ECU has demonstrated an unusual willingness to adopt legalized forms for structuring cooperation.

Thirdly, this is a highly asymmetric grouping driven by the political will of Russia, in economic terms a veritable giant in comparison with other members. Yet, Russia has ostensibly accepted to operate within what appears to be a multilateral framework, seemingly willingly subjecting itself to legalized constraints and challenges. For example, despite being the smallest state in the ECU, Belarus has used the bodies of the organization to hold Russia to its commitments and maximize its own leverage. Furthermore, the very combination between asymmetry and legalization can be viewed as puzzling. As McCall Smith has shown, from a rational functionalist perspective, high relative economic power tends to favour power-oriented rather than rule-oriented dispute settlement mechanisms.[5] Indeed, he argues that 'legalistic dispute settlement is expected only in accords among parties whose relative size and bargaining leverage are more symmetric'.[6]

Fourthly, the deep integration agenda and legalized design have been pursued by a grouping of countries characterized by non-democratic political regimes. This may also be viewed as unusual, given that non-democracies tend not to pursue binding forms of regional integration. As argued by the 'democratic legalism' literature, democracies are

---

[4]   Francesco Duina and Sonia Morano-Foadi, 'Introduction: The Institutionalisation of Regional Trade Agreements Worldwide: New Dynamics and Future Scenarios' (2011) 17(5) *European Law Journal* 561.

[5]   McCall Smith, above note 3.

[6]   Ibid., 149.

more willing to use legal institutions and are more likely to comply with such agreements.[7] This is because, predictably, 'governments with strong constitutional traditions ... are more likely to accept rule-based constraints on their behavior' and 'norms regarding limited government, respect for judicial processes, and regard for constitutional constraints carry over into the realm of international politics'.[8] Similarly, legalization has been associated with the demands of domestic interests and lobbies in pluralist environments, while the new regionalism literature points to integration as a mechanism to 'lock in' domestic reform achievements.[9] For example, it is argued that Mercosur has engaged in close economic cooperation in order to protect democracy in member states.[10] It is plain to see that the political profiles of the ECU members might be expected to preclude these patterns of behaviour.

Finally, even before any consolidation of existing achievements has taken place, the ECU has sought to expand towards more countries in Central Asia, while simultaneously seeking to engage Ukraine. The European Union's dilemma between deepening and widening does not yet seem to resonate in the ECU, which is pursuing both with equal vigour.

In sum, the ECU is a complex phenomenon, riddled with paradoxes particularly relative to existing comparators. Seeking to simplify, ignore or exaggerate some of its characteristics in a desire to fit it into a neat category is, to use Jill Solomon's phrase on another subject, 'reminiscent of the ugly sisters' attempts to squeeze their unshapely feet into Cinderella's shoe'.[11] This is a temptation we have sought to avoid. As discussed in Chapter 1 of this volume, in seeking to 'unpack' and conceptualize the ECU we have been guided by a range of theoretical frameworks. We referred particularly to selected aspects of the political economy of regionalism and the realist, rational functionalist and liberalist perspectives on international relations, particularly where they overlap with

---

[7] See a summary of the argument in Beth A. Simmons, 'Compliance with International Agreements' (1998) 1 *Annual Review of Political Science* 75.

[8] Ibid., 83–4.

[9] For a summary of the argument see Chad Damro, 'The Political Economy of Regional Trade Agreements', in Lorand Bartels and Federico Ortino (eds), *Regional Trade Agreements and the WTO Legal System* (Oxford University Press, 2006).

[10] Andrew Hurrell, 'Regionalism in the Americas', in Louise Fawcett and Andrew Hurrell (eds), *Regionalism in World Politics* (Oxford University Press, 1995) 258.

[11] Jill Solomon, *Corporate Governance and Accountability* (John Wiley, 2007) 182.

international law and comparative law of regional integration.[12] These
frameworks have been useful, yet only partly applicable in explaining the
case of the ECU, as the discussion above illustrates. Thus, engagement
with the insights of area studies has helped our understanding of the
phenomenon of regionalism in this part of the world. On this basis, below
we present our findings as to the nature and constraints of the commitment to Eurasian integration and how these are reflected in its institutional design and development.

3. POLITICAL FACTORS AND THE NATURE OF POLITICAL REGIMES

The non-democratic nature of the political regimes in Russia, Belarus and
Kazakhstan is vital in helping us to understand the driving forces behind
the ECU. In all three countries policy-making and preference-formation
are highly centralized at the top of the political establishment with the
presidential institution being the main locus of power. This means that
the objectives and visions of the President and his system of power are
primary determinants of the country's participation in the ECU.

This is most clearly the case in Belarus, where the justification for
integration is inseparable from the preferences of the incumbent President. Indeed, integration has a role in extending and promoting the
existence of President Lukashenko's political regime. For Belarus,
integration may carry an economic price but de-integration would be
even more costly for the political leadership. A veteran in the 'integration
game', Lukashenko has pursued an instrumentalist agenda. He has been
selective in pursuing the preferred benefits of integration and strategic in
avoiding unwanted commitment, as shown by Frear in this volume
(Chapter 7). While Lukashenko's room for manoeuvre is limited, especially in core customs matters, he clearly prizes flexibility and has sought
to maintain it through mechanisms that range from resorting to the
institutions of the ECU to blocking implementation.

In all member countries, there is little transparency with regard to the
policy-making process, yet it is clear that the input or pressure from
domestic constituencies in procuring or shaping policies has been
limited. Again, the most extreme case is Belarus, where input from

---

[12]   While explanations for *why* countries cooperate and *how* they cooperate
(the role of legal mechanisms in particular) are distinguishable in the literature,
we find that they are closely connected in our case and are therefore approached
together.

domestic actors is restricted to Lukashenko's system of neo-patrimonial balancing between various interest groups in an effort to enhance his power. In Russia, as Cooper shows in this volume (Chapter 5), while the ECU is clearly a priority for Putin, there exists a network of protagonists across various state or non-state bodies. Even for seasoned observers, however, it is difficult to gauge the extent to which they have influenced policy-making. Importantly, even amongst experts there has been little substantive discussion as to the detail of the design of integration or its implications, with many domestic constituencies, such as the liberal politicians, remaining silent. It is particularly telling, for example, that in Russia there was no public debate on the supranational nature of the Eurasian Economic Commission. Thus, despite the claim for wide public support for Eurasian integration, this support has tended to be at a general level. While attitudes in Kazakhstan have been more divided, the political regime is not willing to allow them to constitute an active policy debate and provide an input into policy-making.

An important implication of this is that the demand for regional rules, regulation and policies by market players identified as a key driving force of integration[13] is not a critical factor in the ECU case. Our analysis shows that while there has been some evidence of 'regionalization' as a market-driven, bottom-up process underpinning economic integration,[14] this has not translated into, and has in fact remained separate from, the demand for state-led integrationist policies. States have been the essential building blocks with which the ECU has been constructed.[15] As a consequence, market actors have been restricted in their ability to push for functional considerations of economic costs. Where the perception of such costs has been growing, as in the case of Kazakhstan, its transformation into policy constraint has ultimately depended on the ability of the political regime to balance neo-patrimonial interests and groups in an effort to achieve its primary goals, as discussed below.

---

[13]   Walter Mattli, *The Logic of Regional Integration: Europe and Beyond* (Cambridge University Press, 1999) 42.

[14]   Alexander Libman and Evgeny Vinokurov, *Holding-Together Regionalism: Twenty Years of Post-Soviet Integration* (Palgrave Macmillan, 2012) 63–4. For the distinction between 'regionalization' and 'regionalism', see, for example, Shaun Breslin and Richard Higgott, 'Studying Regions: Learning from the Old, Constructing the New' (2000) 5(3) *New Political Economy* 333, 344.

[15]   This confirms the view by Hurrell that states are key actors in regionalism. See Andrew Hurrell, 'Regionalism in Theoretical Perspective', in Fawcett and Hurrell, above note 10, 67.

Thus, the ECU is a statist initiative in regional integration and as such the liberal perspective, in so far as it emphasizes the role of the plurality of domestic interests in formulating domestic preferences and structuring international cooperation, has a limited application in explaining it. Yet the nature of the political regime clearly matters in terms of the primary role of the leaders' motivations. The centralization of policy-making in the ECU member states is closely linked to the personalization of the drive to integration. Kazakhstan's participation in the project, for example, is rooted in the initial 'ideological' commitment to Eurasian unity propagated by Nazarbaev, who is still frequently referred to by Putin as the 'father of the initiative'. Similarly, it is clear that Eurasian integration plays a key role in Putin's conceptions of Russia's place in the region and in the world, as will be discussed further below. Nevertheless, while providing the comfort of knowing 'who is who', and thus arguably simplifying negotiation processes, this personalization brings uncertainty about the future of a project tied closely to the personality and power basis of the leader.

4. ECONOMIC FACTORS

The motivation of political leaders in the member states is complex and varied. Interestingly, in all member states there has been a noteworthy effort to stress the economic benefits of integration. A more careful examination, however, shows that economic considerations appear to have a limited role in structuring the commitment to integration and its design.

As pointed out, the ECU member states face economic costs associated with integration. Yet there is little evidence to suggest that these costs have been taken into account in the set-up of the ECU regime.[16] While business has been given the opportunity to inform some areas of regulation, as pointed out by Dragneva in this volume (Chapter 3), in

---

[16]   Interestingly, existing reports and studies from within the ECU postdate its launch and/or target its expansion. See Sergei Glaz'ev, 'Real'noe yadro post-sovetskoi ekonomicheskoi integratsii: itogi sozdaniya i perspektivy razvitiya Tomozhennogo soyuza Belorussii, Kazakhstana i Rossii' (2011) 6 *Rossiiskii Ekonomicheskii Zhurnal*, http://re-j.ru/archive/2011/6; Eurasian Development Bank (EDB), *Assessment of the Economic Effect of the Kyrgyz Republic's Integration into the EurAsEC Customs Union* (EDB, 2011); EDB, *A Comprehensive Assessment of the Macroeconomic Effects of Various Forms of the Deep Economic Integration of Ukraine with Member States of the Customs Union and the Common Economic Space within the EurAsEC* (EDB, 2012).

relation to the revisions of the Customs Code of the ECU, the nature of the political systems in general has not been conducive to fostering wide and specific public debates on costs and benefits. In any event, Kassenova reminds us (in Chapter 8) that, given the speed of integration and overlap of processes, a careful economic evaluation would be extremely difficult. Moreover, decisions on the further deepening of integration were made before the benefits/costs of the steps taken were demonstrated or implementation ensured.[17]

This indicates the limited usefulness of purely economic cost–benefit explanations of regionalism in the case of the ECU. Where economic costs have been identified, such as the price Russia pays for Belarus's allegiance, they have often been outweighed by other benefits, primarily geopolitical, as argued below. This is less so the case in Kazakhstan where costs have been high and more difficult to internalize by the political regime, resulting in a more selective position as to the evolution of Eurasian integration. Kazakhstan is vulnerable to these costs and the instability created by them – something that has been noted even by the official regime. In combination with the growing sensitivity over sovereignty, Kazakhstan has been more forceful in its demands and bottom-lines – for example, in relation to the distribution of votes in the Eurasian Economic Commission or blocking the fast progression to a political Eurasian Union. While attached to the symbolism of Eurasian integration, Kazakhstan is most sensitive to the broad developmental benefits that it actually delivers. This might explain why, despite its ECU undertakings, Kazakhstan has not fully departed from its multi-vector policy, as noted by Kassenova in this volume.

Nonetheless, one fundamental economic advantage sought through the ECU that has become apparent is the protection of the domestic economies from the negative effects of the global economic crisis. As noted in this volume, there has followed a strong sense of vulnerability and uncertainty. The ECU has been a vehicle for responding to those external threats. This echoes the experience of Latin America where the economic crisis led it to engage in deeper integration and required a

---

[17]   This seems to be becoming a concern for the Russian officials working on the EEU: see 'The Eurasian Customs Union: What's in it for the EU?', Event Transcript, Carnegie Endowment, 24 October 2012.

greater degree of institutionalization,[18] confirming 'the catalytic importance of external challenge' in the ECU.[19]

Responding to economic interdependence, on the contrary, has been
only a contributory motive for integration. Over the last two decades, the
external trade orientation and development goals of all three member
states have diverged to a significant extent. Until the formation of the
ECU, Russia and Kazakhstan were increasingly less reliant on trade with
the post-Soviet states, with the EU and China being the most important
trading partners.[20] Belarus is equally dependent on the EU and the CIS
market. However, using the gravity model, de Souza argues that Belarus
already overtraded with the CIS by 200 per cent at the expense of trade
with the EU.[21] Thus, while Hettne and Söderbaum argue that 'no
interaction is possible without some *shared* interests to start with'
[emphasis added],[22] the ECU member states certainly do not appear to
share a strong economic reason for integration.[23]

Certainly, there are special cases, such as the energy and defence
industries with their particular structural legacies, especially in the
relations between Russia and Belarus. Yet these special cases do not
necessarily explain the radical steps undertaken within the Eurasian
Customs Union as well as the further integration stages pursued. As
shown by Frear in this volume, much of what has been agreed could have
been done within the Union State of Russia and Belarus (USRB) on a
bilateral basis. More important is the fact that, for the countries which are
already highly integrated, supporting disintegration is a really costly
option. Through its dependency on Russia, Belarus is locked into further

---

[18]   Edward D. Mansfield and Helen V. Milner, 'The New Wave of Regionalism', in Paul F. Diehl (ed.), *The Politics of Global Governance. International
Organizations in an Interdependence World* (Lynne Rienner, 1997) 14.
[19]   Breslin and Higgott, above note 14, 334.
[20]   Julian Cooper, 'Russia's Trade Relations within the Commonwealth of
Independent States', in Elana Wilson Rowe and Stina Torjesen (eds), *The
Multilateral Dimension in Russian Foreign Policy* (Routledge, 2009).
[21]   Lucio Vinhas de Souza, 'An Initial Estimation of the Economic Effects of
the Creation of the EurAzES Customs Union on Its Members', *Economic
Premise No. 47* (World Bank, January 2011).
[22]   Bjorn Hettne and Fredrik Söderbaum, 'Theorizing the Rise of Regionness'
(2000) 5(3) *New Political Economy* 457, 460.
[23]   Interestingly, even where clear shared economic reasons have been in
place, such as the need to manage water resources in Central Asia, integration
structures have remained shallow, ineffective and non-legalized, thus again
pointing to the weakness of economic justifications in the Eurasian region.

integration (but only with limited commitment to implementation).[24] Indeed, the economic costs of disintegration would not only be onerous for both parties, but would have a disproportionate impact on Belarus in general and for Lukashenko in particular.

In this sense, the ECU's membership validates the view that pre-existing political and military alliances with a strong track of past cooperation play a crucial role in motivating countries to engage in economic integration rather than seeking 'economically optimal' partners. In the CIS, the three countries formed 'a coalition of the willing', reflecting the propensity of the states to liberalize commerce with political-military allies, regardless of detailed economic rationale.

5. GEOPOLITICAL FACTORS

We argue that geopolitical factors primarily explain Russia's interest in the ECU and, to some extent, the interest of Kazakhstan. Thus, the geopolitical factors vary in terms of their salience between member countries. This differentiation, in turn, affects the readiness of member states to balance between different justifications, in particular consideration of the related economic costs. It also affects the preference for further integration steps as evidenced in the tensions over the shape of the EEU.

In the case of Kazakhstan, the choice of the Eurasian option is influenced by the unwillingness of the regime to accept the political conditionality attached to the European/Western alternative, as pointed out by Kassenova in this volume. With the participation in Eurasian integration, Nazarbaev has made a 'civilizational' choice in an effort to ensure domestic stability and security in the face of growing regional uncertainty and competition from China. However, as argued, Kazakhstan's choice is not unconditional – it is premised on the continued economically beneficial terms of participation in Eurasian integration.

Geopolitical motives most clearly underpin Russia's membership of the ECU and its terms. As widely observed, the notion of global competition – economic, military and normative – resonates strongly among the Russian political elites. This notion stems from the Hobbesian understanding of world politics as an arena where a constant battle of interests and struggle for domination is played out.[25] A corollary of

---

[24]   Libman and Vinokurov, above note 14, 14.
[25]   Derek Averre, 'Competing Rationalities: Russia, the EU and the "Shared Neighbourhood"' (2009) 61(10) *Europe-Asia Studies* 1689.

Russia's aspirations to being once again a 'great power' is its claim to hegemony in the 'near abroad'. As part of its claim to power status and to dispel the doubt cast on it by many observers, Russia has shifted its focus to a rule-based approach to integration in a renewed attempt to '"advertise" Moscow's international credentials'.[26] This approach – facilitated by Russia's accession to the WTO – clearly styles the ECU as a vehicle for building a 'proper' region in which Russia acts as a hegemonic leader. Eurasian integration projects Russia as a re-emerging modern power in Europe and Asia demanding relations with international partners, such as the EU, to take account of its status within the regional trading bloc.[27] Russia's overarching policy objective in this sense has been spelled out by Putin:

> Our integration project is moving to a qualitatively new level, opening up broad prospects for economic development and creating additional competitive advantages. This consolidation of efforts will help us establish ourselves within the global economy and trade system and play a real role in decision-making, setting the rules and shaping the future.[28]

Russia's perception of itself as a 'major power' is reflected in the readiness to bear direct economic costs, for example, in relation to the developmental priorities discussed by Malle in this volume (Chapter 6), as well as externally, for example, by subsidizing Belarus. With regard to the latter, Russia's integration behaviour is not unique: large states derive political benefits from the commercial gains of allies, as long as concessions strengthen the alliance as a whole.[29] Importantly, this 'generosity' also demonstrates the benefits associated with ECU membership to other potential members Russia aims to attract. Yet, ultimately, Russia's need to balance priorities is conducive to a preference for

---

[26]   On Russia's search for a status on the international arena, especially in relations with the EU and NATO, see Mark Webber, *Inclusion, Exclusion and the Governance of European Security* (Manchester University Press, 2007) Chapter 6.

[27]   Putin visited Brussels in December 2012 as a leader of the nascent 'Eurasian Union' asking the EU to conduct trade relations with the ECU on an interregional basis, showing visible frustration when the EU declined.

[28]   Vladimir Putin, 'Novyi integratsionnyi proekt dlya Evrazii – budushchee, kotoroe rozhdaetsya segodnya', *Izvestiya*, 4 October 2011.

[29]   Edward D. Mansfield and Helen V. Milner, 'The Political Economy of Regionalism: an Overview', in Edward D. Mansfield and Helen V. Milner (eds), *The Political Economy of Regionalism* (Columbia University Press, 1997) 11.

retaining some flexibility in the structure of cooperation, as will be discussed below.

Geopolitical motives underpin not only Russia's drive for deepening integration but also the widening of the regime. The expansion of Eurasian regional integration schemes across the post-Soviet space strongly features on the Russian agenda irrespective of the economic costs. As Cooper shows in this volume (Chapters 2 and 5), in fact Russia does not rely on the ECU exclusively in this effort but is seeking to develop other regional organizations in addition to it or even, conceivably, as back-up options, such as the multilateral CIS free trade area. Amongst the post-Soviet states, only the accession of Ukraine would strengthen the ECU economically, while the accession of new Central Asian members would have mainly symbolic political value. With their small economies and low GDP, the membership of Kyrgyzstan and Tajikistan would be an economic liability for Russia, but would provide Moscow with a foothold in Central Asia, further restrain USA influence, and help construct a bridge with China.

The juxtaposition of the economic and geopolitical motives for expanding the ECU results in tensions. Stressing Russia's high stakes in Central Asia, Malle is optimistic about the prospects for enlargement to Kyrgyzstan and Tajikistan. This, however, is not high on Kazakhstan's agenda. Rather than bringing in two poor and underdeveloped neighbours, Kazakhstan would prefer to turn the ECU into an economically beneficial regime for the existing member states.[30] Kassenova suggests that 'Moscow can continue to entertain broader geopolitical ambitions, but the realities on the ground dictate the more feasible goal of making the relatively prosperous 'core' of post-Soviet space integrate and work'.[31]

This interest in widening the ECU is greatly influenced by Russia's encounter with the EU as a 'normative power' in the post-Soviet space. This encounter has taught Russia important lessons about the high stakes in the region: 'what for Brussels is just one of its "neighbourhoods" is for Russia the crucial test case which will either prove or dismiss the credibility of its Great Power ambitions'.[32] To prevent a loss of influence

---

[30]   Interestingly, for Kazakhstan, the internal fragmentation of Central Asia appears to be of lesser concern than striking the balance between the key external players in the region – that is, the EU, Russia and China.

[31]   Kassenova in this volume [Chapter 8].

[32]   Arkady Moshes, 'Russia's European Policy under Medvedev: How Sustainable is a New Compromise?' (2012) 88(1) *International Affairs* 17.

across the post-Soviet space to other external players,[33] Russia has put a premium on economic integration in the shape of a binding, legalized regime to underpin the commitment to the project and its viability.

The ECU's proposed expansion to Ukraine is driven solely by Russia and reflects both economic and geopolitical motives: it seeks to counter perceived encroachment by the EU, as discussed in this volume by Delcour and Wolczuk (Chapter 10), but also to control energy transportation networks. The arguments and instruments used in the pro-ECU campaign in Ukraine reveal that Russia promotes the ECU as a worthy counterpoint to the EU in terms of economic integration, while explicitly capitalizing on the numerous weaknesses of the EU's strategy in the post-Soviet space.[34] Nevertheless, the quest to win Ukraine raises the questions of, first, the rationale of pressurizing a country which is reluctant to become a member and, second, the possible impact of the membership of such a country on the viability of the regime.

6. IMPLICATIONS FOR THE DESIGN OF INTEGRATION

While the motivation of the different member states for participating in the ECU is strong, it is not without its difficulties, as is shown above. Given that the ECU was formed by a coalition of 'politically willing' rather than economically optimal partners, the ability to bear or balance economic costs with other objectives is clearly an important factor for all member states. Thus, it can be argued that, not unlike the comparative experience of non-Western regionalism, flexibility matters. This, however, is at odds with the ECU's claim to a highly legalized design. Furthermore, there are no significant domestic pressures in motivating the highly centralized political leadership to favour and implement such a design, which the liberal perspective considers important. This seeming contradiction is resolved by considering the limits of commitment reflected in the legal and institutional regime for cooperation, but also the broader socio-legal context in which this regime is placed.

---

[33] James Nixey, 'The Long Goodbye: Waning Russian Influence in the South Caucasus and Central Asia', *Briefing Paper REP RSP BP 2012/03* (Chatham House, June 2012).

[34] Rilka Dragneva and Kataryna Wolczuk, 'Russia, the Eurasian Customs Union and the EU: Cooperation, Stagnation or Rivalry', *Briefing Paper REP BP 2012/01* (Chatham House, August 2012).

Firstly, while the ECU regime clearly features at the top end of legalized coordination (in particular, in terms of delegating decision-making and third party dispute resolution), there is still significant scope for coordination at the highest political, intergovernmental level. For example, consensus remains the primary mode of decision-making within the Council of the EEC as well as the High Eurasian Economic Council. Similarly, political pressure is the ultimate sanction in the event of a lack of domestic compliance with the decisions of the Court of EvrAzES. Furthermore, the only interstate dispute of the ECU era that reached the Court, the oil export duties row between Russia and Belarus in 2010, was ultimately resolved through bilateral, diplomatic means. Thus, flexibility is retained especially with regard to matters deemed sensitive by member states.

Secondly, flexibility is promoted by the very mode of organizational and legal development. As argued by Dragneva in this volume, the ECU and its predecessors have emerged as a result of an incremental approach to institution-building. In general there have been very few radical design innovations, the creation of the Eurasian Economic Commission being one of them. Continuities with past regulations remain and changes are selective. While the impression indeed is of a 'big bang' development, a more careful analysis shows that the 'bang' is more of an 'echo'. Similarly, the lack of a comprehensive design and the reliance on a web of issue-specific agreements is conducive to retaining flexibility. Ultimately the legacy of 'institutional traffic' and its Byzantine complexity suggest no firm boundaries or irreversibility of commitment.

Thirdly, the nature of coordination at the international level cannot be divorced from the nature of statehood and domestic legality. This is a point on which our analysis fully validates the liberal paradigm. We argue that the latest and most ambitious project in Eurasian integration reflects the duality identified at the domestic level between the constitutional-legal and administrative-patrimonial spheres or modes of decision-making, as conceptualized by Richard Sakwa.[35] Analysing Russia, he points out that there exists a constitutional (legal-rational) sphere which is susceptible to violations but nonetheless functions. Indeed, formal legality exists, laws can be sophisticated, and the introduction of best legal norms and international practices in domestic legislation is

---

[35] Richard Sakwa, 'The Dual State in Russia' (2010) 26(3) *Post-Soviet Affairs* 185; *The Crisis of Russian Democracy: The Dual State, Factionalism, and the Medvedev Succession* (Cambridge University Press, 2011) Chapter 1.

viewed as a matter of prestige.[36] Nonetheless, this legality often remains abstract and superficial. In a deeply path-dependent manner, formal laws tend to have a declaratory rather than a regulatory role, and structure the actual behaviour of state and non-state actors only to a limited degree. As Kathryn Hendley shows, law has more often been the instrument of state power than the means for ordering relations.[37]

Formal law coexists with a system of informal legality in the 'neo-patrimonial state'. This duality emanates from the conditions of systemic insecurity, but also reproduces them. In Sakwa's words, 'formal and informal worlds operate at the same time, reproducing dualism at all levels and allowing actors to operate elements of either, but undermining the inherent internal logic of both'.[38] Both are employed by ordinary people,[39] and constitute a pervasive and persistent dimension of the post-Soviet reality. Similarly, both are used instrumentally by state authorities: Putin promotes rule of law policies, particularly in relation to the court system, and also violates them.[40]

The nature of post-Soviet legality prevalent in the ECU member states translates into 'integration behaviour' and is replicated at the regional level. The use of legalized design in constructing the common regime is not surprising. It reflects the institutional learning within the organization, as discussed by Dragneva in this volume. At the same time, legalization aims to adhere to a modern, advanced template for structuring economic integration, often by imitating the EU, a frequent reference point as the most advanced and successful regional regime. Thus, the ECU design represents an expression of the principles of the constitutional-legal state in a regional context but also signals 'modernity' as an aspect of Putin's geopolitical vision for Russia, noted above.

Formal law-based, binding commitments, however, coexist with the mechanisms of informal coordination, instrumental interpretation and

---

[36]   The most recent illustration of this point relates to the reform of the cornerstone of the Russian legal system, the Civil Code adopted in 1994. The Code is currently undergoing extensive changes to modernize it in line with developing best practice and the needs of the business community.

[37]   Kathryn Hendley, 'Varieties of Legal Dualism: Making Sense of the Role of Law in Contemporary Russia (2011) 29(2) *Wisconsin International Law Journal* 233.

[38]   Richard Sakwa, 'Russia: From Stalemate to Equilibrium?', *Eurozine*, 24 October 2012, 3, http://www.eurozine.com/articles/2012-10-24-sakwa-en.html (accessed 8 March 2013).

[39]   Kathryn Hendley, 'Who Are the Legal Nihilists in Russia? (2012) 28(2) *Post-Soviet Affairs* 149.

[40]   Ibid., 168–9.

strategic application that characterize domestic systems. While a techno-cratic lobby versed in WTO parlance and rules may be developing in Russia and populating the ECU institutions, as suggested by Cooper (in Chapter 5), it is unlikely in the short run to overturn the deeper nature of post-Soviet legality without a radical change in the political and eco-nomic institutions of the member states.[41] As Connolly has argued in this volume (Chapter 4), mere membership in regional integration regimes (including joining the WTO) is not sufficient to realize its benefits without effective domestic institutions. In this sense, the complexity of the common Eurasian regime, introducing a layer of additional rules and institutions, presents important challenges.[42] The frequent as well as incremental changes increase the risk of 'grey areas' in regulation, but also introduce uncertainty into the regime. If duality of behaviour is the established post-Soviet response to uncertainty, as Sakwa asserts, this feature of the common regime is likely to perpetuate it. While Russia's membership of the WTO might lead to an improvement in institutional quality,[43] Connolly cautions against excessive optimism in light of the experiences of other post-Soviet states.

Therefore, we find that the ECU presents fewer contradictions than it initially appeared to do. The effects of what can be described as a legalized regime are significantly mitigated by the limitations of the institutional design as well as by the overall approach to organizational development. Importantly, the nature of legality in the post-Soviet world is essential in understanding how flexibility is retained and uncertainty tackled. The analytical framework of the legalization literature, which views the institutional features of regional integration groupings along a

---

[41]   Hendley's findings that legality is more likely to be disregarded by the very rich and the very poor, by the young (the Gorbachev and Eltsin gener-ations), as well as by the supporters of Putin's core policies of the so-called 'power vertical' provides a lot of food for thought: ibid.

[42]   Tarr also argues that by adding multiple layers of (inefficient and corrupt) governance the ECU compounds problems rather than alleviates them: see David Tarr, 'The Eurasian Customs Union among Russia, Belarus and Kazakhstan: Can It Succeed Where Its Predecessor Failed?', *FREE Policy Brief Series* (Stockholm Institute of Transition Economics, 11 May 2012).

[43]   Improvements have been shown to follow under certain conditions: see Sudip Ranjan Basu, 'Does WTO Accession Affect Domestic Economic Policies and Institutions?', *HEI Working Paper No. 03* (Graduate Institute of International Studies, Geneva, March 2008); Susan Aaronson and M. Rodwan Abouhard, 'Does the WTO Help Member States Clean Up?', *NCCR Working Paper No. 201149* (Swiss National Centre for Competence in Research/NCCR Trade Regulation, Bern, November 2011).

continuum between legalized and political methods of coordination, has been a useful starting point in arriving at this conclusion. Yet the ECU shows that the continuum is compressed in the simultaneous realities of the dual state.

It is also clear that flexibility in the Eurasian context has a price. Following Sakwa's logic, the key challenge is whether the evolution of Eurasian integration and the planned improvements in its design will enhance the constitutional-legal state or will intensify the challenge presented by the predatory state, and ultimately tilt the balance towards the latter. Clearly the potential of the Eurasian integration in this respect still hangs in the balance.

7. CONCLUSION

As our analysis demonstrates, the ECU is characterized by multiple idiosyncrasies. It presents itself as an exception to the *zeitgeist* of the second wave of regionalism, rejecting a 'definition of regionalism modelled on the legalism, institutions, and acceptance of supranationality *à la* European integration'.[44] Somewhat paradoxically, it is reminiscent of 'old regionalism' in terms of deep integration, institutionalization and legal design at the very time when the 'EU golden standard' of integration is evidencing major cracks and faces serious questioning.

Yet a comparison with the EU is misleading. Although the ECU has turned into a complex, multi-layered project, in many respects its modelling on the EU is superficial. Despite the formal legalization, the ultimate commitment of member states to be bound is mediated and mitigated by the nature of the political regime and legality in these states. Thus, the unpacking of the ECU requires a flexible 'toolbox' of analytical perspectives and heuristic instruments drawing from area studies, comparative regionalism, international relations and international law.

Without a doubt, the ECU has been an ambitious and fast-developing project. A lot has happened in the first years of its existence and ambitious plans have already been laid for the immediate future within the proposed framework of the EEU: deeper economic coordination, extensive regulatory convergence, codification of the legal basis, and measures to improve domestic institutional capacity. At the same time,

---

[44]   Alberta Sbragia, 'Review Article: Comparative Regionalism: What Might it Be?' (2008) 46 (Annual Review) *Journal of Common Market Studies* 29, 29.

there has been an effort to attract new members, many of whom have a dubious commitment to, and capacity for, deep economic integration in Eurasia.

Therefore, it is highly uncertain whether this rapid pace can be maintained. The project already faces the risks of what could be called an 'integrational overstretch'. This is evident in the pattern of the development of its legal and institutional regime which has suffered under the pressure of the fast-developing political agenda. There is also the risk of diluting the achievements in the field of customs integration by adding more and more areas of cooperation. Sovereignty sensitivities are reawakened in the context of debating a political union, especially in combination with the growing realization of the price of current commitments. Finally, the project is stretched in the context of its simultaneous widening.

Much of the progress so far has been contingent on the personalities of the leaders of the three member states, making the project vulnerable to leadership changes, especially if the costs associated with this overstretch continue to mount. Yet the complex set of preferences and reliance on a combination of legal and political mechanisms to advance integration will not necessarily doom the project. The *Oberge Espaniol* nature of the ECU has already delivered benefits in accommodating the diverse preferences of the member states and may well continue to do so.

The ECU has already achieved a considerable degree of integration, which cannot be undone without serious consequences. Thus, the failure of the ECU may be too costly a price to pay, especially for Russia given its ambitions and the reputational costs involved. If the ECU becomes a well-functioning and beneficial organization for all member states, Russia's credibility will be enhanced on a regional and global scale. Certainly, there is no reason to think that Russia under its current leadership is going to depart from utilizing the full spectrum of instruments available to it on a multilateral and bilateral level to consolidate integration within the ECU as well as to advance it. With the largest state interested in sustaining regional integration, the Eurasian project is likely to persist with or without new members. At the same time, what the proposed Eurasian Economic Union might look like (if at all), who it will include and exclude, or the degree to which it will strengthen domestic institutions is yet to be determined.

Appendix 1: Regional integration initiatives and organizations in the post-Soviet space

Initiative/ Organization	Participants	General status
CIS (1991)	Armenia, Azerbaijan, Belarus, Georgia (withdrew 2008), Kazakhstan, Kyrgyzstan, Moldova, Russia, Tajikistan, Turkmenistan, Ukraine, Uzbekistan	Active
Customs Union (1992)	Belarus, Kyrgyzstan, Tajikistan, Uzbekistan	Abandoned
Economic Union (1993)	CIS members (except Ukraine)	Abandoned
Free trade area (1994)	CIS members (except Russia and Turkmenistan)	Relaunched in 1999
Central Asian Union (1994)	Kazakhstan, Kyrgyzstan, Uzbekistan, Tajikistan (joined 1998)	Renamed Central Asian Economic Union (1998); transformed into CACO (2002)
Customs Union (1995)	Belarus, Kazakhstan, Russia, Kyrgyzstan (joined 1997), Tajikistan (joined 1998)	Transformed into EvrAzES (2000)
Shanghai Five (1996)	China, Kazakhstan, Kyrgyzstan, Russia, Tajikistan, Uzbekistan (2001)	Transformed into SCO (2001)
GUAM (1997)	Azerbaijan, Georgia, Moldova, Ukraine, Uzbekistan (joined 1999, withdrew 2005)	Active; renamed GUAM Organization for Democracy and Economic Development (2006)

Initiative/ Organization	Participants	General status
Free trade area (1999)	CIS members (except Russia and Turkmenistan)	Relaunched in 2011
EvrAzES (2000)	Belarus, Russia, Kazakhstan, Kyrgyzstan, Tajikistan, Uzbekistan (joined 2006, withdrew 2008)	Active
Shanghai Cooperation Organization (SCO) (2001)	China, Kazakhstan, Kyrgyzstan, Russia, Tajikistan, Uzbekistan	Active
Central Asian Cooperation Organization (CACO) (2002)	Kazakhstan, Kyrgyzstan, Tajikistan, Uzbekistan, Russia (joined 2004)	Merged with EvrAzES (2006)
Collective Security Treaty Organization (CSTO) (2002)	Armenia, Belarus, Kazakhstan, Kyrgyzstan, Russia, Tajikistan	Active
Common Economic Space (2003)	Belarus, Russia, Kazakhstan, Ukraine	Abandoned
Eurasian Customs Union (2007)	Belarus, Russia, Kazakhstan	Active; within EvrAzES
Free trade area (2011)	Armenia, Belarus, Kazakhstan, Kyrgyzstan, Moldova, Russia, Tajikistan, Ukraine	Active
Single Economic Space (2012)	Belarus, Russia, Kazakhstan	Active; within EvrAzES

Appendix 2: Post-Soviet countries' applications and accessions to the WTO

Country	Date of application	First Working Party meeting	Date of accession
Armenia	December 1993	January 1996	5 February 2003
Azerbaijan	June 1997	June 2002	–
Belarus	September 1993	June 1997	–
Georgia	June 1996	March 1998	14 June 2000
Kazakhstan	January 1996	March 1997	–
Kyrgyzstan	February 1996	March 1997	20 December 1998
Moldova	November 1993	June 1997	26 July 2001
Russian Federaion	June 1993	July 1995	22 August 2012
Tajikistan	May 2001	March 2004	2 March 2013
Turkmenistan	–	–	–
Ukraine	November 1993	February 1995	16 May 2008
Uzbekistan	December 1994	July 2002	–

Source: Compiled by the editors on the basis of information from the WTO website.

Index

Abbott, Kenneth 8
acquis communautaire 134, 179, 182–5, 187, 189
administrative capacity 62, 75–7, 97, 129, 187
Afghanistan 85, 103, 109, 146
Akeev, Askar 18
Alma Ata Declaration 15
Almaty 20, 29
Area studies 9–10, 208, 220
Armenia 19, 31, 71–2, 85, 87, 95, 105, 181, 185–6, 191
Arsen'ev Progress company 94
ASEAN 66, 69, 72
Asia–Pacific 29, 100–102, 104, 110–12, 115–17
Asia–Pacific Economic Cooperation (APEC) 100–111
Association Agreement 179, 181–3, 185, 190–91, 195, 197–200, 202
    see also DCFTA
Astana 19, 24, 30, 132, 148–9, 153, 156–8
Azerbaijan 18, 31, 83, 87, 105, 135, 181

Balas, Peter 171
Baltic states 15–16, 197
Barabanov, Oleg 116
Belaruskali company 129
Beltransgaz company 131
'big bang' development 35, 205, 217
Bishimbayev, Kuandyk 147
Bolshoi Kamen' 94
Borodin, Pavel 90
Brazil 32, 125
Brussels 97, 133–4, 163, 169–70, 172, 195, 215

Cairns Group 67

CARICOM 72
Caspian Sea 109
Caucasus 76, 84
Central Asia 84, 93, 100–105, 107–08, 112, 117, 140–42, 146–8, 157–8, 160, 174, 177, 207, 215
Central Asian Economic Union (CAEU) 18, 141
centralization 121, 210, 216
Chatham House 17
Chernishev, Sergei 87
China 67, 69, 71–2, 85, 101–04, 107–12, 115–17, 125, 133, 135–6, 142–3, 148–9, 154, 156, 158, 160, 177, 212–13, 215
Chubais, Anatolii 89, 99
Clinton, Hilary 4–5, 84
Collective Security Treaty Organization (CSTO) 85–6, 122, 172
common external tariff 63, 65–6, 125, 127–8, 145–6, 151
common neighbourhood 165, 173, 175, 180, 190–91, 195, 197, 202–3
Commonwealth of Independent States (CIS)
    Charter of 16
    Council of Heads of State and Government 48
    development of 15–18, 31
    Economic Court of 8, 55–6
        see also Court of EvrAzEs; dispute resolution
    free trade area within 16–17, 31, 83, 95, 105, 194, 197–8, 215
Common Spaces 167
Communist Party (Russia) 89
comparative law of regional integration 35, 208

compliance 8–9, 54, 57, 61, 109, 188,
    217
conditionality
    democratic 134, 198–200
    economic 131, 191, 195
    political 134, 163, 166, 213
Connolly, Richard 12, 23, 47, 59, 109,
    172, 177, 187, 219
Cooper, Julian 11–12, 105, 113, 177,
    193, 209, 215, 219
corruption 70–71, 155, 187
Court of EvrAzEs 11, 20, 27, 37–9, 44,
    52, 54–9, 106, 126, 206, 217
    see also CIS, Economic Court of;
        dispute resolution
Customs Code of the Customs Union 2,
    22, 43, 45, 64, 125–6, 211
customs duties 20, 22, 26, 131, 144, 153
    revenues 22–3, 64, 131, 145
    territory 2, 44
    valuation 46
    see also common external tariff;
        tariffs
Customs Union of 1995 (CU–95) 18,
    37–8, 41–3, 48, 140–41

Dalenov, Ruslan 153
Deep and Comprehensive Free Trade
    Area (DCFTA) 165, 182–6,
    190–93, 196, 198, 201–02
    see also Association Agreement
deep economic integration 166, 180,
    193, 204–05, 221
defence industry 81, 83, 93–5, 132, 212
Delcour, Laure 12, 27, 134, 175, 178,
    216
democratic legalism 206
democratization 133, 137, 148, 158
Diez, Thomas 196
dispute resolution 2, 34, 36, 55–8, 109,
    206, 217
    see also CIS, Economic Court of;
        Court of EvrAzEs
domestic reform 70, 81, 179, 207
Dragneva, Rilka 12, 27, 33, 164, 171,
    177, 193, 210, 217–18
dual state 220

Dugin, Aleksandr 92

East–Central Europe 1, 181, 197, 200
Eastern neighbourhood 3, 134, 163,
    165, 173, 181–2, 190
Eastern Partnership 133, 173–4, 181–5,
    187–91, 199
economic crisis 83–5, 107, 112, 115,
    146–7, 193, 200, 211
Eltsin, Boris 18, 82, 84–5, 122–3
Emerson, Michael 167
energy 20, 28, 32, 75, 108–09, 111–12,
    119, 121, 124–6, 128–9, 148, 175,
    180, 182, 185, 193, 195–6, 199,
    200, 202, 212, 216
    subsidies 122, 132, 137
    see also gas; oil
Eurasian Business Council 88
Eurasian Customs Union (ECU)
    Commission of the Customs Union
        21–3, 25, 38–40, 46, 49–53, 57,
        59, 157
        see also Eurasian Economic
            Commission (EEC)
    development of 21–4, 38–41
    enlargement of 26, 103–04, 117, 191,
        215
        see also integration, widening of
    Interstate Council (Highest Organ
        of the Customs Union) 23–5,
        27, 30, 38–40, 43–4, 47,
        49–50, 42–3
        see also High Eurasian Economic
            Council (HEEC)
    legal personality 40, 171
    membership of 40
    treaty basis 38, 40, 42, 45, 47, 49, 51,
        53–4, 57–8
        see also international agreements, in
            ECU
Eurasian Development Bank 124, 131
Eurasian Economic Commission
    (EEC)11, 39–41, 43, 57–9, 67, 75,
    86–8, 97–9, 126, 130–31, 157,
    170, 206, 209, 211, 217
    acts 50–51
    Collegium 25, 30, 51, 54–5

composition 25–6, 53–4
Council 25, 51, 53–5, 217
powers 53–4
voting rules 54–5
see also Eurasian Customs Union,
    Commission of the Customs
    Union
Eurasian Economic Community
    (EvrAzES)
    development of 19–20, 37
    Integration Committee of 19, 37, 39,
        51–2
    Inter–Parliamentary Assembly of 20,
        27, 37–9
    Interstate Council of 19, 27–8, 37–9,
        52, 57
    reform/liquidation of 41
    see also Court of EvrAzEs
Eurasian Economic Union 3, 11, 27–30,
    40–41, 45, 59, 62, 102, 106–07,
    109–10, 115–16, 137, 157, 159,
    164, 169–71, 202, 205, 213,
    220–21
Eurasian integration
    asymmetry 5, 7, 32, 81, 97, 129, 195,
        206
    deepening 3, 34, 77, 82, 98, 100, 106,
        191, 207, 211, 215
    researching 6–11, 207–08
    widening 3, 82, 98, 191, 207, 215,
        221
    see also Eurasian Customs Union,
        enlargement of
Eurasian Party – Union of Patriots of
    Russia 90
Eurasianism 92–3
European Bank for Reconstruction and
    Development (EBRD) 69, 73
European Commission 157, 170–72
European Free Trade Area (EFTA) 26
European Neighbourhood Partnership
    Instrument (ENPI) 188–9
European Neighbourhood Policy (ENP)
    165, 173–4, 176, 181–2, 187,
    189–90
European Studies 1, 11

European Union (EU) 1, 15, 32–3, 48,
    54, 72, 91, 96, 104, 107, 110–11,
    179, 206, 212, 218
    and Belarus 122, 125, 128, 133–7
    and ECU 4, 6, 12, 29, 169–72, 176,
        180, 220
    enlargement of 73, 173, 183, 187, 200
    and Kazakhstan 143, 148, 156, 158
    and Russia 163–8, 173–8, 180, 190,
        214–5
    and Ukraine 190–203
exports 66, 69, 74, 84, 108, 117, 122,
    125–8, 131, 140, 150–51, 153,
    158–9, 168, 185–6, 193–4, 201,
    217
    see also imports
Exxon 111

Far East 94, 96, 100–102, 111–17
Foreign direct investment (FDI) 68–9,
    73–5, 95, 145
four freedoms 24, 169
Frear, Matthew 10, 12, 172, 193, 208,
    212
free economic zone (FEZ) 149
    Khorgos 149
frozen conflicts 187

Gaidar Institute of Economic Policy 90
Gaidar, Yegor 89
gas 27, 84, 97, 101, 108–11, 114, 117,
    121, 126, 128–9, 131–2, 141, 144,
    146, 148, 153, 155–6, 174–6, 193
    see also energy; oil; pipelines
Gazprom 131
geopolitical motives/interests 10, 98,
    101, 105, 110, 115, 117, 132–3,
    137, 147, 156–9, 187, 196, 204,
    211, 213, 215–16, 218
Georgia 16, 18, 71–2, 83, 181, 184, 186,
    188
Germany 167
Glaz'ev, Sergei 3, 21, 86, 88, 90–91, 93
Gref, German 84
grey economy 131, 136
GUAM 18, 83
Gumilev, Lev 92–3

hard law 41, 174, 190, 202
harmonization 20, 22, 25–6, 28, 53, 97,
        190, 205
Haukkala, Hiski 12
hegemony 5–7, 35, 197, 214
    normative 164, 166, 176
    'smart' 5
Hendley, Kathryn 218
Hettne, Bjorn 212
High Eurasian Economic Council
        (HEEC) 39–41, 53–5, 217
    see also Interstate Council (Highest
        Organ of the Customs Union)
High School of Economics (Russia) 90
Hoagland, Richard E. 148
'holding together integration' 10

imports 63–4, 66–9, 73, 109, 121,
        127–8, 145, 151–2, 155, 185, 192,
        194, 201
    see also exports
India 85
Institute of Contemporary Development
        (Russia) 92
institutional design 7–8, 10, 35–6, 41,
        47, 49, 59–60, 208, 219
    and credibility of commitment 8, 183
    and flexibility 8, 204, 206, 208,
        215–17, 219–20
    and uncertainty 8, 211, 219
institutional learning 35, 58–9, 218
intellectual property rights 61, 77, 184
interest groups 9, 209
international agreements
    in CIS 2, 42, 48
    codification 30, 45, 59, 220
    domestic effect 44
    in ECU 30, 39, 41, 43, 46–7, 57–8
        see also Eurasian Customs Union,
            treaty basis
    in EvrAzEs 37, 40
    monitoring implementation/
        enforcement 52, 54, 56
    'spaghetti bowl' of 42, 44
international law 28, 40, 42, 47–9, 192
    literature 1, 6, 7, 11, 35, 298, 220
international relations 1, 6–8, 207, 220

liberal perspective 8–9, 207, 210,
        216–17
    rational functionalist perspective 7–8,
        206–7
    realist perspective 7, 207
Iran 85, 109
Ishaev, Viktor 113
Izborskii Club 92–3
Izvestiya 29, 142, 146, 148

Japan 102, 112–13
Jiabao, Wen 143, 149
Jingtao, Hu 149
Just Russia party 88, 90

Karin, Yerlan 156
Kassenova, Nargis 10, 12, 103, 108,
        172, 211, 213, 215
Katzenstein, Peter 204
Kazan 17
Kelimbetov, Kairat 25
Keohane, Robert 7
Khabarovsk 113
Khristenko, Viktor 25
Komsomol'sk–na–Amur 94
Kozmino 111
Kozyrev, Andrey 140
Kuz'minov, Yaroslav 90
Kyoto Convention on the Simplification
        and Harmonization of Customs
        Procedures of 1999, 45
Kyrgyzstan (Kyrgyz Republic) 3, 18,
        20, 24, 27, 31, 63, 66, 85, 94–7,
        104–06, 109–10, 116–17, 137,
        140–41, 158, 160, 215

Latin America 32, 135, 211
legality 9, 35, 42, 58–9, 217–20
    formal law 9, 218
    informal mechanisms 218
    see also dual state; rule of law
legalization 8, 35–6, 202, 206–07,
        218–20
Leonard, Mark 173
Levada Centre 91
Liberal Democratic Party (Russia) 88–9
liberal empire 89, 99

see also Chubais
liberalization
  of barriers to FDI 74–5, 145
  of trade 67–8, 76–7, 127, 152
  visa 182–3, 188
loyalty 119, 122, 137, 202
  see also political allegiance
Lukashenko, Aleksandr 10, 17, 27, 30, 119–24, 126, 128–30, 132–8, 174, 208, 209, 213
Lutsenko, Yuriy 198

Maastricht criteria 25
Malle, Silvana 12, 93–4, 96, 177, 214–15
Mann, Michael 76
Mansurov, Tair 20–21
Massimov, Karim 148
Mau, Vladimir 90
MAZ Automobile factory 129
McCall Smith, James 206
Medvedev, Dmitrii 29, 64, 88, 92, 191
Medvedkov, Maksim 87, 98
Mercosur 5, 32, 62, 67, 69, 72, 207
Middle East 135
Minsk 20, 27–8, 119–20, 122–9, 131–8
modernization 3, 102, 128, 136, 142, 158, 171, 175, 180, 184, 193–4, 196, 198, 200, 202
Moldova 18–19, 31, 83, 87, 95, 105, 175, 181, 184–6, 188, 191
Mongolia 85
Mordashov, Aleksei 87
Moscow 16–17, 20–21, 26, 28, 82–4, 88, 95–9, 116, 122–4, 126, 128–9, 131–3, 135–7, 140, 148, 156–8, 163–5, 168–9, 172–7, 202, 214–15
Moscow State University 17, 28, 92, 140
multi–vector policy 103, 117, 147, 156–7, 159, 197, 211

NAFTA 5, 32, 62, 66, 69
nationalists 107, 115, 120, 154, 159
Naryshkin, Sergei 27, 87, 98, 156
NATO 1, 91, 163, 168, 172

Nazarbayev, Nursultan 10, 16, 20, 26–30, 56, 110, 139–42, 144, 146–8, 156–7, 159–60, 178, 210, 213
  and the Eurasian Union idea 17–18, 28, 140, 210
New Zealand 26, 31, 111
non–tariff
  barriers 26, 65, 69, 143, 146, 152, 182, 184
  regulation 53, 64, 219
  see also sanitary and phytosanitary standards
normative power 1, 180, 196, 202, 215
Nur Otan Party 156

oil 66, 84, 101, 108–11, 117, 121–2, 126, 128–9, 131–2, 135, 144, 146–8, 150, 153–6, 217
  see also energy; gas; pipelines
oligarchs 5, 121, 132, 194
opposition 29, 89, 124, 130, 134–5, 155, 198
Orange Revolution 24, 173–4
Organization for Economic Cooperation and Development (OECD) 74, 97
Orthodox Church 132

Pakistan 85
Partnership and Cooperation Agreement (PCA) 166–8, 190
Partnership for Modernization 167
Party of Regions 199
Pavlovskii, Gleb 82
pipelines 108, 111–12, 117, 129, 131, 147
  see also gas; oil
political allegiance 123, 211
  see also loyalty
political regime 9, 206, 208–11, 220
  authoritarian 120, 174, 204
  neo–patrimonial 5, 9, 209
  non–democratic 204, 206, 208
  semi–authoritarian 9
Popescu, Nicu 173
privatization 70, 74, 82, 89, 114

Prokhanov, Aleksandr 92
protection of property rights 109, 114
Pskov 92
public opinion 81, 91, 115, 124
Putin, Vladimir 3, 5, 22–3, 29, 30, 64,
    84–6, 88, 93, 96, 98, 100, 107,
    110–11, 113, 115, 123, 132, 141,
    156, 160, 164, 168, 169, 176, 191,
    193–5, 209–10, 214, 218

Rakurs 151
Rapota, Grigorii 21
Recently Acceded Members (RAM) 67
regional trade 34
    agreements 65, 67, 69, 72
    blocs 72–3, 77
regionalism 11, 204, 208, 211, 216
    comparative 220
    new 1, 207
    old 1, 220
    second wave of 1, 10, 220
regionalization 209
Rodina Party 86, 90–91
Rogozin, Dmitrii 86, 90–91, 95
Rosnano state corporation 89
Rosneft 111
rule of law 5, 9, 10, 70–71, 101, 130,
    187, 218
rule–based integration/regime 2, 5,
    34–5, 57, 59, 180, 196, 199–200,
    207, 214
Rumas, Sergei 25
Russian Chamber of Trade and Industry
    87
Russian Union of Industrialists and
    Entrepreneurs 87

Saakashvili, Mikhail 188
Sakwa, Richard 217–20
Salamatov, Vladimir 88
Samara 17
sanitary and phytosanitary standards 23,
    26, 77, 128, 146, 189, 194
    see also non–tariff barriers,
        regulation
Savitskii, Petr 92

security 28, 33, 83–6, 93, 98–99, 101,
    103, 104, 106, 110–12, 120, 146,
    148, 172, 180, 213
Shanghai Cooperation Organization
    (SCO) 85, 143, 149
Shoigu, Sergei 113
Shokhin, Aleksandr 87–8
Shukeyev, Umirzak 155
Shuvalov, Igor 22, 25, 86
Siberia 100–102, 111, 113–14, 116–17
Simmons, Beth 8
Single Economic Space (SES) 21, 24–6,
    28–30, 32, 39, 40, 44–6, 51, 53,
    55, 59, 77, 84, 97–9, 103, 109,
    115, 119, 122, 124, 126, 129, 133,
    136–7, 139, 147, 150, 153,
    155–60, 205
Sino–Russian Eastern Petrochemical
    Company 111
Slepnev, Andrei 87
Slutskii, Leonid 87
Snidal, Duncan 8
Söderbaum, Fredrik 212
soft law 179, 190, 197–8
Solomon, Jill 207
Soskovets, Oleg 88
sovereignty 5, 8, 28, 32, 42, 59, 120,
    123, 133, 147, 155–6, 164, 177–8,
    211, 221
Soviet Union 2, 5, 32, 42, 81, 84, 89, 91,
    96, 100, 157
    see also USSR
Starchenko, Tat'yana 22
State Duma 27, 87, 89–90, 98, 156
Suleimenov, Timur 151
supranational delegation 2, 34, 47, 51,
    53
Syria 26

Tajikistan 3, 18–20, 24, 27, 31, 37, 52,
    63, 85, 96–7, 104–06, 109–10,
    116–17, 141, 158, 160, 215
tariffs 53, 63–5, 68, 105, 107, 126–8,
    144–5, 147, 151–6, 159, 172, 194
    see also customs duties; common
        external tariff
taxation 126, 141, 144, 153

Tianjin 111
trade turnover 107, 125, 141–3, 150
transparency 35, 58, 61, 205, 208
Treaty of European Union 181
Trubetskoi, Nikolai 92
Turkey 157
Turkmenistan 16–17, 31, 105, 108–10,
    117, 141
Tymoshenko, Yulia 198

Ukraine 3, 16, 18–19, 24, 26–7, 31, 40,
    66–7, 71–2, 83, 85–6, 93–9, 105,
    137, 165, 173–6, 180–81, 183–6,
    188, 191–202, 207, 215–16
Union State of Russia and Belarus
    (USRB) 18, 30, 90, 119–20,
    122–5, 127, 129–30, 132, 212
United Russia party 88
United States 110, 117, 135
    see also USA
Urals 101
USA 33, 96, 148, 215
    see also United States
USSR 5, 15–16, 18, 29–30, 42, 81–2,
    84, 89, 91, 93–94, 178
    see also Soviet Union
Uzbekistan 18–19, 31, 85, 94, 105,
    108–19, 117, 141

Valdai Discussion Club 114
Valovaya, Tat'yana 87–8, 90
Venezuela 135
Vietnam 26, 31, 71–2, 111
Vinhas De Souza, Lucio 212
Visa Liberalization Action Plan 188
Vladivostok 110, 113
Voronin, Yurii 86

Wolczuk, Kataryna 12, 27, 134, 175,
    178, 193, 216
World Bank 145
    Governance Indicators 70–74
WTO
    and Belarus 4, 61, 171
    and CIS free trade 31, 105
    and Eurasian Economic Union 28
    and EvrAzES 19–20
    and Kazakhstan 4, 61, 142–3, 145–8,
        150, 159, 171
    and Kyrgyzstan 105, 109, 116
    and Tajikistan 24, 27, 109, 116
    and Ukraine 201
WTO and Russia's accession 61–3, 77,
    87, 89, 98, 167, 170
    and ECU 3, 22–3, 26, 34, 37, 45, 47,
        61–2, 64–5, 67, 206, 214, 219
    effect on Belarus 65–9, 74–5, 125,
        127–8, 134
    effect on institutional quality 70–73,
        219
    effect on Kazakhstan 65–9, 74–5,
        139, 144, 152, 154
    and groups within WTO 67
    impact within Russia 73–5
    implementation of undertakings 33,
        62, 76–7, 97, 171

Yabloko Party (Russia) 89
Yanukovych, Viktor 174, 193, 199, 201
Yurgens, Igor' 92

Zaporozh'e 86
Zavtra 92